JOY and SORROW

The story of an Exclusive Brethren survivor

Joy Nason

'One joy scatters a hundred griefs' – Chinese proverb

Publish-_Me!_

First published 2014 by
Publish-Me!
PO Box 205 Haberfield NSW 2045
www.publish-me.com.au
info@publish-me.com.au
T. +61 2 9362 8441

Cover photograph by Peter Cooke

For the National Library of Australia Cataloguing-in-Publication entry
please see www.nla.gov.au

ISBN: 978-0-9942691-6-4 (pbk)
ISBN: 978-1-9252815-6-9 (hbk)

Contents

Foreword

On the death of her mother, who was misled until the end that she was living among the "saints", Joy Nason tried to contact her brother to talk about the funeral.

When she finally tracked him down and asked on the phone about the arrangements, his response was as cold as misguided religious belief can get: "Do you have a particular interest in this matter?"

Joy grew up in the Exclusive Brethren. By the time of her mother's death, she was "out," her mother and brother were "in". But it's around death and bereavement, the mechanics of family fealty and funerals, that this particular religious cult is at its most brutal. Joy missed the service.

The aptly named *'Joy and Sorrow'* is the story of a woman who was raised by the deluded, but at a young age achieved the clarity of sight to leave. Twice.

Her life story is remarkable. It gives painful, but sometimes hilarious insight, into life inside this closed sect. In the 1950s, a stricture against taking pride in singing resulted in them routinely intoning their hymns woefully out of tune.

Another edict declared that mental illness could be cured by prayer. This had the effect of dozens of "poor demented souls" suddenly appearing in the ranks of Brethren meeting halls. One young Brethren man was ceremonially escorted from his mental institution and back into the fold, then memorably rushed out again as he divested himself of his clothes.

But hilarity was rare; cruelty was routine. There was the mortal fear instilled in the young, including young Joy, that they would miss the "rapture" for their childish sins. They endured the burning of books and the killing of pets when one world leader, James Taylor Junior, decided they fell foul of some Bible verse or other.

By far the cruellest of the edicts was Taylor's "separation, or eating matter" in the early 1960s, which dictated that members of the cult could associate only with other members. It split families in two, parents from children, brothers from sisters, and has continued to do so down the decades.

But Joy's book is not just about the Exclusive Brethren. It would infuriate them – who believe they are at the centre of everything – to know that they have been a part of her life, but not the dominant part.

She has been a lover, a traveller, a wife (several times), a mother, and extremely successful teacher and administrator. The Brethren would hate her success and her happiness.

Joy – aptly named – is a living, breathing counterfactual to Exclusive Brethren propaganda. A woman who has lived life, lived it fully, and achieved her three score and ten years without the help of their punishing God. This book is her testament to a life well lived.

© Michael Bachelard
February 2015

Michael Bachelard is the Investigative Unit Editor at Fairfax's *The Age* newspaper. Michael was chief Indonesia correspondent for Fairfax from 2012 to 2015. He's a former political reporter and workplace reporter and has won a number of awards, including a Walkley. Michael is the author of 'Behind The Exclusive Brethren'.

Dedication

This book is dedicated to the memory of my parents, Joseph Edgar Nason (1902-1984) and Hilda Stonall Beresford (1901-1991) and to my seven siblings, Donald, Mildred, Beryl, John, David, Janet and Edward, whose lives were all affected as a consequence of being born into the Plymouth Brethren religious fundamentalist sect.

> *'People tell you the world looks a certain way. Parents tell you how to think. Schools tell you how to think. TV. Religion. And then at a certain point, if you're lucky, you realize you can make up your own mind. Nobody sets the rules but you. You can design your own life'.*
> **Carrie-Anne Moss**

> *'Life is like a hand of cards – it's not the cards that matter, but how you play the hand that counts. You can't win by folding, and sometimes you must take chances in order to win'.*
> **Anon**

Explanatory Notes

The religious fundamentalists of this narrative are a group known as the Exclusive Brethren. I have variously referred to them as the Church, the Flock, the Brethren, the Exclusive Brethren or the EB. In 1830, John Nelson Darby was a prominent church leader in Plymouth, England when the group was called the Plymouth Brethren. By 1848 a division led to two main branches being established – one became known as the Open Brethren and the other the Closed, or Exclusive, Brethren.

Many significant divisions continued since that time, with the present day Exclusive Brethren being followers of the Taylorite/ Hales branch, which from about 1960 has developed most of the features characteristic of high-demand organisations, popularly known as cults. The Exclusive Brethren, in 2014 renamed the Plymouth Brethren Christian Church (PBCC), number around 40,000 adherents, living mainly in the UK, USA, New Zealand and Australia. An internet search will show a huge amount of information regarding the past and present history of the Exclusive Brethren documented on the internet in various websites. *Wikipedia* gives a concise and factual account.

Some names have been changed to protect identity.

Prologue

They're here. Again. I don't need to hear their silent footfall in the hallway, I can sense in every fibre of my being that they are walking stealthily, searching, looking for me, waiting to pounce. How many are there this time I wonder - one? Two? I could outwit two - at the most. It's too late to hide now, they're getting nearer - I know it. Too late to crawl under the bed to conceal myself from these intruders. I lie motionless, hardly daring to breathe, sure that the loud thumping of my heart threatening to burst my ear drums can be heard by my assailants. This time, if they find me, I'll beg them to let me go - I'll do anything they ask. I am so still, maybe they'll give up, go away, leave me alone.

But no, they're getting closer - right next to my bed now - always these same faceless, nameless men, who represent to me images from my past. They'll grab me, they'll take me and I will be powerless to escape their clutches. Then my screaming begins, I scream and scream again, but my voice seems caught in my throat, is it a silent scream? I don't know, but I must keep crying out for someone to help me, or I will surely die.

Then a human voice comes to me through the darkness - it's OK, it's OK, it's OK - over and over, until it reaches my consciousness. Oh my God, not again - it's my long-suffering husband shaking me out of my nightmare. I lunge for the bedside lamp, he begs me not to turn it on - tries to convince me there is no-one in the room. I react cautiously, I don't really believe him, there must be someone there trying to get me, it was so real. Finally I say - "Was it the voice?" Yes, he replies. Then I know it was my recurring nightmare. I dare not close my eyes again just yet; I've known the nightmare to return.

I'll get up and walk around, until my thumping heart subsides, my body calms.

I've lost count of the times I've had the same nightmare over many years. They occur less frequently now – but I know full well the sound of 'the voice'. I've never heard my own screaming of course, but my mother suffered similarly throughout my childhood, and once you hear the howling, banshee noise emanating from this sort of nightmare, you never forget it. As a young mother myself, I awoke once to find my school-age son shaking me, shouting to get through to me, his eyes wide with terror. He said the chilling sound of me in a nightmare will haunt him for the rest of his days.

The first time my husband heard it, he tried to hold me in a comforting embrace. Big mistake – I thrashed around like a wild thing, practically knocking him out. Now he routinely wakes me with calming words: if he's lucky he'll convince me not to leap out of bed and turn on the lights, then he has a good chance of only a slight disturbance to his slumber.

As for me – I'm left to ponder – how did this all begin? Is it possible a nightmare gene can be passed down through the generations? Of one thing I am certain – I have lived well, laughed often and loved much: the universal measure of success, which judged in the clear light of day, can be considered quite an achievement. In the darkness of the night however, when the subconscious takes over, if you grew up on a diet of hell-fire and brimstone sermons convincing you that if you turned your back on God's one true Flock, the Grim Reaper surely awaits you at the end of your days – this is enough for a lifetime of nightmares.

Come with me now on my journey.

PART 1
1943 to 1952

1

Beginnings

The deck of cards is shuffled, cut and your hand is dealt – before you are capable of conscious thought or have even taken your first breath in this world. This is when our life's journey begins – when we have no part in deciding where we are coming from or going to.

My advent into the world was pure chance, never entering my parents' calculations. I was a 'change-of-life' baby for my 43 year old mother, whose first-born child was then almost 20. I was an afterthought, the eighth child following a long break since number seven – another mouth to feed for a working-class, Plymouth Brethren family, struggling to make ends meet in war-torn Britain. Nevertheless, in my parents' eyes, I was a miracle. My arrival at Bristol Southmead Hospital in 1943 was in the midst of the Second World War bombing blitzes on the city and some years after a serious cancer scare had resulted in my mother's mastectomy.

From the outset it seems I was destined to a perplexing existence – could I have been dealt a 'confusion' card? Confusion seemed part and parcel of my earliest years. For a start no one could agree on my proper name. I was baptised 'Myrtle Joy' but was referred to as 'Girlie-Joy' or merely 'Girlie' during my childhood in England. Years later I saw a letter written by my eldest brother towards the end of the War. He sent it to my mother from Italy where he was serving in the British Army as a transport driver for the Royal Army Service Corps. In the first paragraph he asks how 'little Myrtle' was getting along. Good grief – Myrtle was an actual person!

I tried to bury Myrtle for years, or at least sweep her under the carpet. A ghastly memory surfaces. A school-yard chant: 'Moytle the Toytle with the Poyple Goydle'. The resulting tears I shed on my mother's breast were evidently sufficient reason to go with the flow as Girlie.

Findmypast.com records Myrtle Nason on the passenger list of the migrant ship *SS New Australia* on departure from Southampton in 1953, but a metamorphosis occurred. By the time I started school in Australia, both 'Myrtle' and 'Girlie' had disappeared and Joy had taken their place.

In my twenties when my life's journey took a major U-turn, I wanted to return to the land of my birth. In the process of applying for an Australian passport, a copy of my British birth certificate winged its way across the world from Somerset House in London – and there was Myrtle staring me in the face again. Oh how I loathed that first given name. I seriously considered an official name change and found you can alter your last name with a minimum of fuss by producing a marriage certificate or similar document, but changing your given name is much harder.

At that time international airline tickets could be written with a first name conveniently deleted, so there was little point in going to the considerable effort necessary to produce deed poll documents to obliterate 'Myrtle' forever. It seemed simpler to ignore it and so I went about my life for the next 30 odd years with Joy being the only name legally required on any document other than my passport.

Forces were at work that eventually caused my little ruse to be exposed. The '9/11' terrorist attacks in the USA had world-wide consequences. Security measures enforced since that terrible event mean no one from the four corners of the globe can have an airline ticket written that does not exactly match the birth certificate name. Back came 'Myrtle'.

The wonders of technology linking flight reservations to accommodation bookings then led to the mortifying experience of entering a fancy hotel room in a foreign destination with new husband in tow, who was quite happy with a Joy in his life, only to be greeted with a giant plasma screen flashing: 'Welcome Myrtie and Pete' - the typo being the icing on the cake! From then on, with my propensity for getting in a muddle and other curious quirks, my husband invariably declares it is the 'Myrtie' factor at work.

In his old age my father proudly proclaimed to me one day that I was cleverly christened Myrtle Joy to give me two meanings - Joy and Sorrow. He even got that wrong - Internet research assures me Myrtle is, and always has been, merely a tree. I shouldn't be too harsh on my dear old dad however, steeped as he was in his daily Bible readings, he was probably confusing my name with one of the Three Wise Men's gifts to the baby Jesus: 'myrrh' in Arabic means bitter. My etymological delving also revealed that the evergreen shrub Myrtle was sacred to Venus as a symbol of love - if I'd known that before, I may have viewed my dreaded moniker less disparagingly.

So, in the words of Dickens' David Copperfield 'I am born', an inauspicious beginning perhaps but my recollections for the most part are of a happy childhood. Has the passage of time dulled the memory? Or did I instinctively play my 'optimism' card from the beginning? To this day I endeavour to perceive the glass half full. The 'trust' card I was dealt has served me well throughout my life, despite many warnings that being trusting simply equates with being easy to fool.

Bristol in the World War of the 1940s was not a particularly enviable place to be, yet I've always thought I was there when the 'lucky' card was dealt. Being the youngest by a long way in a brood of eight children, I was as spoilt as any other baby in a family and shielded from most of the grim realities of wartime existence.

An infant, wrapped tightly against the cold and darkness of a blackout, carried swiftly down the steep steps leading to the safety of the air raid shelter in the back garden, has no memory of the frightening warning sirens and whistling bombs that gave most of my family nightmares for the rest of their lives.

We lived in a semi-detached Council house at No 7 Uplands Road, Fishponds, Bristol. It was a traditional 'two-up two-down' dwelling, surrounded by street after street of similar non-descript houses typical of the times. Various social housing references confirm my recollection of the premises:

> Downstairs the front room was the parlour and the back room the
> kitchen where the family cooked, ate and spent most of their time. There
> was usually a small extension at the back in which was the scullery.
> Upstairs were two bedrooms, one for the parents and the other for the
> children and perhaps an extra small bedroom in the "back addition".

These Bristol Corporation houses were made to last. Only luck prevented instant demolition during the blitzes, but since then apparently nothing has affected their structure. *Google Earth* zooms in to show the row of tenements unchanged from the day they were built, my old home being instantly recognisable to me.

There is no denying which side of the tracks I was born on. I have the Bristol Corporation Rent Book for 1943, the title page headed: '*Conditions of Tenancy of Houses for the Working Classes*'. The fortnightly rental for our house at 7 Uplands Road was the sum of £1.9s.10d. A sub-section of the Housing Act, 1938, under the heading '*Overcrowding*' is printed on the inside cover:

> 'The permitted number for this dwelling is Eight persons. In counting
> the number of persons, each child under ten years of age counts as half
> a person, and a child of less than one year is not counted at all.'

So little Myrtle was entirely overlooked in their equation.

There was never the full complement of eight children under the one roof at any time. When I was born, my eldest brother, Donald, had already left to join the Army and my eldest sister, Mildred, had also moved on; though the circumstances were shrouded in mystery and never openly discussed. We rarely saw her and I used to imagine she had run away with a handsome sailor. 'Millie' was a talented student at school and both she and her teachers were disappointed when she was not permitted to further her studies. I learned later she married against our parents' wishes, but was to regret her hasty decision.

Some years passed before the third sibling, Beryl, was accepted for nursing training. It must have seemed like a golden opportunity for her – a chance not only to escape the drudgery of our family's Spartan existence, but to better her prospects. Young working-class girls then could never aspire to much more than a life in menial occupations if they did not marry.

I have my sister Beryl to thank for a first-hand account of those far off days. In 2006 after reading one of my travel journals, Beryl wrote and urged me to consider writing a story. I told her I might write about our family one day. I was well into this manuscript in 2011 when, in a search for material, I unearthed the forgotten notes that my sister had sent. I am so thankful she wrote to me then with her remembrances of life in Bristol as Beryl later moved to a care home as she battled dementia.

In reading Beryl's account, written in her 80th year in a shaky hand, I am struck by her positive take on our situation in Bristol, hardly mentioning our poor circumstances. Beryl seems to have cheerfully accepted her lot in life, maybe because everyone in our family's immediate circle would have been in the same situation. She even reports my brothers' suits were purchased from a well-known and very posh city store. Such extravagance surely could only have been made possible with the assistance of a benefactor from our Church.

Memories of 7 Uplands Road, Fishponds, Bristol – by Beryl Nason

Saturday Afternoons

Sometimes we had quite a treat. A tea-meeting held in a Brethren hall where in the interval, big trays laden with wonderful cakes were passed down the rows of people all sitting down in their Sunday best, we children all watching the mouth-watering cakes on their way and hoping the tray would not be empty by the time it reached us.

The ladies all wearing a hat and their hair in a 'bun' at the back. The little girls also dressed in their best clothes and wearing a hat – with their hair duly plaited and tied at the ends with a neat ribbon. Knee high socks and lisle stockings well worn at heel and carefully mended.

Sunday Mornings

The boys' shoes being cleaned and polished in the kitchen, then dressed in suits bought from Horn's Outfitters, the best shop for men in the city. The long march to The Meeting Room began – not a car in sight – just a few children playing on the deserted streets and pavements. Bibles being held tight. Home again to a cooked meal and occasionally to meet some German prisoners-of-war at tea-time.

Sunday Afternoons

'The Searchings' were brought out and some set questions answered looking up things in our Bibles. The Searchings was a small Magazine which always appeared at weekends. Dad would sit at the small pedal harmonium in the front room and play a few of his favourite hymns from the 'Golden Bells' Hymn Book.

Holidays

A visit to Weston-Super-Mare was quite an event, donkeys being ridden up and down the sand, crowded with children with buckets and spades making sandcastles. Vast stretches of mud could be seen if the tide was out but avoided as the quicksand was quite a dangerous place to walk. Weston-Super-Mare was a short train ride from Bristol.

Closer to home, within walking distance we would enjoy a picnic in the summer holidays at Eastville Park Estate or at Snuff Mills – a wood with a river running through and a lake where the boys would do a spot of 'pond dipping'.

War Time

Our family, minus John, David and Edward, who were evacuated to mid-Wales in Auntie Winnie's care, were all huddled in the back porch watching searchlights quaver in the sky over Bristol city – hoping bombs did not come any closer or we would need to go to the bottom of our garden and get into the Anderson's air raid shelter. I had not long been discharged from Winford Orthopaedic Hospital, Bristol where I was having treatment for curvature of the spine. Many patients were being discharged in order to make room for war casualties.

Mother was often busy in the allotment, cultivating peas, cabbages and potatoes to add to our meagre rations. We were allocated coupons for many foods, particularly meat and butter. Bread was a rather strange colour – greyish – not white. Bananas were non-existent. We did try 'whale meat balls', but once was enough. Hens kept in a run in the garden provided us with extra eggs, which had to be declared in the ration book.

An Uncle of ours kept a pig in a sty at the end of the lane by his house near Coventry – proving our rural roots! Uncle was such a kind and loving man, I always enjoyed a visit to his home. There was always food in plenty, cooked on the gas stove by Auntie. To entertain us, Uncle would often sit down at the piano and strum along with the lid of the piano raised for maximum effect.

Auntie Winnie used to send us wonderful parcels full of goodies and also carefully picked and wrapped primroses which gave me a great deal of pleasure.

Dad was exempt from being called up as he was working on an important job – driving 'Pool Petrol' lorries – during the war. One day Dad gave me a lift in a lorry and as we veered around a bend, my gas mask fell out of the door which had sprung open – there was very little traffic about and I was able to jump out and retrieve it safely.

Dad had strange 'food crazes' – once we were given nothing but dates to eat every day. I was so glad this craze didn't last long. There was a grocery shop near where we lived run by two lovely Christian ladies – they were very generous and we were often benefited by them from their cooked meat counter.

Growing Up

Bicycles and motorbikes were typically being repaired in the back garden by the boys. I remember having a ride on David's motorbike and lived to tell the tale. Then an ancient Austin 7 appeared parked outside – a door handle tied up with string – have a lift in it who dares!

One by one we 'fled the nest'. Donald went to Coventry where he joined the Fire Service and experienced the blitzes, Mildred got married, I began nursery nurse training at Downend Babies

Home, Bristol. John joined the RAF and went to Hong Kong as a technician. David 'joined up' and went to Egypt. Janet, Edward and Joy sailed away with Mother to join Dad who had gone on to Sydney to make a new life there.

2

Family History

I have scant details of the history of the early Nason and Beresford families. There are no documents of my forebears to guide me and scarcely any written information, apart from a genealogy chart prepared by a cousin some years ago. The compiling of elaborate family trees and discussing one's lineage wouldn't have occurred to anyone when I was growing up.

Except on rare occasions, my family did not trouble themselves with niceties such as posing for the staged studio images typical of that era and which are usually part and parcel of family history. When all you can think about is where your next meal is coming from, a collection of portraiture would be viewed as a scandalous waste of money. For that reason, I look on the few family photographs that have survived as precious.

That any documents or photographs were saved is a miracle, considering the circumstances of our family, governed by a religious cult whose teachings meant no great store was set on earthly history. I consider myself fortunate to have the few items that my father was left with on the breakup of his marriage, which I salvaged when I was his sole carer at the end of his days. In my mid-twenties when I walked out of the church, I walked out on my old life forever and the door was closed on any opportunity of reminiscing. Our family would have amassed a mountain of anecdotal evidence at least, denied to me because I turned my back on the one true flock.

My mother was born in Leamington Spa, Warwickshire, on 29th November 1900. From all accounts she had a sad upbringing. When she was only five, her mother died of TB (the dreaded 'consumption' as it was termed) shortly after giving birth to my Auntie Winnie. My grandfather, Herbert Beresford, later married one Emily Woolley and then a son, 'Bertie' completed the family. In 1905 the new stepmother would have done her best to care for the two little motherless girls, but my mother was always to regard her childhood as loveless.

The pattern of perceived adversity was to follow my mother throughout her life. The Nason family were God-fearing, hard-working farming folk but my mother clung to the notion that the Beresfords were more refined and a cut above a rural family. Both families belonged to Plymouth Brethren communities, where a social pecking order was firmly established. My mother and her generation never questioned the prevailing class system. Her apparent sense of 'marrying beneath her' came through to us children in no uncertain terms, much to the detriment of harmonious family relationships.

In later years, I was to watch the movie *Sons and Lovers*, a 1960 British film adaptation of the D H Lawrence novel, and marvel that it could portray so accurately the dysfunctional bondage that typified my mother and father's relationship. Despite this, that they loved each other was never in question.

When my father died in 1984, I learned from his death certificate that his place of birth was Pillerton, Warwickshire, England where he was born on 22nd November 1901. Only one photograph exists of my father from this era, taken around 1912, showing the Pillerton village schoolmaster and his charges staring fixedly at the camera. Even as a youngster and despite his comparatively short stature, from the look of determination on his face, you can tell you wouldn't want to mess with my father.

The place name 'Pillerton' was unknown to me and it was not until 1997, while visiting the UK, that I made the pilgrimage to where Dad was born. On a brilliantly clear and crisp autumn day in the Warwickshire countryside, it was quite emotional to find my father's birthplace. The adjoining villages of Pillerton Priors and Pillerton Hersey are picturesque rural communities, the graveyards full of tombstones with 'Nason' inscriptions. That fits in with hazy bits of family history that my forebears were farming folk – but in Stratford-on-Avon just seven miles along the old Roman Fosse Way from Pillerton, is a puzzling piece of the past.

On my travels in 1997, after the obligatory tourist stop at Anne Hathaway's cottage, I decided to step inside the Stratford church where William Shakespeare is buried, to see for myself a startling discovery made by a sister of mine a couple of years previously.

There on the wall, inches from the illustrious Bard's tomb, is an impressive plaque dedicated to the memory of *'John James Nason, Justice of the Peace, Thrice Mayor of this Ancient Borough, 30 years Churchwarden of this Collegiate Church. Died 29 April 1917, aged 84, Great-Grandson of Stephen Nason, Vicar of Stratford-upon-Avon, AD 1763-87'*. What a thrill to see the evidence of such notable namesakes.

My mother's only sister, our eccentric Auntie Winnie Beresford, bless her heart, looms large in family folklore. The story goes that one of my brothers, in a brave attempt to escape a local bully, used a dire threat: 'I've got an 'ammer at 'ome and an Auntie Win'! My sister Beryl mentions her kindness to us and her gifts of food parcels were legendary. These parcels included 'dripping', which with lashings of salt was quite palatable and went a long way towards saving us from starvation both during and after World War II.

The following anecdote written by my brother John underlines what an important part Auntie Winnie played in our lives:

'We children were most unkind to Auntie Winnie, as she could be what we would call a funny old stick, but looking back, she was so very good to us during the War. She was at one time head cook to Lord De L'Isle and Dudley at Penshurst Place in Kent. In 1940 when all children had to be evacuated from the large cities, she was head cook to a retired Major in a lovely big Manor House in mid Wales, and arranged for us to go there for safety. We had a wonderful time there in the country. I was the eldest *at that time and one day I led the others on a walk. I was so cocksure that I knew the way, and took one of my famous short cuts. Hours later a distracted Auntie Winnie and posse found us miles away, dinner gone cold and me in disgrace.'*

Unquestioned acceptance of the class stratification system in England was another given. If your station in life was working-class, that is where you stayed. It was as ingrained as your religion. My mother constantly referred to 'The Gentry' in reverential terms and through our Auntie Winnie, who had 'gone into service' as a teenager, we felt privileged to have an insight into another world.

Auntie sent us reams of cuttings from the social pages of newspapers featuring stories of her employers from the 'Upstairs/ Downstairs' realm she was part of. I could never watch an episode of the British TV series 'Downton Abbey' first screened in 2010, without thinking of my Auntie Winnie. In the 1940s, it seemed we were basking in the reflected glory of our Aunt who had risen through the ranks from Scullery Maid to achieve the pinnacle of her career – Head Cook in the homes of The Gentry. They weren't any ordinary parcels of dripping!

Auntie Winnie never got over the heartbreak when in the early 1960s my mother was forced to cut off any contact with her. Our fundamentalist religious group had by then commenced their descent into cult territory. My misguided mother held tenaciously to her unquestioned obedience to the sect's increasingly bizarre edicts until her deathbed, with many dire consequences.

I was particularly thankful to reconnect with my Auntie and her daughter Elizabeth in the 1970s after I had left the Exclusive Brethren. In recent years, I have become very close to my cousin and her husband, enjoying many happy times visiting them. My cousin inherited her mother's culinary skills and for many years she and her husband ran a guest house in Cwmbach, the Wye Valley, Wales. It was a gourmet experience staying there.

My father's first driver's licence, dated 1922 and issued in the County of Derby, has survived the years intact, despite his domestic upheavals and oceans traversed. It is a demonstration of my father's determined character that he obtained a licence at age 23 when he was not much older than the horseless carriage itself and aspiring to own one would have been the stuff of dreams.

Also saved are all the rent books from when my father and mother married in 1923 in Coventry until their final move from Bristol after the War. These books, now fragile with age, their columned pages filled in a spidery hand, open a little window of history for me on the years before I was born.

During this period, the rent rose from about 10 shillings a week to just over £1. No doubt the Public Housing authorities, as is the practice today, calculated a small percentage of income to arrive at a fair rental. In 1923 at each rent collection a stamp duty of 'tuppence' had to be paid in the form of actual stamps pasted into the book, over which the rent collector signed his authority to ensure they could not be re-used.

They are a mute testament to a typical family, like many thousands of their working-class brothers and sisters, battling against the odds during the worldwide depression of the early 1930s closely followed by the devastating Second World War.

The various addresses on the rent book covers, with such sanguine street names as Beech Tree, Elm Tree and Pine Tree Avenues mean nothing to me, but are poignant reminders of another life, and confirm my brother John's recollections which he sent to me for this story, of the family's constant moves mainly between Bristol and Coventry. My father continually tried his luck and started again at different locations – but the cycle of persistent poverty was never broken.

3

My Early Years

Memories of my early years in Bristol are hazy but I have a profound recollection of a moment of joy that brightened the daily grind of the Council house in Fishponds. One day, the postman's knock sent my mother scurrying to open the door while I hid in the hallway behind her skirts. Were my ears deceiving me? The brown paper parcel was addressed to me! Tensions were high as I tugged at the knotted string (yes, cutting string was sacrilegious), then finally I tore open the paper to reveal a beautifully dressed porcelain doll.

I had never seen anything so precious in my short life and when the realisation sank in that it was actually mine, I was overwhelmed with emotion. It was a gift from my blind Great Aunt Eliza Woolley who lived in Coventry. I'll always remember how I felt at that moment – there was only me and my doll in the world.

Other memories of those days are of sharing a bed with one or more siblings, and, depending on the climate, throwing another overcoat on the bed for warmth. In keeping with British tradition for the working classes, Friday night was bath night. In winter, ablutions for the three youngest children took place in a tin tub filled with hot water and placed in front of a blazing coal fire in the living room, where a huge blackened kettle forever bubbled on the swivel hob, thus achieving even further economy by not heating the freezing bathroom upstairs. This was one ritual where I did not get lucky. Being the youngest I scored the last of the bath water – a murky accumulation of the weekly grime of my older siblings.

Whichever way you view it, we lived on 'Struggle Street'. Should I ever want an aide memoire, I need only look at a small photograph taken when I was at Hillfields Park School in Bristol, showing my hair adorned in rags. Other little girls in my class may well have sported similar 'hair ribbons'. Using every last strip of material from a discarded garment exemplified the lengths the population went to in the drive for economy brought about by post-war scarcity.

'Gullible Girlie' was a prime target in my earliest school days. I well remember the horror of standing in line for my first compulsory school health checkup, while some older boys nearby took great delight in telling me a tale of the nurse retrieving their swallowed tongues with a big hook. By the time it was my turn to go in I was a quivering mess, jaws locked in terror, much to the bemusement of the nurse. The painless check-up was all over in five minutes, but my reaction was how lucky it was that, being a small girl, I didn't have to endure the torture that the bigger boys experienced. It never occurred to me they were conning me.

I have unwanted memories of some mealtimes at Fishponds, Bristol. An ominous silence often descended, if any of my brothers would squirm or snigger during the lengthy ritual prayer my father offered up to the good Lord for his bountiful gifts. Dad's 'Amen' would immediately be followed by the chilling words to the offender: 'You've had your dinner'. I can hear it as though it were yesterday. The boys knew better than to argue and would silently slink away.

The punishment of foregoing the evening meal was a far harsher penalty to a hungry lad than any of the 'back of the hairbrush' beatings dished out with monotonous regularity by my tyrannical father for perceived misdemeanours. I don't recall if we were then permitted to eat the extra servings going wanting as a consequence of bad behaviour. In fanciful moments, I like to dream our mother contrived to salvage a morsel from their plates to give them when my father wasn't looking.

From all accounts, food or lack thereof, does seem to be an overriding theme. My older siblings have told me about lining up for a gruel-like broth available at the school for poor families. But the worst I remember was the semolina. I was put off semolina for life after my father somewhat mysteriously produced a whole sack of the stuff, which my mother proceeded to serve ad nauseum, albeit in various disguises, until every grain had been used.

I grew up with food rationing coupons and meagre meals; watching my mother many times as she carefully divided a boiled egg to share with my brother or sister. Fresh fruit and vegetables were seldom seen. The small garden allotments traditionally situated at the rear of British council houses represented a lifeline and were hoed and planted with no respite for lying fallow. The history of Allotments in the UK goes back over a thousand years. In 1943, the year I was born, the wartime 'Dig for Victory' crusade was at its height and allotment numbers peaked at 1,400,000. A recent upsurge of interest in home grown food crops has meant allotments in the UK are once again in high demand.

At a tender age I could recite one of my mother's many maxims on cue:

'Oh, do not throw upon the ground
The crust you cannot eat
For many a little child would think it just a treat
For wilful waste brings woeful want
And I may live to say
Oh, how I wish I had that crust that once I threw away.

You never shake off these notions when you learn them at such an impressionable age, and to this day I cannot bring myself to throw away food leftovers until they have been stored in the fridge for 24 hours at least.

The food shortage persisted, but in post-War Britain the whole nation was in the same boat, so we felt no different from anyone else. My mother did her utmost to relieve the monotony of those dreary times by insisting we 'pack a picnic' on Saturdays when weather permitted and traipse off by bus and foot to various local 'beauty spots'.

One such place was called Snuff Mills, also mentioned in my sister Beryl's account and I too have a pleasant memory of bluebells in profusion and sweet smelling grass. Snuff Mills is a park in the Stapleton area of north Bristol, purchased in 1926 by the Corporation of Bristol as "a pleasure walk for citizens of Bristol" and restored in the 1980s by the Fishponds Local History Society. Today, Snuff Mills is still a popular site for locals and visitors who come to enjoy the tranquility and natural surroundings.

Memories of my early years are coloured with the consequences of the evangelical zeal of Christian fundamentalism. Whilst I was too young for the whistling bombs and air raid sirens to emotionally scar me, slowly but surely the idea of the Devil getting me if I sinned became well established.

I vividly remember the thunder and lightning that accompanied a sudden storm late one afternoon, which my mother pronounced was God's punishment on sinners. Not just any sinners – to be exact it was the Council maintenance workers who had been in our house that day. Goodness knows how they had offended my mother's puritanical sensitivities, but to my devoutly God-fearing mother they were sinners and the thunderstorm was proof positive that God was speaking to their souls.

As the thunder crashed overhead and I shivered with fright in the arms of my sister Janet, who did her best to soothe my fears, my mother's 'comforting' advice was to remind me that so long as I didn't sin I need never dread the wrath of God. Being an impressionable child, it's no wonder this left me with a life-long terror of thunder storms.

The prospect of incurring God's wrath by way of a lightning strike, (which much later morphed into a fear of flying) was further entrenched in my teenage years in Australia, when the preachers of fire and brimstone would quote the Bible in thunderous tones from the pulpit: 'God commandeth the lightning where it should strike'. They tenaciously clung to the conviction if they frightened the 'bejesus' out of the flock, we would be saved from the torments of hell. To this day, I take obsessive precautions to ensure I am not caught out in a thunder storm but luckily, popping a little pill works wonders for air travel.

We children were left to our own devices and made our own entertainment, mostly innocent fun. On one memorable occasion however, a childish game of hide and seek with my cousin Elizabeth who was visiting us from Wales, came to a sticky end when I snatched too eagerly at a makeshift drape. As a consequence the house brick precariously holding the curtain came crashing down squarely on my head. I frightened my small cousin half out of her wits by promptly following the brick to the ground and lying motionless beside it.

My mother deemed a dash to the local Southmead Hospital would be prudent. We must have looked a curious sight as I was hustled up the street to the bus stop, with my mother firmly holding a moistened towel on my head. I still remember being nearly suffocated by the stiffly starched uniform of the casualty ward nurse who clamped a large rubber sheet over my head while a doctor stitched up the nasty wound. They then sent me packing with stern words to be more careful in future. This little accident has come in handy over the years to laugh off any temporary lapses in sanity I might display.

4

My Father's Emigration

Lack of worldly wealth did not equate with lack of guts and determination on my father's part. During the war years in Bristol, his employment with a petroleum company necessitated the dangerous undertaking of driving fully laden petrol tankers from the Avonmouth Docks to the Filton military airfield on the outskirts of Bristol.

One of my earliest memories is of being lifted up to sit with my father behind the wheel of one of these massive vehicles - what a thrill for a tiny child. By the time he left England in 1952, he had improved his lot and was a 'semi-skilled fitter' for the Bristol Aeroplane Company at Filton.

My hand is trembling and tears are threatening now, as I read one of the testimonials he received in 1950 in his quest to migrate to Australia. The letter, yellowed with age, is addressed to The Chief Migration Officer, Australia House in London. In typical British understatement, it reads:

> 'Mr Nason worked for the Power Petroleum Board, Cardiff as a Driver for five years, 1943 to 1948. During that time he gave every satisfaction . . . etc.etc. His work was carried out frequently under most arduous conditions, very considerable disturbance being created by bombing.'

Before we leave recollections of my father and the war years, one vivid memory stands out above the rest. The unrelated combination of my father belonging to a religious sect and also being a weekend coach driver, resulted in the not inconsiderable feat of him getting permission to regularly commandeer a coach on Sunday evenings. He drove to the prisoner-of-war camp on the outskirts of Bristol and collected as many of the poor souls as wished to come with him to church. They listened to a sermon of the Lord preached at them in a foreign tongue and Dad then drove them back again.

My sister Beryl's account also mentioned these prisoners-of-war. We enjoyed a unique and cordial association with these sad German soldiers over quite a period of time – sufficient to learn a smattering of the language and for my father to be presented with a treasured 1888 edition of Martin Luther's translation of *Die Bibel*[1], which is still in my possession.

I was allowed to accompany my father on these evangelical missions fairly frequently. One such occasion was around Christmas time and the crunching noise of the prisoners' boots as they left the coach and marched along the frosty paths to their sleeping quarters and the haunting sound of their guttural voices united in singing a Christmas carol in German, left such an indelible impression on me, my skin has goose bumps now as I write. I need only close my eyes to hear the refrain *'Stille Nacht, heilige Nacht'* stirring the still night air.

The wheels of fate were inexorably turning, with our father planning the family's migration to Australia, a country that, to my small mind, was as far off as another planet. No way could I have even found it on a map. Indisputably, my father had a propensity to 'up sticks' and relocate, whether on a whim or as a result of his frequent quarrels with the Brethren hierarchy is anyone's guess.

The Government campaign to populate Australia with sterling British stock was at its height in the post-war era. My father would have been lured by the prominently displayed Australia House posters, extolling the virtues of living in Australia. Even at 52, with

---

1   Die Bible: The Luther Bible is a German language Bible translation from Hebrew and ancient Greek by Martin Luther. The New Testament was first published in 1522, and the complete Bible in 1534.

virtually no financial or family backup, the prospect of wiping the slate clean and starting a new life on the other side of the world, proved irresistible to my father.

My father's ambitious plan to leave England in 1952 and send for his wife and children to join him in Australia one year later, was viewed by our close-knit religious community as a hazardous undertaking. Worse still, it was flying perilously close to flouting God's pre-ordained path for our family – but nothing was going to stop my Dad playing his cards and taking his chances on winning.

By then, five of my siblings had flown the coop. Eldest brother Donald demobbed from the Army and married, eldest sister Mildred married with three young children, next sister Beryl employed as a nurse away from home, next brother John in the Air Force and shortly to be married and lastly, brother David scheduled to be called up for National Service duty, from where he would follow us to Australia. Only Janet, Edward and little Girlie-Joy were still at home. From eight to three dependent children in a less than a decade left my father free to pursue his dream of emigration.

The testimonials from his employers to the Australian Migration Office served their purpose and Dad eventually received his passport and emigration papers. There was another item he secured which he would have prized more highly than any government-issued official document. This was the 'Letter of Commendation' from the local Brethren church, without which seal of approval, no one in the Exclusive Brethren community world-wide was permitted to change domicile to even another part of the country, let alone overseas.

The original curiously worded letter is dated February 1952 from the Briar Way Meeting, Fishponds, Bristol, addressed to 'The Saints, Sydney, Australia' and counter-signed by two 'Brothers in Christ' Messrs Carron and Chapman. God's passport gave my father the green light to escape his deprived existence in England. He could not have foreseen how despicably these same self-styled 'Saints' would treat him in the twilight of his life.

In the latter days of his life, my poor deluded father repeated the cycle of selling up and moving on. He undertook several voyages across the globe and back, starting afresh in the Bristol area, then returning to Australia, in his fruitless search for peace – a legacy of the cruel doctrines of the EB, in particular their inhumane practice of separating even husband and wife if one partner fell afoul of the regime. In the 1970s Dad was excommunicated for his temerity to dispute the world leader and consequently he lost his wife of 60 years to the church.

He died in Sydney some years later, a broken-hearted, lonely man. My Dad had his faults, an explosive temper being one of them, but notwithstanding his rantings, he loved my mother. We children could attest to his strict observance of the Bible principle 'spare the rod and spoil the child', but he never laid a finger on my mother.

In post-war Bristol, the perishingly cold conditions in the Council houses were legendary and could well be one of the reasons my Dad yearned for warmer climes. I clearly remember the constant mantra to his long-suffering wife, 'No more dead fingers in Australia'. Yet this promise of a better life sorely tested my mother's resilience as she faced the daunting prospect of leaving half her family and the only life she had ever known many thousands of miles behind. It must have been some small consolation to her that Australia was one of the 'pink' bits in our World Atlas.

One misty and miserable winter's day in February 1952, a poignant scene was played out on a cold, grey platform at Temple Meads Railway Station in Bristol. The farewell to my father, who was on his way by train to join the *SS Mooltan* departing from Tilbury Docks, London as a fare paying passenger to Australia, was a significant milestone in the chain of events that was to irrevocably change the fate of our family.

True to form, I skylarked with my brother, oblivious to any sense of occasion, but I did manage to stand still long enough to wave goodbye to my father until all we could see was a distant outstretched hand disappearing into the enveloping fog. As my mother sought traditional British comfort from a cup of tea in the railway tearooms, to my shame, I remember being sufficiently insensitive to pester her as to why she was crying.

The routine of my life did not noticeably change with the departure of my father, but it would have been a major upheaval for my mother. Despite his best intentions, my father could only leave a paltry sum in a bank account to cover our expenses. While I have no way of confirming the figure, family hearsay at the time put the amount at £100. With no guarantee when our Dad would make enough money to send any back to England, my mother must have had nightmares over how long she would have to eke out that one hundred pounds. Despite limited employment prospects, she secured a part-time office job at a nearby factory to supplement the family income and achieved the feat of keeping the wolf (or the bailiff!) from the door for the duration.

For many years, a battered tea caddy on the sideboard had been the sole receptacle for our everyday expenditure. The small amount earmarked from my father's pay packet for housekeeping was placed in the tin and had to last my mother an entire week or longer. I have memories of mother lifting the lid only to find the caddy empty.

Left to her own devices, out went the tea caddy, my mother reasoning if she was now in charge of family finances, she did not want to be reminded of the dreaded housekeeping tin. Were we eligible for any social welfare benefits to assist us in those dark days? I have no idea.

After my father's departure, wanting to make the most of what little time she had left in England, my mother took me with her on a farewell journey to family and friends around Coventry and Birmingham where she grew up. I don't know why my sister and brother still living at home didn't feature in this visit, but I was more than happy to have my mother to myself.

I have fond memories of this grand goodbye tour. I was only nine and had rarely seen any of these relatives before. It seemed to my small mind they 'killed the fatted calf' many times over in honour of our visit. It was the first time in my life I had experienced an abundance of food and being too full to eat. I recall the mortification of having to decline a delicious looking pudding, desperately worried

I was letting my mother down by appearing to be ungrateful - to say nothing of the sinfulness of rejecting God's bountiful provisions.

My mother's leave-taking visit meant a great deal to our relatives and friends and they were full of talk about our impending departure to the ends of the earth. My mother mastered the art of a diplomatic response to the continual question 'Are you looking forward to going to Australia?', to which she steadfastly replied: 'Well, in a way'. Poor soul - saying 'Yes' would reflect badly on the family and friends we were leaving behind, and saying 'No' - saints preserve us - what if my father got wind of it!

A Coventry relative who deserves special mention is my father's brother. I was terrified of visiting his house as my Uncle seemed a gruff old man to me and to cap it off, had the singular peculiarity to us city kids, of keeping a pig in his back yard. My mother did nothing to dispel fears of my uncle, almost encouraging my cringing behind her skirts. My Aunt was a kindly, cheery soul yet she seemed treated with disdain by my mother, who apparently believed Aunt was of Romany Gypsy descent. Another example of misguided bigotry - in my opinion to lay claim to Romany Gypsy ancestry adds an enviable element of mystique to family folklore.

My sister Beryl put quite a different slant on my Uncle, describing him as a cheery, kindly man, who liked nothing better than strumming a tune on his well worn 'Joanna' as he termed his piano. In later years, I was able to rekindle the association with the Nason cousins in this family when I took my young son to visit them in Coventry. They were charming, hospitable and welcoming. Any past misunderstandings were laid to rest.

Given her life's circumstances, it is small wonder my mother's hair became prematurely white. Lack of dental care, as well as the frightful diet she endured, also caused the loss of all her teeth. There was no money to replace them, so her gums must have been rock solid before some kindly elder in our church took pity on my mother and donated the cost of a replacement set of teeth. What a relief to our family when the ghastly gummy look was gone.

Nothing could alter the fact that the years had not treated my mother kindly. My mother suffered motion sickness to such a degree, I swear she would even throw up on the local bus going to the shops. When we were returning by coach from Coventry to Bristol at the end of our farewell tour of the relatives, we were not far along the road from Coventry, when mother had to lurch from her seat, get the driver to stop the coach, while she staggered off to heave her heart out at the roadside.

The acute embarrassment of it all got to me, and I started to cry with silent tears rolling down my cheeks. A well meaning fellow passenger came and put her arms around me and said 'Don't worry, Granny will be OK'. She got more than she bargained for when my tears turned to sobbing wails at the shame of my mother being mistaken for my Grandmother.

5

Farewell to England

Despite, or could it have been because of, the absence of my father, there seemed an improvement in our circumstances.

I scored a 'hand-me-down' handbag to call my own. On its first outing, I remember skipping happily down the road to church (a considerable change from the usual dragging of feet), dressed in my 'Sunday best' and swinging my handbag, until my brother Edward brought me down to earth by telling me sharply to stop showing off.

I even became the proud owner of a scooter – no matter that it sported a touch-up paint job and had been reconstructed by the combined efforts of my brothers.

The last family Christmas before we left England was the only Christmas I can remember with no shortage of food and gifts – a rare treat. Brother John was on home leave from Hong Kong, dashing in his Air Force uniform and laden with presents for the family, strangely the most memorable being a pair of 15-denier nylon stockings for my sister, who was totally overwhelmed.

This was 1952 and I was not to experience another such festive Christmas occasion until 20 years later, when I was freed at last from the bonds of Exclusive Brethrenism who held that Christmas be viewed as a Pagan festival. A group of young 'Ten-pound Poms' who were my friends near where I was flatting at Neutral Bay in

Sydney, cooked up a storm and celebrated with all the trimmings. We dubbed it the 'Orphans Christmas' each of us being separated from our immediate families – my friends by the tyranny of distance and me by the tyranny of bigotry.

As a new year opened in 1953, a chapter closed on the Nason family's life in England. The crucial letter arrived from Australia and the die was cast. My father had found work and lodgings for us so we were booked to leave the country on the 28th of January. My mother packed up the last of our worldly possessions, bade her sad farewells to the children and grandchildren who she was, for all intents and purposes, leaving behind forever. With the three youngest of her brood she stoically set off to join her husband in the furthermost corner on the globe.

In the weeks before our departure, we had one last visit to my sister Mildred and her family in Devizes. I felt very close to them, especially my eldest nephew was only four years younger than me and my nieces were dear little toddlers. As Devizes was not far from Stonehenge, we went there, clambering over the stones and thoroughly disrespecting the sacredness of the site. There was no such thing as a cordoned-off area at this historic monument in those days.

My eldest brother, Donald and his wife Doris, also had the foresight to organise an overnight trip to London for us, so at least we could say we had been to London to see the Queen before we left England forever. I only vaguely recollect this important flying visit, Buckingham Palace and Madame Tussaud's Waxworks being two memories, along with everyone huddled together, sleeping in the car by the roadside overnight. The luxury of paid accommodation in London was out of the question.

In our jet setting age, a visit to the Colonies Down Under is a mere commonplace – the journey measured in hours, and achieved with a minimum of fuss to mind or body. In the England of my childhood, I vividly remember a rare visit by my Uncle and Aunt from Liverpool to our house in Bristol, being accompanied with all the fanfare of aliens from another planet.

Oh, the fuss as they arrived in their unpretentious Austin sedan, helping them inside for the reviving cup of tea which was considered essential after surviving such a long and arduous journey – all 130 miles of it! This being the prevailing sentiment of the time, no wonder my mother viewed her impending journey to Australia, a distance of some 10,500 miles an awesome undertaking which filled her with trepidation.

At last, on a bleak winter's day at the end of January 1953, all my siblings came to Southampton to witness our exodus on a migrant ship aptly named the SS *New Australia*.

As with my father's departure just one year previously, I'm sure I was oblivious to the import of the occasion, but I do treasure the slightly out-of-focus snapshot capturing the scene. It was the only time in the entire history of our family that all eight children were to be in the one place together – it must have been an extraordinarily emotional moment for my mother. We took other 'jolly' photos. My mother recalled later that we needed any distraction to 'pass off the parting' as she put it.

The boarding formalities were a blur to me, then suddenly there we were on deck, straining to catch a last fleeting glimpse of our loved ones and excitedly reaching for the flying streamers. The *New Australia* blasted its mighty foghorn, the streamers snapped and floated in the breeze, the gap widened between sea and shore and the ship's bells signalled full steam ahead to transport us across the vast oceans on our journey to a new life.

Photos Part 1

Hilda Nason with her six youngest children, 1943;
Beryl, John, David, Janet, Edward and baby Myrtle Joy

Mother and Father

Joseph Edgar Nason, Back Row, 2nd from left. Pillerton, circa 1912

Joy School photo Aged 6

L to R Back row: Edward, Donald, John, David
Front row: Mildred, Janet, Mother, Joy, Beryl

The SS New Australia departing Southampton, January 1953

PART 2
1953 to 1968

6

My Journey to Australia

The next part of my journey begins on the Shaw Savill & Albion Company's vessel *New Australia*, my home for just over four weeks from 28th January to 1st March, 1953. What tumult of emotion must have filled every heart, from the gut-wrenching anguish of farewell to the eager anticipation of a new future, as my family, along with 1,580 fellow migrants, embarked on this voyage. Here was the chance to make a fresh start, to seize the opportunity of playing a winning hand. I wonder how many in this hodgepodge of British citizenry made a success of their life as New Australians?

On our passenger list was a group of 'orphans' sent to Australia by the Fairbridge Society - you'd have to say they'd been dealt a lousy hand of cards so far. The children were part of a child migration scheme made infamous years later as the 'Leaving of Liverpool' kids. Many were not orphans, yet were dispatched without the knowledge or permission of their parents. In a shipboard postcard sent *en route* to her own little grandchildren left behind in the UK, my mother mentioned that she'd talked to some of them. No doubt she had particular empathy for their heartrending plight, cast adrift and left in the hands of fate.

Peter Plowman's 2006 publication *'Australian Migrant Ships 1946 to 1977'* gives an insight into the history of the *'New Australia'* and the prevailing political policies of the post war era. The immigration debate raging in Australia then aroused similar passions to those of today, the parochial element of the population always viewing newcomers as interlopers.

Plowman writes that in 1945, Arthur Calwell was appointed Minister for the newly created Department of Immigration and he coined the famous slogan 'populate or perish'. In his first speech to Parliament as Minister, Calwell launched the government's Immigration Policy, in which he emphasised the security aspect of immigration as well as the economic advantages:

> 'We cannot continue to hold our island continent for ourselves and our descendants unless we greatly increase our numbers. We are but seven million people and we hold three million square miles of this earth's surface. Our first requirement is additional population for reasons of defence and for the fullest expansion of our economy.'[2]

What the government wanted was an intake of 70,000 migrants a year and it was hoped all of them would come from Britain. Susan Chenery in her article 'Stolen Childhoods' in the Sydney Sun Herald on 12 June 2011 wrote:

> 'When bleak post-war Britain answered Australia's call for "good white British stock" to build its population, it saw an opportunity to empty overflowing institutions of the innocent victims of poverty, illegitimacy and broken homes.'[3]

To cope with the transport of this human tide, the government came up with a scheme to convert old passenger liners into a flotilla of migrant vessels. The *New Australia* was considered an unusual looking vessel, with austere accommodation but it had originally been one of the most luxurious liners in the world. Launched as the *Monarch of Bermuda* in 1931, its sister ship was the *Queen of*

---

2   The SS New Australia departing Southampton, January 1953
3   Susan Chenery, 2011, 'Stolen Childhoods', Sydney Sun Herald, 12 June

Bermuda and the pair were known as the 'millionaire's ships' during the 1930s. In 1939, the *Monarch* was requisitioned by the British Government as a troopship, the luxury fittings were removed and quarters for 1,385 men installed.

In 1947, during yet another refit, the once stately *Monarch of Bermuda* was gutted by fire and the hulk towed away to Rosyth Dockyard in Scotland. At any other time, it would have been sold for scrap. However, passenger ships were in short supply to provide Australia with its huge influx of migrants, so it was rebuilt, the cost being shared equally by the British and Australian governments. It was renamed the *New Australia* and placed under the management of Shaw Savill Lines.

Accommodation for 1,600 persons was installed, in mainly 6-berth cabins with no air conditioning. All cabins contained two-tier metal bunks and wardrobes, but no washbasins. Instead, they had a large number of communal facilities. So, from being one of the most luxurious liners ever built, it was now the epitome of austerity. From early 1950, it carried thousands of British migrants to Australia.

Immediately after my voyage, the *New Australia* entered a new phase of her history and was pressed into service as a troop carrier. On 5th March 1953, less than a week after we disembarked in Sydney, the men of the 2nd Battalion Royal Australian Regiment, boarded the ship to be taken to Korea. The *New Australia* then variously served as either a troop or migrant carrier for the remainder of her working life, before eventually being sold to Spanish ship-breakers in 1966.

I remember sleeping accommodation for the sexes being strictly segregated on the *New Australia*, families being separated on embarkation – cabins for fathers and sons to the left please, mothers and daughters to the right! Couples forced to sleep apart considered themselves lucky if they were allocated a cabin with someone empathetic. A bit of planning and a wink and a nudge meant a mother would disappear with her daughters and be discreetly occupied elsewhere, so a husband and wife could have some privacy. Despite her Victorian values and religious fundamentalism, my mother was a compassionate soul and did the right thing by the young family whose lot it was to share our cabin. At the time, I was blissfully unaware that the whispered negotiations and mysterious knocks at the door heralded a conjugal visit.

Much to my chagrin, my mother did her very best to uphold our religious observances throughout the voyage – my embarrassment at her insistence on mumbling 'grace' at mealtimes, being nothing compared to my fit of pique when, on our first Sunday in the tropics, we were denied the simple pleasure of purchasing an ice cream from the ship's shop. This system of belief, where it was considered a sin to enter a shop on the Sabbath (well, Sunday equated with the Sabbath in the Christian creed), proved impossible for my parents to let go of for their entire lifetime.

Even when I visited my father at the end of his days, in a nursing home, excommunicated from the church that had taught him the beliefs he clung to, we took a walk around the block one hot weekend, and nothing would persuade him to yield to the temptation of entering the corner store to buy an ice cream on a Sunday.

My research tells me that on embarkation, each family received a little yellow leaflet, outlining our planned route from Southhampton, through the Suez Canal, along the coast of East Africa, into the harbour of Colombo, Ceylon and on to Western Australia. I have no memory of seeing the leaflet, but how positively exotic the itinerary must have seemed to us working-class Britishers. The brochure listed in detail the countries and points of interest that were viewed from the *New Australia* with the ports of call being Aden, Colombo, Fremantle, Melbourne and Sydney.

Tales of rough seas around the Bay of Biscay were legendary, and as the itinerary listed this right after the English Channel, I am instantly reminded of my mother succumbing to seasickness, which never left her until our first night on dry land at the end of the voyage. I clearly recall the ghastly heat on the lower decks, with the pervading stench of vomit. The martyr in my mother, or the British tradition of a stiff upper lip, meant she endured the suffering rather than choose the sensible option of taking motion sickness pills.

Despite this, Peter Plowman's description of the 'epitome of austerity' obviously depends on your point of view. To my small mind, conditions on the *New Australia* were anything but austere - particularly the abundance of food. A startling side effect for me however was caused by the over-supply of Arnott's Assorted Cream biscuits, seemingly at every meal sitting. You could scoop up handfuls of these sickly sweet little numbers and with me not knowing when enough was enough, a classic case of aversion therapy resulted. Since that epic voyage I have never again been able to stomach an Arnott's cream biscuit.

Other snippets of our journey surface, a fancy-dress parade being one. Our family wouldn't dream of joining in the worldly pleasure of 'dressing up', but I do remember the excitement of watching the parade. One creative family marched along covered in the ship's all too familiar 'vomit receptacles', on which they had painted pictures of swooping birds. Their sign read: 'The Return of the Swallow' - clever!

During the voyage my nomenclature wasn't the only thing to undergo a change on this journey - my precious teddy bear's true identity was also cruelly revealed. My mother had allowed me to take my bedraggled and more or less hairless bear aboard the boat, believing this small tangible comfort would outweigh the taunts of my older siblings that a child of almost 10 should need a toy to take to bed.

My brother decided the time had come to point out that my bear was in fact a rabbit (Don't you know anything - ever seen a bear with long ears and whiskers?). Apart from the fact that I never forgave him, you get the gist that my life's confusion continued.

I was not the only family member teased on this voyage. My sister Janet, aged 17, developed a crush on a handsome young Quartermaster and we taunted her mercilessly. In my search for material to write my story, I found in my father's possessions, a battered photograph album which used to belong to my sister. There are pages of inscriptions written in my sister's hand but most of the photos had been removed except for a tiny black and white one of the Quartermaster on the SS *New Australia*. It was a heart-warming memory - I'm glad he posed for my sister's camera; it meant a lot to her to have that photograph.

I also well recall the *New Australia* slowly negotiating the narrow Suez Canal. My mother seized upon this chance for a history lesson to impress on her three youngest children how privileged we were to behold the Biblical lands of the Pharaohs. And there was Mount Sinai in the distance – my mother could not pass up this heaven-sent opportunity to remind us of the story of Moses and the Ten Commandments!

While the itinerary leaflet stated 'passengers can go ashore at Aden', by the time we got there, some sort of uprising or other prevented anyone leaving the ship but we had all the excitement we needed, leaning over the deck and watching the little launches wallowing in the waves far below. How envious we were of families with sufficient spare cash who could haggle with the foreign-looking vendors in turbans, yelling out the prices of their bargains to us from the water. The curiosity was fever pitch as purchases were hauled aboard in baskets by pulling frantically on ropes. Goodness knows how they were attached, it was way too complicated for me to work out.

Then on to Ceylon – where, through the wondrous workings of God in this far-flung outpost of the British Empire, an ancient lady, one Mrs P, actually belonged to the Exclusive Brethren flock! With God's passport (the magical 'Letter of Commendation' to any Saints gathered worldwide), we had entrée to a mysterious tropical paradise, the home of this 'Saint' in Colombo.

All I can remember is the fierce heat and humidity and having to be on my best behaviour for at least an hour or more, while we were entertained in this alien environment. For once, we became the envy of our fellow passengers by actually going ashore in one of the ship's motor launches during this brief port stop to take up this unlikely dinner invitation. One of the few perks of being an EB!

Fremantle was next, our first steps on Australian soil – God's passport ensuring we were welcomed for the day into the bosom of the Brethren at Stirling Street, Perth. Warmth pervades my memories – from the oppressive heat in the church hall to the warm feeling of being among our own kind once more.

7

The Wonders of Our New Home

Next stop was Sydney, our final destination, where my father awaited us. The itinerary says we docked at Melbourne, but migrant ships were sometimes known to skip ports and maybe this happened in 1953 as I have no memory of stopping between Perth and Sydney.

Sunday 1st March, 1953 dawned bright and clear and while the *New Australia* hove to outside the Heads to await the pilot boat, feverish activity and excitement was the order of the day below decks. Families queued up in the public areas before daylight to complete the necessary disembarkation formalities. The queues moved forward at snail's pace, with children darting from their mother's side to race up on deck to report if the famous Sydney Harbour Bridge had yet appeared on the horizon.

The tension and impatience during this interminable bureaucratic procedure was palpable. The adults couldn't leave the queue and if we docked before all the wretched forms had been signed, they'd miss out on seeing the Harbour and the Bridge as well. Many passengers knew that on landing they were to be whisked away by train to remote destinations in country New South Wales with not much chance of returning to Sydney.

Finally, patience was rewarded with our first glimpse of the Harbour Bridge - what an impressive, unforgettable sight, a symbol of strength and stability if ever there was one for this ship's cargo of human flotsam and jetsam still in recovery mode from World War II.

At last the *New Australia* manoeuvred into position at Pyrmont Wharf, and there we were on deck, niftily securing a spot between some posts so our father waiting on shore could pick us out more easily. Our arms nearly dropped off from waving once we spotted each other and my father had a camera at the ready to capture the moment. Once the ropes were secured, Dad wasted no time racing up the gangplank to greet us. The long separation was over. We faced the prospect of a brighter future with hope in our hearts.

The drive from Pyrmont to our new abode in suburban Enfield passed in a blur but I clearly remember being blissfully happy when I awoke the following morning to the first day of my new life in Australia.

I was up with the sparrows, a habit I have had all my life, the glorious sun pouring through the windows beckoning me outside. I stood in the garden, gazing around at my strange surroundings, firmly believing our temporary lodgings in Enfield, were akin to paradise. I ran back into the bedroom I shared with my sister and shook her awake, saying excitedly 'Isn't it lovely, Jan?' But I'm sure my poor sister did not quite share my enthusiasm at this ungodly hour.

That day was a Monday and we went *en famille* to the local shops. The sight of our first Australian butcher with an array of various cuts of meat displayed in the gleaming front window was so overwhelming; the notion that we had indeed reached the Promised Land was further fixed into my impressionable mind. Our butcher's shop in England had sawdust floors and empty windows, the butcher disappearing somewhere into the bowels of the backrooms when you asked for perhaps a pound of sausages.

Our initial lodgings in Enfield were with a Brethren family – one Mr Roy and his daughter. Mr Roy was a rough diamond who hailed from Tasmania and I'm sure he deliberately alienated himself from my mother with his uncouth manners, especially his practice of boiling a pot of potatoes and pumpkin, mashing them together and eating forkfuls of said mash straight from the pot. Fresh from

England, where pumpkin was considered pig's food, this was another thorn in my mother's side. Mr Roy had a propensity to exaggeration – why, even the apples in Tasmania were as big as coconuts according to him.

Mr Roy didn't exactly endear himself to me either; he took great delight in telling terrifying tales of storms he had witnessed in Tasmanian bushland where lightning ripped the bark off trees. With my ingrained fear of thunderstorms, I made up my mind on the spot never to visit Tasmania and run the risk of being struck by lightning, thank you very much.

It was to be the year 2000 before I eventually went to Tasmania, on a weekend trip with my husband Pete. By then, the years had erased any memory of the erstwhile Mr Roy and bark-shredding thunderstorms were the last thing on my mind.

I don't know if Sydney was in the grip of a heat wave when we arrived in 1953 but we little English flowers suffered from the heat. I was bowled over by it, so much so my mother took pity on me and let me acclimatise at home for a few days before packing me off to the local school. That was another black mark we gave to the much maligned Mr Roy; he couldn't stop himself warning us with monotonous regularity that if we thought it was hot in March, heaven help us when the real heat started come December.

What a culture shock awaited me at Enfield Primary, which was my place of learning for two years. Many of the boys went to school barefoot; attempts to encourage them to take school seriously enough to at least turn up in shoes being met with strong resistance. The winds of change were in the air however, and by the time I left Enfield School, bare feet were in a minority. Lukewarm bottled milk at recess and weekly swimming lessons were two other novel experiences I quickly became accustomed to.

Less than three months after our arrival it was my 10th birthday – what a far cry from any of my previous anniversaries. My father had hidden exactly ten Cadbury's Milk Chocolate bars around the house and garden and I have joyful memories of the search until all ten were found. Certain domestic tensions behind the event were lost on me – I later realised my mother could hardly bear the extravagance after so many poverty-stricken years in England but my father had a point to prove.

The strict religiosity of my family ensured two embarrassing incidents happened to me at Enfield Primary School. There was a popular radio quiz show in Sydney hosted by Jack Davey and it was considered an honour to be chosen to participate in the children's segment. I must have shown precocious proclivities because not long after my arrival, my teacher proudly announced my name as a candidate. Now came the stumbling block. Parental permission was required, which was dismissed out of hand – no way would a little Brethren girl be tainted by anything to do with the evils of radio.

Then at the end of the year, I was thrilled to be given a bit part as an angel in the school nativity play (it was out of the question that I'd be Mother Mary but that bothered me not one jot). For some reason, official permission to take part was not sought from my family. I relished the thrilling experience of flitting around on stage with my classmates. At the end of the night, my father came backstage to collect me. Oh, the humiliation of having my 'make-up' scrubbed off by my furious father, telling me in front of my fellow little angels that the lipstick could be removed from my lips but it could never be removed from my conscience.

Embarrassing situations continued on the home front too. Mr Roy's back garden was enormous and included a large chicken run. There was an arrangement whereby a next-door neighbour shared the chook management and the eggs. One day I was helping collect the eggs when an aggressive rooster suddenly leapt upon a nice plump hen, with much ensuing squawking and flying feathers. To me the hen was in deadly peril, so I shouted to our neighbour at the top of my voice: 'Come quickly. Please stop these chooks fighting'. A muttered 'They're not fighting' was his perplexing reply. I was left in the dark, with the uneasy feeling I had said something wrong which the grown-ups wouldn't explain to me.

My tendency to confusion went hand in hand with a good dose of gullibility and naivety as well, not helped by my family's arcane notions that discussing any topic remotely connected with the human body was taboo. I was not far off puberty before the realisation dawned on me that a woman has two breasts, and that the single breast my mother had as a result of her mastectomy was not where babies came from. Not so incredible when you consider the only evidence I had to go on was my own, skinny, late-developing body. Any adult females, apart from my mother that I ever came in close contact with, clung to Victorian notions and contorted under roomy outer garments to change from daywear to nightwear and vice-versa without a centimetre of flesh ever being revealed to my curious eyes.

There was ample opportunity for enlightenment. Not long after my arrival in Australia, I was grocery shopping with my mother when my stage-whispered observation that a lady walking by must be a greedy piggy to have such a bulging tummy, was merely shushed. Sex talk was strictly forbidden in our household, including any basic 'birds and bees' information. So that evening at mealtime when I earnestly recounted the story, I was bewildered by the embarrassed silence around the table. No one seized the day to reveal said lady was pregnant and, thus, my ignorance continued.

Fast forward to 2010, I am with my five-year-old grandson on a bus returning from an outing to the zoo, discussing the possible infirmities of the people depicted on the disability stickers, for whom we should forfeit our seats. Clearly the wheel-chair and walking-stick figures had bad legs. However, a roly-poly figure presented puzzlement, but for mere seconds only, when the dear child astounded me by suggesting knowingly: 'maybe the lady is going to have a baby'. Ah, the difference a couple of generations makes!

My biological knowledge didn't improve for some time. In my first year of high school, a lecture on human reproduction was announced and we were given permission notes to take home for parental signature. I was totally humiliated when I discovered I was the only girl in my class where permission to attend was withheld. The reason given by my mother was that any such instruction should be limited to the confines of the family home. Like 'Lettis Leaf', a comic strip character of the time who was the greenest girl in her school, I was the last person who should have been denied this lecture. No 'birds and bees' talk ever eventuated.

Growing up in a closeted household had its drawbacks all right. No wonder I had a lot of catching up to do when I finally cast off my chains and launched myself, trustingly but cluelessly, into the alien territory that was the outside world. In hindsight, I was breathtakingly naïve.

For the time being at least, our new life in Australia met all our expectations – my mother no longer had 'dead fingers', my school days were happy enough, my sister Janet secured office work at the well-known CSR company at Pyrmont and my brother Edward commenced his electrician's apprenticeship with Warburton & Franki in Kent Street, Sydney. Most important of all for my father, things were sailing along smoothly at the nearest Brethren church in Croydon Park. I tended to think we had merely swapped one boring set of bible meetings for another – except that in Sydney, we kept awake by vigorously fanning ourselves in the hot weather, whereas in England we used to sit shivering in the cold pews.

In those days, most of our neighbours attended some place of worship, so as we made the weekly walk to our local church, I didn't feel much different to my school friends who went to Sunday School. I knew the Brethren were strict but they were not far removed from, say, the Baptist religion, except that we didn't have the wireless and I couldn't go to the movies. We were still in regular contact with all the family we had left behind in the UK, whether they were attached to a Brethren gathering or not. This fairly normal state of affairs was to be short-lived; by the end of the 1950s, a change of leadership set the Exclusive Brethren on a terrible path of destruction as our Church descended into Cult territory.

My father worked tirelessly to better his status in life and by 1955 achieved the egalitarian Australian dream of owning his own home. There seemed no class barriers in Australia; hard work meant you could be as good as the next person.

The house loan approval may well have been smoothed because one of the 'Saints', a Brethren elder, was a bank manager with the

Bank of New South Wales in Ashfield. The Brethren always looked
after their own; but I'm sure my father would have been considered a
safe bet anyway. By the time I started high school, we had moved to
Croydon Avenue, Croydon - our home until 1959.

8

Lessons Learned

No-one was more surprised than I, when I was selected to attend Fort Street Girls High in Sydney. Only the best and brightest from primary school were chosen so I just knew they had made a terrible mistake and I lost no time in proving it. My tenure at Fort Street from 1955 to 1958 was an unmitigated disaster. I was a teacher's worst nightmare – my report cards read like a broken record: 'could do better if concentrated', 'very disappointing result', 'must learn to pay attention in class' – on and on *ad nauseum*.

The only ray of hope was in composition and comprehension, with my English teacher, the erudite Helen Palmer, daughter of well-known Australian author Vance Palmer, praising my work and predicting I would be a writer one day.

That was not sufficient to save me. After repeating First year (which I perceived as a mark of failure in itself, although my June birth date did mean the first time around I was six months younger than anyone else in the class), when there was no improvement by the end of my second year, I knew the writing was on the wall. There was no salvation forthcoming on the home front either in the way of homework help. School studies for a girl of that era in a religious household came a poor second to bible studies.

One year at Fort Street, on taking my report home to be signed, my mother took pity on me when she saw I had ingeniously folded the report so only the square-inch signature block was left exposed. She signed without a word. The reason for this contrivance was my place: 137/137 - bottom of the year - I've never forgotten the number. I was so ashamed and terrified of being found out. I had stuffed up my hand of cards big time and folded without a fight.

There were only two other Brethren girls attending Fort Street while I was there and I lost contact with them after I left the Church. Hopefully their Fort Street experience was not as dismal as mine.

A lifeline was thrown me midway through third year in high school. A young Brethren girl from another locality told me she was leaving school after the half yearly exams and was enrolling in a business course. Faster than you could say 'Jack Robinson' my mind was made up - I was outta there! My 15th birthday was in June 1958 - 15 was then the legal school leaving age, so I set about convincing my parents I should leave school, do a secretarial course and get a job. Money still being in short supply, my family didn't take much convincing.

School approval might have been a harder nut to crack but for the fact that the Fort Street teaching staff probably breathed a collective sigh of relief at getting rid of a problem pupil. My exit interview with the formidable Headmistress, Miss Lilian Whiteoak, was a nasty experience. Miss Whiteoak succeeded the famous Fanny Cohen, who ruled the Fort from 1929 to 1952. I was ushered trembling into Miss Whiteoak's august presence with my signed parental form giving notice of my departure. She scanned this contemptuously and pronounced in icy tones: 'You're making a terrible mistake'. I had no answer, but inwardly I was thinking the terrible mistake was my being selected for Fort Street in the first place.

Miss Whiteoak was right up to a point. At times during my working life I was disadvantaged by the lack of an Intermediate Certificate but I learned to fudge job applications, hoping that 'Secondary Education - Fort Street High Selective School' would be sufficiently impressive to distract prospective employers from noticing the absence of a formal qualification.

It was decades later, on being accepted to study a Masters degree at Sydney University, before I got over that particular inferiority complex, at the same time scoring a triumph over the Exclusive Brethren into the bargain. One of the EB's more bizarre edicts in the 1960s was banning University attendance. I well remember listening to the rationale given by the Elders that Higher Education would lead to someone being able to 'look down on another brother or sister of the flock'. What rot. As usual, the flock were too brainwashed to realise that considering the pinnacle of J S Hales' academic achievement at the time was Accountancy studies, obtaining a superior qualification to the Australian head honcho would not be tolerated or even contemplated. Anyone with the desire or ability to progress beyond a vocational certificate could forget their aspirations.

Back in 1958, there was still the tricky question on the home front of how to pay the Business College bill. The expense of a traditional one year's course was way beyond my parents' capabilities. Luckily the wonderfully innovative Williams Business College in George Street, Wynyard came to the rescue. WBC offered the only self-paced program in Sydney at that time, with the guarantee that if a student worked hard it was possible to complete a basic shorthand/typewriting course in six months instead of twelve.

I knuckled down as though my life depended on it. No more 'could do better if concentrated' comments: I took to shorthand like a duck to water and the practice of a plywood-square-niftily-fitted-over-the-typewriter-keyboard-and-knuckles-rapped-with-a-ruler trick, made sure touch typing became second nature too. When I finished the course at year's end with sufficient skills to be sent on interviews, doors started to open and, for once, my parents were proud of me.

In 1965 I went back to Williams Business College to do a refresher course and, according to the then Principal, Mr Laurier Williams, an internal Pitman shorthand test I passed at 170 words per minute was one of the highest speed transcriptions he had seen at the college. I was over the moon with my 150 wpm external Certificate awarded by the Commercial Education Society of Australia (CESA) for Hansard dictation – look at me now Fort Street!

Shorthand is similar to learning another language. Once you have mastered the technique and with continued practice, become fluent, the art never leaves you. I keep a notebook handy for times when I have no computer access and write all my notes in shorthand – it just happens without me giving it any thought.

At the same time I learned sign language for the deaf, as there happened to be quite a contingent of the hearing-impaired in the Brethren fellowship, both in Sydney and Melbourne. A dedicated group of interpreters was always on hand to translate the church services to our deaf brethren in a little area set aside in the meeting room. Interpreting long, boring meetings was a labour of love, selflessly and tirelessly undertaken by mostly older, single 'sisters'. Good Brethren girls aspired to join the ranks of these interpreting ladies and if you became fluent enough to get on the Roster, you got in the Elders' good books. My sister Janet made it to the Interpreting Roster. I don't remember any male interpreters; it seemed to be the province of spinsters.

While I was not to attain the exalted status of an official interpreter, I did become quite proficient in conversing with the deaf and as a result, enjoyed a warm friendship with a hearing-impaired family in Melbourne. I stayed in their house in Melbourne on more than one occasion and sometimes they would stay with us on visits to Sydney. They had eight children and every single member of that family was 'stone deaf' as it was then termed. I was there just after their eighth child was born and I remember feeling sad as the mother banged two saucepan lids together and watched expectantly to see if there was any reaction from her youngest child. There was none.

They were a wonderful, happy family – maybe I empathised with them because there were eight children like in my own. I loved the atmosphere in their home, they made me feel totally at ease and I kept in contact with them until I left the Church. My friendship with the family was completely natural and I have no memory of any associations of disability. They had courage in spades but were to fall foul of the extreme edicts of the Exclusive Brethren. A 'hearing' young man in the Brethren fell in love with one of the girls and was forbidden to marry her – the Bible verse condemning 'unequal yokes' being the justification. What cruelty in the name of religion.

But getting back to shorthand! My unexpected success in secretarial studies was not only the beginning of a challenging and rewarding occupation leading to a career in education, it was a pipeline to the outside world which provided me with the confidence and courage I later needed to make the life-changing decision to leave the Exclusive Brethren.

As I write, children born into this extremist sect are kept in ignorance literally from cradle to grave. All are educated in Brethren operated schools, work in Brethren businesses and inter-marry. Brethren also have their own Mortuary and Undertaking licences to serve the Flock when they shuffle off their mortal coil. When I was there we had our own midwives too.

The years 1955 to 1959 at Croydon Avenue provided plenty of milestones for me. My brother David arrived in Australia at the conclusion of his British National Service in the Middle East, bringing me great delight – I loved my brother and had missed him. My mother was so proud when David quickly landed a job as an Engineer at the Burrinjuck Dam near Canberra and we had the rare treat of a weekend away to visit him on site. I remember him waiting for us by the side of the road to lead the way. There he was, wearing a pair of maroon corduroy trousers, shockingly worldly to the Brethren way of thinking but I thought he looked so suave.

No one was happier than me when David officially joined the Brethren church and in 1957 he married a much respected 'sister'. Memories come flooding back looking at the family photo taken to mark the occasion. My sister Beryl made her only visit to Australia, made possible because she was on a year's working holiday as a nurse in New Zealand and 'crossed the Ditch' for her brother's wedding.

Beryl, as well as my older sister Millie and brother John in England, had moved away from the EB fellowship years before. In 1957 the EB rules still permitted contact with family members who had left the Church, so Beryl was allowed to attend her brother's wedding.

Also in the wedding photo is my brother's new father-in-law. What a story he could tell – the poor man was hounded out of the Church years later when he confessed to being a secret smoker. Smoking was considered a high-level sin by the Brethren, the reasoning being that if you breathed in smoke you couldn't breathe in the Holy Spirit. Nicotine-related illnesses never rated a mention!

Consuming alcohol was not considered a sin however. Don't know how they worked it out but imbibing spirituous liquids was not only encouraged but became more or less compulsory over the years, leading to all sorts of alcohol related issues. Whisky dependence characterised James Taylor Jnr, the Cult chief, at the height of his infamous leadership and allegedly caused his early demise in 1970.

As in many religions, there was a pecking order of sins and everyone knew the hierarchy as far as the Holy Trinity was concerned. Some sins could be forgiven by The Father and/or The Son – but Heaven help you if you sinned against the Holy Spirit – you were automatically damned for all eternity. Trouble was, no actual list existed categorising various sins, so you spent your life in mortal terror that you might have committed a Holy Spirit sin. Being 'luke-warm' was a Holy Spirit sin (they got it from the Bible somewhere about God spitting people out of His mouth if they were neither cold nor hot) – fence-sitters need not apply! Threatened with such dire consequences you'd have thought that would be enough to make any secret EB smoker go cold turkey.

My brother's new family had another terrible cross to bear. The whereabouts of his wife's mother was never openly discussed but years later, when the church leaders decided mental illness was a figment of the imagination and could be cured by prayer, she was released after many years in a psychiatric institution. She went to live with my brother David and his family, on the south coast of New South Wales.

What a commotion that wacky edict caused when all these poor demented souls suddenly appeared at the Brethren gatherings. There were no exemptions to this ruling, so it was quite an eye-opener to discover that not only the rank and file had 'skeletons in their closets' so to speak, but also many an Elder had a mad aunt.

On one notable occasion, a young man with a mental condition who had been sheltered by his family was produced at a large Brethren gathering in Brisbane, Queensland and ushered with great ceremony to a seat in the front row with the Elders. Not far into proceedings, he started to take off his clothes, which prompted fervent prayers to the good Lord for intercession in this distressing situation. When it became evident that the power of prayer may not prevent the youth going the full Monty - he was hurriedly escorted out. It was rumoured that his medication was resumed forthwith.

9

Breaking Away

While we were at Croydon Avenue, Dad's business improved: he had motor vehicle traders' plates and delivered new cars straight from the Homebush Ford factory to various country dealerships in New South Wales. His first contract was with Mr Earl an Elder of the EB, who had the Ford franchise in Manuka, Canberra. My father must have thought he had struck the jackpot, motoring along the pleasant highway between Sydney and Canberra in a brand new car, when the last job he had as a driver entailed him risking certain death from bombs dropping on his loaded petrol tanker in the height of the Bristol Blitzes.

But no matter how well my father played his hand of cards, eventually he couldn't win against the powerful cult the EB became. For the time being however, no one rocked the boat and so long as we conformed, we had the persona of a typical Brethren family, as a photo taken at home in Croydon shows.

The fear of God's wrath descending on me increased dramatically during those years in Croydon. I became more aware of the Brethren's teachings and my own shortcomings. The worst thing was the dread of the Rapture happening and my being left behind. For the uninitiated, the Rapture means The Second Coming of Christ, when all those who are saved from their sins supposedly ascend into heaven in the twinkling of an eye. Sinners stay right where they are. This tenet of faith was used as a powerful weapon by our preachers to keep the Flock on the straight and narrow.

The brainwashing was such, my mother only had to be a few minutes late home from the shops, or the house might become suddenly quiet, for naked terror to overtake me – sheer, unadulterated panic. You could only breathe safely again when you had laid eyes on any Brethren person, family or not, who was such a good individual you knew they must be Saved, so the Rapture couldn't have happened or they wouldn't be standing there – unaware of how comforting was their sheer bodily presence. You couldn't let on to anyone of course, you suffered in silence, because if you admitted you'd been scared witless because you thought the Rapture had happened, it would be tantamount to admitting you knew you weren't saved from your earthly sins! Thankfully, these illogical 'panic attacks' vanished when I left the Brethren.

One phobia I developed in Croydon, is still with me. It was my job to collect the Bibles and hymn books from the hatstand in our hallway for our Sunday before-church home prayers. As I went to pick up the Bibles one morning, I noticed what seemed like a tassel over my eye. I looked into the hatstand mirror and there was a enormous Huntsman spider on my head – it must have been hiding in one of the hats. Bibles flew in every direction and my screams could have been heard for miles, because being a little English girl, I'd been warned about the deadly, dangerous spiders in Australia. So now I had arachnophobia to add to my list!

No use telling me they're harmless, as my husband Pete found out early in our relationship. One night a Huntsman decided to take up residence on the wall above my bathroom door, so Pete was summoned on a 30-minute car trip from Pennant Hills to North Sydney. No amount of reasoning could persuade me it was OK to use the bathroom until Pete arrived, did the impressive jam jar-over-the-spider trick and tossed it outside.

In 1958, my brother Edward married an EB girl who lived at Maroubra. What a fun family she came from. I relished the open atmosphere of visiting their house, conditions at my home seemed boring in comparison. I have no photos of my brother's wedding but I remember my new sister-in-law was a clever seamstress and she made me a beautiful dress to wear for the occasion.

I have a 'Guardian Angel' story from those days. I sometimes went to Maroubra after school to meet my Brethren friend, Jane, and wait until my brother's family arrived home. On one such occasion Jane and I were walking along the beach front at Maroubra (a delightful change from the dull streets of Croydon), when I noticed a man in a parked car behaving strangely.

I didn't say a word to Jane, because I didn't even know what he was doing. It dawned on me years later he was masturbating vigorously as we sauntered slowly past, but I just thought he was having trouble with his trousers. Minutes afterwards, as I walked up the hill alone to wait at the empty house until the family came home from work, the same man drove by, turned his head and stared at me. The fates were kind to me that day and that psycho just kept on driving.

In 1959, I was thrilled to have my first job, as a junior typist in the office of a fluorescent lighting company at Darlinghurst. My father had grave misgivings regarding its location but I knew nothing of Darlinghurst's proximity to Kings Cross and its reputation as a red light district, so I ignored him and commenced to learn about a world outside the confines of the Exclusive Brethren. I yearned to go to the movies, cut my hair and have a good time like everyone else. The Exclusive Brethren rules were becoming more restrictive than ever but no amount of hell-fire and brimstone preachings could suppress my inner rebellious streak.

I fell prey to the charms of a work colleague, old enough to be my father, who would sometimes drive me home from the office, park in a secluded spot then have a passionate petting session. The Devil has got me now, I thought, as I put on my most innocent expression walking in the door after one of these titillating trysts.

Around that time I made a wonderful friendship with Nora from a Brethren family recently arrived from Scotland. She had a Brethren boyfriend, Tom. Nora was about my age and we were as thick as thieves – I felt I had a soul mate at last. We saw our first movie together in 1959, The Angry Hills, starring Robert Mitchum at Hoyts Cinema in George Street – the suspense of the movie was nothing compared to the trepidation of being found out. My list of sins was growing.

Among the more daring of our exploits was skipping various church services. We were allowed to sit together in the back rows and became adept at using a toilet break to slip away, chat over a milkshake at a nearby café, and return in time to nonchalantly mingle with the Flock as they emerged from the meeting hall. I don't think my mother suspected a thing.

A very narrow escape however made me think twice about wagging meetings. The occasion was the most important date on the EB calendar – the annual Sydney 3-day Fellowship Meetings, held on the Labour Day long weekend in October. The imposing location was none other than the Sydney Town Hall – hired out exclusively by the Exclusives every year.

Nora and I beat a hasty retreat as usual from the restrooms, enjoyed the thrill of our illicit hour or so of freedom and breathed easily again when we rejoined our families exiting the Town Hall. This time however, my mother was sombre and clearly some sort of appropriate response was expected to her questions about the service I had ostensibly just attended. I gave the vaguest of replies, to which she sternly said: *'God was speaking to you in that hall when He saw fit to take our Brother Mr S'.* Hells bells – one of the Elders on the platform had suddenly collapsed and died – stretchered out under the shocked and hushed gaze of the 2,000 strong congregation and I'd missed everything!

It would be close to 50 years before that ghost was laid to rest for me. My dear friend Sophie, a fellow EB escapee, and I were both members of a Community Choir in Sydney and enjoyed participating in many uplifting choral recitals. Sophie happened to be the granddaughter of the above sadly departed Mr S and as a small child had witnessed the distressing spectacle of her grandfather's very public demise.

One October afternoon in 2007 we took our places on that very stage of the Sydney Town Hall for a concert of classical music. Both of us held our heads high, our voices raised in song – but our hearts were full of emotion as we respectfully remembered Sophie's grandfather and the associated triumphs and tragedies of the intervening years – our life journeys taking us a world away from the bleak and scary scenario of 1959. The choir exorcised that Sydney Town Hall ghost.

Another excruciating memory was how the Brethren murdered hymn tunes in church. Singing was 'A Cappella', instrumental accompaniment being forbidden. After a hymn was chosen by a brother, tunes were raised randomly by any male voice courageous enough to start off. The congregation would then join in. Often a wrong tune would be started that didn't match the hymn. Quelle horreur! We would falter to an uncertain stop after a couple of stanzas and sit there attempting to stifle nervous giggles, until the situation was retrieved by another tune being started.

Women had to be 'silent in the assembly' so in those days, the idea of a sister giving out a hymn or, however musically inclined, raising a tune, was unthinkable. It was almost de rigueur for a hymn to be sung out of tune, after all we were told it was wrong for pride to be taken in the act of singing – it was the lexis heard by the Lord that mattered.

One of my brothers was the proud possessor of a reel-to-reel tape recorder which the elders gave permission to use at fellowship meetings. Proceedings were transcribed and published as our 'ministry books' - prescribed reading for the faithful flock. My brother recorded the hymns as well. It was the cause of much mirth at home to play back the first and last verses of a long hymn, and hear the congregation en masse droning out a dreadful dirge at least an octave lower at the end.

We mechanically used our well-worn hymnal 'Spiritual Songs for The Little Flock' – selected 1856 latest edition 1962 – noting that even the words must not be governed by poetry, according to the original editor Mr John Nelson Darby, one of the first prominent leaders of the Brethren. I quote from his preface: 'something at least of the spirit of poetry is needed, though not poetry itself, which is objectionable, as merely the spirit and imagination of man.'[4]

What chance would singing a rousing rendition of a hymn have with that admonition ringing in your ears? Small wonder choral music is now particularly meaningful to me and I treat it with the respect it deserves. I savour the opportunity of discovering the joyfulness of losing yourself in the sheer pleasure of singing, whether a sacred song or classical composition.

In 1959, things came to a head for me when Nora and I hatched a plan to escape the Exclusive Brethren. Her boyfriend Tom had a racy MG, far too worldly for Brethren standards, sufficient reason in itself, I imagine, for him to ditch the church. I was to meet Nora and Tom on Liverpool Road, Croydon at the top of our street one night, and we were to begin our adventures. I crept silently out of the house at the appointed hour without being detected. (In a conciliatory mood later, my father was to comment that I could take up a career as a cat burglar!)

I hurried to the getaway car and we sped off through the darkened city streets and over the harbour bridge to a safe house we'd hastily arranged. I will never forget the exhilaration of that glorious ride to freedom with my two friends – no matter that I was perched somewhat precariously in the back of the two-seater MG.

In hindsight, the escapade was doomed to failure from the outset – for me at least. I had planned nothing beyond packing a handful of clothes and creeping out the house at midnight. At the ripe age of 16, I was destined to come to a screeching halt sooner rather than later. Nora and Tom were better prepared and together had a far greater chance of survival. My liberty was short-lived; from memory it was no more than a week before my father, with the aid of the police, tracked me down at a job I'd got through the Centacom employment agency (I wasn't clever enough to give a false name) and frogmarched me back home in disgrace with my tail between my legs.

---

4   John Nelson Darby, 1962, 'Spiritual Songs for The Little Flock' – selected 1856 latest edition 1962

Coming events cast their shadow before them however, as during our week of freedom, Nora and I found a room in a boarding house in Shellcove Road, Neutral Bay, where in 1970, I was to form lifelong friendships with a group of wonderful girls, just doors away from the scene of my embarrassing false start.

In 1984 when I was living in Kirribilli, my sister Janet's son, my nephew Michael, escaped from the Exclusive Brethren when he had just attained his 16th year. He tracked me down, turned up on my doorstep and memories of my first escape attempt at the same tender age came rushing back.

Sixteen may be the legal age of consent, but I was desperately worried for my nephew and begged him to consider returning to his family and leaving much later when he would be better equipped to handle the vicissitudes of life on the outside. To his great credit, he took no notice of me and against all odds, has made the transition to a happy and successful life.

Back in 1959, it was a major trauma for my entire family to endure the shame of my running away, however in those days I was permitted to live at home while God was supposed to be working hard on my soul to bring about a repentant state. During this process I had many 'priestly visits' as they were termed, from the elders as they urged me to confess my sins - sexual misdemeanours being the top of the list.

When I finally broke down and admitted an encounter with the opposite sex, they lit on it like a duck on a June bug and grilled me shamelessly in their attempts to extract the gory details – the perverts! After they established there had been no sexual intercourse, one of them had the gall to ask how did this miracle happen? I could not answer them – maybe I was just lucky.

One of my local elders was none other than Mr John S Hales, who was infamously to become the Exclusive Brethren leader, or Man of God to use one of his many and varied titles, decades later. His dire warnings frightened me to death, the 'God commandeth the lightning where it should strike' threat being the worst. Among other things, JSH declared that my friends Nora and Tom would not stay together, according to him they were doomed to a path of destruction, God would see to that. Contrary to Mr Hales' predictions, Nora and Tom are still committed Christians and amongst the privileged minority in our society whose happy marriage has endured to this day.

I was determined not to re-join the Brethren and I held out for several months but eventually they wore me down and I decided there was nothing for it but to accept the error of my ways, turn over a new leaf and become a sober sister of the Church. I have to admit that as a young teenager with little or no resources at my disposal, there was no way I could have made it in the outside world on my own. My parents were delighted, we picked up where we left off and the final chapter in my Exclusive Brethren journey began.

An aside to my 'Getting right with the Lord' meant I had to come clean about all sorts of sins committed while I was briefly on the outside. I had secured an excellent job as a junior stenographer at the Sydney office of the pastoralists, The New Zealand and Australian Land Company, where I was to work for 10 years. I later became the personal assistant to the general manager, with whom I was to maintain a lifelong friendship. An employment agency had hinted that firms usually didn't employ girls as young as 16 for worthwhile positions, so why not say I was older? I took my chances using this subterfuge and sure enough, I was promptly hired.

After officially returning to the Brethren Fold, this lie weighed heavily on my conscience. I'll never forget summoning up every ounce of courage and approaching Mr W F Bradley, the office manager who had interviewed me, to tell him I had a confession to make. He quickly sat me down in his office and I blurted out that I had put my age up to get the job.

Mr Bradley couldn't believe his ears. Later I overheard him relating the story to a colleague amidst howls of laughter, as evidently he had leapt to the conclusion that I must have been fingering the till. Far from being sacked, he told me I'd proven my maturity and they kept me on at the same pay.

10

Descent to Cultdom

1960 was a significant year. Our family had moved up in the world and now moved to 44 Boyle Street, Croydon Park. It was a bigger and better house and we felt quite respectable. 1960 was also the start of the darkest period in the history of the Exclusive Brethren and my story until my final departure in 1968 is overshadowed by these events.

The rationale of my narrative is not to give a dissertation on the perceived evils of the Exclusive Brethren. My purpose is this: if, by sharing my story, even one person feels empowered to escape any cruel or unjust regime that may be holding them prisoner and makes a bid for freedom, then the world will be better by one.

The internet will provide the reader with everything anyone could possibly want to know on the subject of the Exclusive Brethren. One website, Wikipeebia.com, includes a poignant 'In Memoriam' section dedicated to the memory of suicides directly attributable to the cruel dictates of the EB regime – another section 'Horror Stories' is also particularly emotional.

A present-day David and Goliath saga was played out in 2009, when the wealthy and powerful EB church, through their Bible and Gospel Trust, brought a multi-million dollar lawsuit against Peebs. net in the USA in a desperate move to silence criticism by closing the website down, albeit on flimsy grounds. The Flock must be kept in ignorance after all – wouldn't do for anyone to stumble across the truth while 'illegally' surfing the internet. An out-of-court settlement closed this particular case and the website is still operational, with some small concessions as to privacy being won by the EB.

The history of the Exclusive Brethren is the subject of many books. Highly recommended are:

Behind the Exclusive Brethren, Michael Bachelard, Scribe Press 2008 and Behind Closed Doors, Ngaire Thomas, Random House 2004.

To give some idea of the surreal circumstances controlling every aspect of my life in the 1960s, the following extract from an article detailing the rise to power of the new leader, Mr James Taylor Jnr, summarises the situation at that time:

'James Taylor Jnr was to have a major influence on the Exclusive Brethren over a controversial 10 year period and beyond. At a conference in Central Hall, London, in 1959, a major confrontation developed between James Taylor Jnr and Gerald Cowell from England. Cowell maintained a moderate view of associations with 'unbelievers'. However, at the conference, James Taylor Jnr advocated a new radical doctrine of separation from the world; from family, from friends, from work mates and from school mates not amongst the Brethren.

A major schism developed and many families, particularly those with non-Brethren relatives elsewhere, left the Brethren. Taylor was established as the worldwide leader and Cowell was 'withdrawn from' (ex-communicated) less than a year later. The Brethren had always shunned most forms of commercial entertainment but now a stricter regime applied. Movies, radios, TV, books and magazines, cinemas, dancing, bars and hotels, restaurants, holidays and parties were forbidden. Professional associations, a university education, voting, keeping pets or celebrating Christmas were not permitted and eating and drinking with 'non-Brethren' was expressly forbidden.

Over the next 10 years until his death in 1970, James Taylor Jnr issued a
continual stream of 'directives' that regulated the behaviour of the
Brethren in exacting detail; prohibitions against women working,
wearing slacks, using make-up or cutting their hair; prohibitions relating
to facial hair on men and rules about working on Saturday or Sunday,
required attendance at meetings, bans on public swimming, life
insurance and organised sport. The list of rules, compiled later on the
internet, numbered in the hundreds.[5]

The impact of this hard-line absolute dictatorship was horrendous
and immediate. In every part of the EB world, families departed in
droves if they did not explicitly follow the directives of the Leader,
the above James Taylor Jnr who resided in Brooklyn, New York. In
Australia, Brethren defections were not as many as in some countries
closer to the hub of the leadership. JT Jnr's henchmen in Sydney
were powerful and effectively prevented negativity from coming to
the ears of the faithful Flock in Australia.

Viewed now some 40 years down the track, it is almost impossible
to believe not only the gullibility of the church members but the
unquestioning obedience to any order given by the Leader through
the local hierarchy. New directives came fast and furiously and were
increasingly bizarre, but the Flock fell over themselves like lemmings
in a macabre contest to show utter devotion to 'Our Beloved Brother
JT Jnr' as he was commonly termed.

In 2006 when I was interviewed by ABC TV's *Four Corners* for
their investigative program 'Separate Lives'[6] which exposed the cruel
practices of the 'shadowy sect' as they were termed – there was one
over-riding theme: the unquestioned obedience by the Flock to the
dictates of whoever was acknowledged to be the Universal Leader at
any time.

It's obvious to me now – anyone unfortunate enough to be caught
up in a cult has no idea they are in a cult – only a miracle giving you

5   David Tchappat, 2009, Breakout: How I escaped from the Exclusive Brethren,
    New Holland Publishers
6   Four Corners Separate Lives", 2006 ABC TV

a pipeline to the outside world can enable you to even contemplate an opposing thought or deed. The EB's official label is an 'opposer' to describe anyone who dares to question the supreme authority of their Church.

All works of fiction were banned under the new rules in 1960. I can remember my self-righteous feelings that were fanned by the flames of our household's backyard bonfire. Enid Blyton – out you go! *Wind in the Willows* – pffft! Nothing escaped the purging burn, so there was no chance of the enlightenment of George Orwell's *Animal Farm*. When I got to read this novel not long after my escape, my incredulity increased with every page I turned – why wasn't this book titled 'The Exclusive Brethren'? It described their whole sorry history in prescient detail.

In 1960, with my recent attempt to leave the Brethren fresh in my mind, I was swept along in the feverish current of the day, brainwashed with the whole congregation. In fact, like a reformed smoker, no one was more zealous than me and I became the epitome of the 'subject sister', a status all female members of the EB strove to achieve.

It is mortifying for me to recall my complicity in getting rid of our family cat (who admittedly was in his declining years), when the 'No Pets' rule was introduced. This edict was a corker! Naturally the EB leadership had a line from J N Darby's edition of the Bible to back up the latest weird decree: *'Without are the dogs' Revelation 22:15* being the justification trotted out on this occasion. If only the internet was around then, because it tells me the full verse actually is: *'Outside are the dogs, the sorcerers, the sexually immoral, the murderers, the idolaters, and everyone who loves and practices lying'*.

No one would have been brave enough to argue that the word in J N Darby's *'translation from the original languages'* was wrong. In truth, if you kept your pet *outside*, wouldn't that spare it the veterinarian's needle? You would have been excommunicated on the spot for daring to question the infallibility of our beloved JND's version of the Bible in an attempt to keep your pet.

Pity the poor old souls whose only true companion was a beloved moggy or devoted dog. But they knew the score - have your pet put down or be excommunicated from the Brethren. Most chose the former option, not so incredible really when you think of the web of Fear, Finances and Families - the 'Three Fs' that above all else meant total subjugation of the rank and file.

If you were faced with losing all contact with your family, and you may well have a Brethren-financed mortgage, plus you believed you risked eternal damnation if you defied an edict - what might be the result? The moggy would draw the short straw.

Another incident resulting from the 'No Pets' pronouncement happened to an EB family who lived a few doors away from us. One of the daughters had just purchased some goldfish and had proudly set them up in a nice glass bowl - then came the directive. What to do? Perhaps the local pet shop might refund the money if the goldfish were returned quickly enough. After a short delay pondering this problem, my friend eventually put the fish in a container, went to the shop, but she didn't get her money back. As he dropped them back into the fish tank, the owner insisted the fish had grown too much and he wouldn't get the same return for them as for baby goldfish, so my friend went away empty-handed.

When I did my research for the ABC TV *Four Corners* interview in 2006, I tried to find out if this 1960s mass extermination of EB animals had come to the notice of any veterinarian authorities but surprisingly I drew a blank.

Little Brethren children at the time were consoled in their tearful farewells to their unsuspecting and trusting animals, by being fed the line that the Rapture was imminent - what if it happened tomorrow for instance - who would feed the poor animals left behind? This blatant trickery of course worked like a charm on young, innocent minds.

The harshest directive of all was the instruction to terminate any association with outsiders, particularly the sharing of food or drink, irrespective of whether they were your closest family or merely acquaintances. The faithful Flock obeyed the call, although a significant schism did occur over this edict, which became known as 'the separation or eating matter'.

It was a blanket rule - 'outsiders' meant just that: anyone who was not in the Exclusive Brethren fellowship. In so many instances, your relatives were practising Christians who just happened to go to other places of worship. It should be noted that a feature of EB doctrine has always been the belief that they are the only assemblage on earth who are God's chosen people - therefore complete heathens were viewed in a far more considerate light than members of other religions. The most diabolical label of all was reserved for the Roman Catholics. If it was necessary for the Elders to mention them at all, the only acceptable term to use was: 'She who is called Jezebel' and you knew exactly who they were talking about.

So the message went out - the Exclusive Brethren would from henceforth be 'in the world' but 'not of the world' - no matter what the cost. This caused a flurry of unwelcome media attention at the time, as word got around that families were being divided by this little known and secretive sect. A journalist from *The Sun* newspaper snapped me on the Sydney Town Hall steps on one of the last occasions the EB three-day fellowship meetings were held at that venue. It must have been the October long weekend of 1961 or 62 and although I have searched various archives it has never come to light. *The Sun* article, with my picture on the front page, was shown to me at work the following week. I had quite a bit of explaining to do.

The whole separation issue was a nightmare and, to my shame - as I had turned over a new leaf and was now a 'true believer' in every sense of the word - I joined the madness and wrote to my family in England telling them I could no longer have any association with them, either in writing, on the telephone or in person.

I suppose my mother's blind devotion to the church eased the pain she must have felt on penning her letters to her own much loved offspring. I remember her reminding me that the more we suffered on earth, the larger our crown of glory would be when we eventually reached the Pearly Gates. The Pearly Gates is my expression; mother would have used proper EB-speak such as when we 'joined the Lord in Heaven on Judgment Day'.

The hurt was irreparable and I can't even begin to imagine the heartbreak for my mother's only sister, Auntie Winnie, who saved our family from starvation during the dark days of World War Two. On one of my visits to England in the 1970s to see Auntie Winnie and other family members, I made a point of telling them how sorry I was for the pain of separation they had been forced to bear. It was some consolation to clear up this unfinished business and, as I was welcomed by the warm embrace of my English relatives, I marvelled that no one blamed us personally. To them it was obvious that my family in Australia had suffered the misfortune of being totally brainwashed by the clever tactics of the Exclusive Brethren leaders.

Meanwhile in the '60s, as we lost contact with our overseas relatives, in Australia our family was growing. At the beginning of 1963 my eldest brother Donald and his wife Doris arrived from England amid much fuss. They had decided to immigrate to Australia and as they were officially in the EB fellowship, it must have been of great consolation to my mother coming so soon after losing contact with her other children in England.

Donald and Doris were unable to have children and were quite well off by our standards. They travelled to Australia by plane and I remember the excitement of standing on the tarmac at Mascot awaiting their arrival. In those days, a speck in the sky was the only indication that the plane was actually due to land, then they came straight down the steps, walked into the terminal to collect their luggage and greeted us within minutes.

Now there were five Nason children residing in Australia – all EB stalwarts, and the three in England henceforth ceased to exist for us. Notwithstanding, they were never far from my mother's mind as she steadfastly remembered them in her daily prayers in expectation of her just reward in Heaven.

For the remainder of the '60s I had a lot to do with Donald and Doris as they bought a house near us in Croydon Park but my enduring memory of them is from the 1980s after I left the church. They had moved to the outer Sydney suburb of Kellyville, much favoured by the Brethren and I experienced the trauma of being denied access to my mother when she was living in their house.

In 1964 to our delight, my sister Janet married. I knew Janet's sole desire was to be a good Brethren person, settle down, get married and have children. She had no other aspirations.

11

Questions of Conscience

Before long grandchildren started arriving on the scene, bringing joy and warmth to our family. I adored my little nieces and nephews and by the time of my eventual departure in 1968 there were 12. My brother David had three boys and one girl, Edward two boys and three girls and Janet two boys and one girl. There had been a tragedy in 1965 which greatly affected us all. Janet's firstborn were twins, a boy and a girl. The little infant boy departed this life when he was only eight months old, never having fully recovered from a difficult and premature birth.

I admit to having a family favourite and that was my niece Robyn. Coincidently her second name was Joy, and she and I had the closest of bonds. I have never before or since experienced such strong reciprocal feelings from a little person and I have no explanation for it. I can hardly bear to recall my grief as towards the end of the '60s I came to the inescapable conclusion that I must break my ties with the church – knowing that this decision spelt the end of my relationship with my entire family in the EB, my favourite niece included.

A typical family photograph taken in 1967, only months before I left the Brethren, shows me with my father, mother, sister and brother, their spouses and seven of my nieces and nephews. Unsurprisingly, little Robyn is sitting on my knee. It is a moment frozen in time –

my life as it was in the confines of the EB church – my life before I marched to the beat of a different drummer.

In 2001, my sister Janet's daughter, Abigail, who was born after I left the Brethren, escaped the church and I met her soon afterwards. She was then approximately the same age as my sister was the last time I saw her and as Abby walked towards me, the family likeness was so strong, my mind played tricks on me and I thought it was actually my sister Janet!

Abby quickly wrote out a family tree as it then stood. No less than nine more nieces and nephews had been born after my departure and I now had the astonishing total of 50 great-nieces and nephews – not one of whom would have known of my existence and I certainly did not know of theirs. Any form of birth control is strictly forbidden in the Exclusive Brethren, so they breed like rabbits, thus ensuring the succession of the Cult.

I learned that my niece Robyn was now herself a mother with eight children. Not only that, but a double tragedy had befallen her – first, the accidental death of her eldest child when he was only 18 months old in 1985. He was run over by a car in the driveway of the family home. Later, her husband was tragically killed in a road accident in 1996. My heart went out to my niece. I was given her address and wrote a carefully worded letter expressing my fondest feelings. As I expected, my letter was unanswered and I have no way of knowing if she read it.

As for my Brethren and family life in the 1960s, it was not all doom and gloom. I had many lovely friends who I remember fondly to this day and happy memories of enjoying various social occasions such as were permitted within the parameters of allowable activities. Entertaining at home was a weekly ritual, followed by sing-songs around our old pedal organ, using of course, hymns from 'Spiritual Songs for The Little Flock'.

Anything bordering on 'worldly' pleasures was banned, but in the Brethren circles our family mixed with, the warmth of love and understanding permeated and we knew the closeness of fellowship in the truest sense of the word.

I have a well-used 'Visitors Book' bought when we moved to Boyle Street in 1960 and I made sure no-one who dined with us left the house without signing. It reads like a virtual 'Who's Who' of the Brethren assemblage of those times – I found it in my father's possessions and it saddens me to see the abrupt end in 1968. The last entry is July, just before the fateful date of my departure. My parents didn't have the heart to continue the Visitors Book after I'd gone.

An entry in August 1962 is particularly significant – it is signed by a family friend, who I think of as a true saint. A few years later she was to provide a safe haven for me the day I finally escaped the Brethren. This is a very emotional topic for me and I will return to it.

Other highlights of Brethren life were weddings. My young friends and I loved weddings, as every girl does; one such occasion in 1961 being particularly memorable. It was a forced marriage for the most ludicrous of reasons. The bride-to-be, Rachel, an English girl, was already betrothed to her much-loved boyfriend in the UK, but she was directed by the Brethren elders to break off this engagement and fly to Australia to marry someone else. If the EB hierarchy decided to meddle in matrimonial arrangements, for whatever reason, you had Buckley's of beating them. Rachel was in a Catch-22 situation, the EB would not allow her current relationship to continue, so she had little choice but to obey and take her chances.

Rachel was then 21, and after much water passed under the bridge, the Fates would decree that on her 70th birthday in 2010, she asked me to give a speech at a very glamorous event organised to celebrate her special milestone. The party was held at a function centre in the Royal Botanical Gardens in Melbourne and I was the only other former EB present. A quote from my speech follows and describes the event in 1961:

'Imagine with me if you will, the cloistered environment of a packed church hall of a fundamental religious sect (not unlike the Amish) and a group of wide-eyed teenage girls, of which I was one, on tenterhooks to catch our first glimpse of a mysterious overseas visitor who had flown all the way from England for her arranged marriage to take place in that

hall in Sydney that night. Absolutely our first known contact with a jet-setter. We were all agog with the intrigue of the occasion. My recollection of the tyrannical circumstances culminating in that event have faded with time, but the private pain Rachel endured, would have destroyed a lesser person.

The moment came; Rachel was escorted to her seat in front of the congregation – gasp – there she was, looking simply stunning, you can imagine the impact on us naïve, dowdy, girls. Back then we believed to look remotely fashionable was a mortal sin even for a bride. But at just 21 Rachel had thumbed her nose at convention and dressed stylishly in the most gorgeous, russet-coloured taffeta number, lustrous hair immaculately coiffed (in contrast to our daggy 'buns' or, if you were daring, 'French-rolls') Rachel looked effortlessly glamorous – and she has not lost her touch over the years.'

The only other consistently bright spot in the 1960s was my working life with The Land Company. I loved my job and got a lot of satisfaction from it. EB directives at one stage meant I had to resign and take up an office job at a company of roofing contractors with offices in Glebe owned by a Brethren family. For some reason which is unclear to me now, I had a reprieve and was allowed to leave this Brethren firm after only a few months. Mac, my loyal boss at The Land Company agreed to take me back, bless his heart.

In 1964, when I was 21, many bizarre decrees in the EB were firmly entrenched. For instance, birthday celebrations had been banned for years – the reason covering this rule, in Brethren-speak, was because it 'remembered the first man' – the first man in this context meaning your original sinful state. My 21st birthday came around and at my workplace, the office staff knew better than to organise so much as a little cake to share, everyone being well aware of the 'no eating with sinners' rule I was governed by.

One of the executives was so incensed at the idea that I could not celebrate my coming of age, he marched into the office on the 10th of June, thrust out his arm for a handshake and said in forthright tones: 'I don't care what anyone says, I'm congratulating you on the occasion of your 21st birthday'. Dear, kind man – little did he know that I was so brainwashed I didn't feel sorry for myself, I only felt sorry for him. He was lucky I shook his hand – to shake an outsider's hand equated to saying 'hail-fellow-well-met' – a no-no in EB terms.

In 1966 I was asked to be 'bridesmaid' at the wedding of one of my best friends who lived in Newcastle. A photo shows me dressed in a suitably sober-coloured Brethren outfit, but with a daringly bright hat. Standing next to me was the bride's brother, looking distinctly uncomfortable. I used to dream that maybe he fancied me, but I was never to have a Brethren boyfriend or arranged marriage – a situation that caused me concern.

I was convinced I was destined to be left on the shelf, and I only ever had one date with a Brethren boy and that was when I was still in my teens. He was visiting from interstate and we went on a secret ferry ride to Manly. Visiting such a worldly destination was against the rules then and swimming was out of the question even though it was a hot summer's day. I have an unpleasant memory of his sweaty embrace, probably caused by a combination of nerves, guilt and temperature. He went back home and I never heard from him again. I thought there must be something wrong with me and worried constantly about it, but for whatever was wrong with me at that time I am now truly thankful!

My home and church life was a roller coaster of emotions, mainly full of fear and anxiety for the future. My father was in constant trouble with the Elders and was a source of great embarrassment to our whole family. He was always questioning the latest rules, and was branded a trouble-maker. This led to ructions on the domestic front at home – Dad's short fuse was hard to contend with at the best of times but when he was at loggerheads with the Brethren elders, Dad would go on the rampage at home and Heaven help anyone who got on the wrong side of him. At least I learned the masterful art of walking on eggshells.

I once was the unwitting cause of my father being found out for a serious breach of the fellowship. Dad made routine deliveries to a motor dealer in Queanbeyan who, unlike Mr Earl of Canberra, was not an EB member. On this particular delivery the car had broken down *en route* and Dad arrived exhausted in the evening, the only return train to Sydney leaving late that night. The dealer offered my father a meal before he went off to get his train and he accepted. His dilemma was to dine and risk excommunication from the EB or decline and thus unnecessarily offend the kindly car dealer. I guess Dad must have let slip something to my mother – two and two were put together and the guilty secret was on everyone's conscience.

Somehow a Brethren elder, Dr D J Martin, a Macquarie Street dental surgeon, must have got wind of the incident. I had become slightly friendly with one of his younger daughters, and I was flattered to receive an invitation through her to dine at their home one evening – invitations to dine with the hierarchy of the EB being rare at my family's end of the socio-economic scale.

However, DJM cleverly conned me. Over dinner he asked me several leading questions about any matters my father might have on his conscience, which I answered in all truthfulness, naively believing this would go no further. What a shock for me later that same evening when, before an audience of several hundred at the mid-week Bible meeting at Ashfield, DJM solemnly announced he had a matter to charge our Brother Mr Nason with – could he deny that he had accepted a meal at the table of a worldly sinner?

My father being the honest man he was, could not deny the charge, he was 'shut-up' on the spot as was the custom in those darkest of times, he stood up and made the grossly humiliating walk down the stairs and out through the hushed congregation of the assembly – and I was the one who had dobbed him in.

What mixed emotions I had . . . would I ever come to terms with what I'd done? But, in the eyes of the EB, exposing a 'sin' regardless of your relationship with the sinner, automatically had the Brethren seal of approval. My Dad never raised any question of my blame. He was restored to full fellowship privileges when he had satisfied the requirements of penitence after what seemed like an interminable period of grovelling to the Elders. Life in the Nason household at

Boyle Street, Croydon Park returned to normal. Thankfully Dad lived long enough for me to eventually apologise to him and put the matter right.

On several occasions during my life with the EB, there would be a rash of 'confession sessions'. One such period was during the mid 1960s, the vivid memories of which have never left me. You knew you were in for a torrid time when the hell-fire and brimstone teachings started to accelerate and the Elders would warn that God was on the lookout for backsliders and sinners – and the only means of repentance was by confession.

Sure enough, it wouldn't be long before we'd have so-called 'special assembly' meetings after the mid-week Bible services. In the grip of Cult fever in the 1960s these purges hit new heights and also caused the highest attendance rate at the Ashfield meeting hall that anyone had seen in years. Nothing like a sex scandal to make the faithful forget their tiredness or whatever normally justifiable excuse there was to miss a meeting.

The Elders would announce that such and such a brother or sister were seeking forgiveness for their sins, which would then be reported in graphic detail over the public address system. Brethren-speak textbook language was used however, which mightily confused most of us early on. The words 'fornication' and 'adultery' became common-place, and I slowly realised the term 'uncleanness' or 'indecency' covered a wide range of sexual gropings or whatever. Depending on the circumstances, the person might be forgiven on the spot, be 'shut-up' until the Elders deemed they were repentant, or be summarily excommunicated, with the resultant traumatic implications for that entire family.

The EB hierarchy milked these episodes for all they were worth. In the shocked and hushed silence immediately following one of these assembly meetings, an Elder would grab a microphone and in the most theatrical of performances, urge anyone else in the congregation who had sins weighing on their conscience to come forward and come clean! Nothing to fear – roll on up, let's hear your sordid stories, we'll get our thrills and you'll be forgiven. You could almost see those perverted Elders salivating.

One night this led to a tragicomedy, excruciatingly embarrassing for the person concerned, who surely would live with the memory until the end of his days. We were all literally quaking in our shoes, as the Elder spruiked for confessions over the microphone. You could have heard a pin drop - the pause seemed like an eternity.

Then we froze. Shuffling up from the back rows, head bowed, came this terrified, shaking figure. He was a well-liked young family man and our hearts went out to him. He was encouraged to the front; I can remember the Elder's words as though it were yesterday: 'Come forward, dear Brother, the Lord is with you, helping you to confess. Seize the opportunity to be cleansed. What is your sin, dear Brother?'

There was a collective intake of breath when the poor fellow said one word into the microphone: 'Sodomy'. The Elder lost no time and the interrogation continued: 'When did the sin take place, where were you, how many times?', etc, etc. Then came the final question - the poor man was over a barrel - the Elders knew there was no way he could avoid answering this one: 'Who was the act committed with dear Brother?' A stunned silence followed his simple reply: 'No one, I was alone in the field behind my house'.

There was a hurried whispered consultation of Elders on the platform, the poor man was ushered outside, then the congregation were told we could all go home, as there had been some error. Huh? That's what comes of keeping the Flock in complete ignorance - and I have to admit at the time I hadn't got a clue what was going on. I only knew that Sodomy was mentioned in the Bible in such a way that it had a very high rating on the sin scale. It would be years after I left the Brethren before it dawned on me that the sin being confessed that evening was the evil of masturbation!

On a more serious note, anything confessed in these Purges was considered to be completely in the hands of the Elders for forgiveness or otherwise. The infallibility behind this reasoning lay in the Bible verse (John 20:23): *'Whomsoever sins ye remit: they are remitted; whomsoever sins ye retain: they are retained'*. There is no doubt whatsoever that the Brethren Elders took it on themselves to forgive criminal acts that rightly should have been reported to the authorities. The EB firmly believed they were the highest court in the land.

There was a particularly nasty case of a grandfather who allegedly sexually molested his two small grandchildren. The most disgusting thing about this incident was, in deciding on this man's forgiveness, we were told the little girls 'liked it and wanted more' the implication being it was their fault. Poor little mites. I hope that man rots in Hell.

The annals of history record that obsession with sex goes hand in hand with religious fervour. The Exclusive Brethren were no different when I was there in the 1960s and it cannot be disputed that religious organisations today, are equally guilty. In 2011 a Minister of the Uniting Church went on record as saying: 'Old obsessions mean the church has this thing that you can only have sex to have babies. It all goes back to that'. (*David Marr, Sydney Morning Herald, article 'Faiths rule on sex from staffroom to bedroom' 12 February 2011*).

If proof is needed of this theory, look no further than the 2013 Royal Commission into Institutional Responses to Child Sexual Abuse set up by the Australian government to inquire into and report upon responses by institutions to instances and allegations of child abuse in Australia. The establishment of the commission followed revelations of child abusers being moved from place to place instead of their abuse and crimes being reported. There were also revelations that adults failed to try to stop further acts of child abuse.

During the late 1990s and early 2000s, allegations of child sexual abuse in Australia surfaced in the Roman Catholic Church and a number of other religious and non-religious institutions. Some of these allegations led to a number of convictions, trials and ongoing investigations into allegations of sex crimes committed by Roman Catholic priests and members of religious orders. Some of the allegations relate to alleged incidents that occurred during the 1950s, others in more recent times. There were calls for a Royal Commission since the late 1990s.

How different our society might be today if we were to reach adulthood blessed with the freedom of reasoned discussion on life's issues, unfettered by religious rulings. Obsession with sex and belief in the infallibility of ancient writings would have no place. The EB were masters at slavish devotion to literal translations of the Bible – unquestioned obedience to the sacred texts a foregone conclusion.

The words of Bertrand Russell are inspirational:

> 'Religion is based, I think, primarily and mainly upon fear. It is partly the terror of the unknown and partly the wish to feel that you have a kind of elder brother who will stand by you in all your troubles and disputes. A good world needs knowledge, kindliness and courage; it does not need . . . a fettering of the free intelligence by the words uttered long ago by ignorant men.'[7]

---

7   Bertram Russell, 1927, "Why I am not a Christian" lecture on March 6, 1927 to the National Secular Society, South London Branch, at Battersea Town Hall. Published later that year in pamphlet form.

12

The Final Departure

It's all very well to have the wisdom of hindsight but at the height of the 1960s EB Purges, I was a brainwashed soul, living in dread of God's wrath. Exactly when the warning bells rang for me that I was not cut out to be a subservient Exclusive Brethren sister for the remainder of my days, I cannot say with any degree of certainty. However, once the seeds of doubt were sown, they grew to a full crop of misgivings that I could not dismiss despite how hard I tried.

I finally came to the conclusion that I wasn't a fit and proper person to belong to the Exclusive Brethren. I believed I didn't measure up to their stringent standards. Time after time I would shake so much sitting next to my mother in the meetings, I was sure she would notice. I was terrified that my sins might warrant a confession and figured I'd rather die than let this happen.

At this stage the sum total of my 'sins' was simply an overwhelming urge to taste life in the outside world. I worked in this world daily, I loved my job, I liked being friendly with my workmates but knew this was frowned upon by the EB. I became attracted to a male colleague, and no matter that it amounted only to harmless flirting, it was enough to put the fear of God into me.

Towards the end of 1967, an announcement was made that our beloved brother James Taylor Jnr from New York was to arrive in

Australia to lead fellowship meetings in August 1968. Not sure why the lengthy notice. Immediately and irrevocably, I made up my mind I would no longer be a member of the Exclusive Brethren by that date. I knew with absolute certainty that I would not be able to withstand the enormous pressure to be totally committed to the Brethren movement that would result from a visit by the World Leader.

But this time I would play my cards right. No way would I stuff up my hand like I did back in 1959. I would consider my moves long and hard. My overriding concern was my mother. I loved her deeply and as she was the most staunchly devoted Brethren person it was possible to be, I knew my defection would break her heart. I had to plan my exit in such a way as to soften the blow to the utmost of my ability.

The ensuing months were the most traumatic of my life as I grappled with the enormity of my decision to finally reject the EB Cult, which this once kindly Christian group had unquestionably become. At that time, the Brethren believed in 'dead separation' and to forsake the one true Flock meant you were an apostate. A similar practice is observed by Orthodox Jews, when a garment is rent and the excommunicated person is forthwith and forevermore considered dead to the religion. My resolve to leave never faltered but the implications were horrendous.

Outings with my little nieces and nephews became precious moments, knowing my days with them were numbered. I hardened my heart to thoughts of the grief I would cause my family and friends; emboldened by the certainty that my personal freedom meant more to me than anything else in this world. To this day, I am grateful I had the courage of my convictions and have never regretted my decision.

On a practical note, I had so much to plan. Where would I go? What immediate steps would I take on leaving home? Thank goodness I had my wonderful job; people who are employed by the Brethren have so much more to lose. I had to secretly rummage through my mother's belongings to find the last letters from my brother and sisters in England because they were the only family members I would be able to contact and I had no idea of their addresses. Incidentally, this is when I found the parcel of carefully preserved letters written by my eldest brother Donald in World War Two asking about little Myrtle.

There was no way I would do a 'midnight flit' this time. I would find some means of preparing my parents for my final departure and when the day came, I would fully inform them of my decision. In 1968, the EB had increased the number of meetings we were supposed to attend to seven days a week, and three times on Sundays. I started cutting down on my attendance, missing meetings, making deliberately poor excuses.

Before long my mother smelt a rat, so I took the next step and started to criticise the Brethren way of life. To do this was considered unthinkable but it was the only way I knew of preparing my family for the fact that I might leave the church. My mother was devastated at the thought that her youngest child was not totally committed to the EB. I missed more and more meetings and both my parents were deeply concerned.

Then came crunch time. There was a special meeting once a month called the 'Care Meeting'. It was absolutely non-negotiable to miss this assemblage. In the four weeks between the July and August Care Meetings, I made my final plans.

I contacted the family friend previously mentioned in my Visitors Book, who herself had recently departed the EB. I told her of my decision to leave and quite simply asked if she would give me a roof over my head, when the day came. She unhesitatingly gave her consent, a brave thing for her to do, when you consider the unwelcome attention this would bring her.

In the days leading up to the August 1968 Care Meeting, I surreptitiously loaded my car with as many of my possessions as was possible without arousing attention. I attended no meetings during that week, leaving no doubt in my parents' mind that I was seriously unhappy with the Brethren. On the Friday night, I sat down and wrote a long letter to my mother, explaining as gently and fully as I could, my reasons for leaving the church and where I would be staying in the first instance.

On the Saturday morning my parents got ready to leave for the Care Meeting - and the game was up. As soon as I said I was not going with them, their faces told the story; to miss a Care Meeting was the equivalent of giving your final notice. They set off for the Ashfield meeting hall planning, I guess, to try and talk sense into me when they returned. They knew the whole armoury of the Elders would now have to be enlisted in the battle to fight for my lost soul.

As soon as the coast was clear, I put the letter to my mother on the kitchen table and moved like lightning to pack my car to the roof with whatever belongings I could take in one load. There would be no question of me returning that day to collect any more of my possessions. I would be far too traumatised to come face to face with my parents until several days had passed to allow me to come to terms with the enormity of living life exiled from the Brethren.

How can I describe my emotions as I drove away from 44 Boyle Street that last time? I guess only adrenalin kept me going along the highway towards my place of refuge with the former Exclusive Brethren family. I recalled the gap widening between sea and shore as our migrant ship, the 'New Australia', transported us on our journey to a new life in 1953. Then, as now, the gulf between my old and new life could not have been more unbreachable.

In the ensuing weeks, I ran the whole gamut of Brethren tactics to get me to return to the Fold. They used every trick in the book, contacting me alternately with threats and then enticements to return, but nothing shook my resolve. The family who had given me refuge showed true compassion, giving me as much comfort and support as it was possible to give.

One of the hardest moments was the night my sister Janet and her husband waylaid me. They were waiting at the railway station where they knew I would be arriving on my way from work. My latest nephew, Michael, had arrived in the world only six weeks previously and here was the new baby in his bassinet being shown to me with the words: 'This is the nephew you will never see again'.

I already knew my other nieces and nephews had been told Aunty Joy was wicked and they would never see me again. There was nothing I could do about it – I had no option but to walk away, taking one last look at the infant in his basket. Michael was the same child who 16 years later would turn up on my doorstep in Kirribilli, himself having just escaped the clutches of the Exclusive Brethren.

Without a shadow of doubt, my toughest test happened about three weeks after I left. I contacted my mother and told her I would be returning to collect the rest of my belongings I hadn't been able to fit into my car. We arranged a time and I knocked on the door. Oh, I can barely type these words as I recount the shock of seeing my poor, dear mother as she opened the front door. She looked like a wizened prune and I was appalled. I blurted out: 'What's wrong Mum?' and she replied she had been fasting in the hope of getting me to repent and return to the Brethren.

That moment in 1968 was burned into my soul. It was hard to live with the knowledge that my actions had caused such pain for my mother. From then until the 2006 ABC *Four Corners* documentary on the Exclusive Brethren, I had always laboured under the delusion that my mother had consumed no food or drink whatsoever during her fast – she looked so dreadful. I knew she had fasted on occasions before, when she did not eat or drink anything.

After the *Four Corners* program went to air, the ABC received a letter from lawyers acting for the Brethren accusing me of lying. It was pointed out that my mother would have died after partaking of nothing for this extended length of time. The EB may or may not have been correct, but in any case as there was no evidence to go on, thankfully, the ABC chose to ignore the accusation. The overriding factor to me was having been so traumatised by the events, I had carried the load of guilt about my mother for all those years. It is typical of the EB's mind-set when in damage-control mode, they would clutch at straws and stop at nothing to save face – regardless of their guilt.

So in the hallway of my former home, my mother stood aside as I collected my belongings like one in a dream. We knew the rules, knew the consequences of my abandonment of the Church, knew the finality of the moment – knew this meant we would be separated for ever. I was not permitted to embrace my mother – so I turned and left her and drove away.

Exclusive Brethren procedures being part of my very existence, I had no need to be formally advised that at the next monthly Care Meeting, my case would be brought before the congregation by the Elders. Some peremptory discussion may have taken place and the conclusion reached that there was clearly no hope of our Sister seeing the error of her ways. Then the solemn pronouncement would have been made that the Assembly had no option but to sorrowfully withdraw from our Sister Joy Nason.

I was now officially an outcast and that chapter in my life was closed.

Photos Part 2

Joy (front row, centre) at Fort Street Girls' High School, 1955

The Nason family, Croydon, 1958
Front Row: Janet, Father, Mother. Back Row: Joy, Edward

Bridesmaid at EB wedding 1966 (Joy far left)

My family in 1967 the year before I left the EB. I am holding Robyn.

PART 3
1969 to 1991

13

Watch Out World – Here I Come!

I wasted no time in sampling 'the Fleshpots of Egypt' as any pleasures of the outside world had been referred to in my previous life. I went out after work and at weekends, going to the movies, experiencing the Club scene, learning to drink and dance and generally having an exciting time - unfettered by EB restrictions.

Given my abnormally sheltered existence up to this time, I had a lot to learn. My friends were understandably anxious lest I get into all sorts of strife, but nothing was going to hold me back now. By the end of that year, while not wanting to seem ungrateful to the family who had stepped in the breach in my time of need, I decided to spread my wings and rent my own flat. This was another steep learning curve and vital in terms of my personal development.

A descent into destruction is often a self-fulfilling prophecy for anyone escaping the confines of a cult - you have no reasonable standards of behaviour or moral codes to go by, the outside world represents an evil place and to your innocent eyes it is indeed an alien environment. Many cult escapees, in their first flush of freedom, go overboard and end up on the path to ruin, thus playing out the dire predictions of their former venerated leaders that the Devil will ensnare them.

I was lucky in that I had a responsible job which kept my feet on the ground somewhat, plus an inner determination to make a success of my new life and prove the Exclusive Brethren wrong. I also had a dream of locating my 'lost' relatives and visiting them in England, which gave me motivation for the future.

For the moment however, I considered myself a 'wild child', believed I was a sinner in the eyes of God and didn't care. I immediately shortened my skirts by at least 6 inches and even bought a pair of jeans. If the Devil had got me, the sin of appearing in men's apparel (an excommunicable offence in the EB) was the least of my worries.

Getting a boyfriend was now high on my list. I made the assumption that experimenting with sex was par for the course and I wanted to be like everyone else. I now officially belonged to the wicked world that I had been warned about my entire life and never imagined for one moment that qualities such as chastity might actually be valued in this milieu. Weren't these virtues the province of God's one true flock? Wasn't that why the Exclusive Brethren were the chosen few who would be raptured to heaven? These beliefs had been instilled in me from the cradle, so the notion persisted that the church I had forsaken had a monopoly on righteous living. It would be years before the realisation dawned that various dubious practices, including sexual promiscuity, were not necessarily the norm.

I was 25, a virgin with little experience of the opposite sex. The sole outing to Manly with a Brethren boy and the brief trysts during my first office job at aged 16, were buried deeply in the recesses of my mind. Not a whole lot to go on in my mid-20s by anyone's reckoning.

I have no memory whatsoever of how I met my first 'date' in 1969, but I do remember the awkward fumblings in the back seat of the young man's car, when on perceiving my ignorance he proceeded to explain various sexual terms, accompanied by a practical demonstration. In my naivety I believed him when he pronounced he had 'done the deed'. I never saw him again and it turned out the silly fool was as ignorant as I was anyway.

My next date some weeks later was a rather sweet person who treated me to dinner before taking me back to his place. I reassured him it was OK to 'go all the way' with me as I was an experienced woman of the world. This encounter was vastly different – a real bed for starters and I didn't need to be told afterwards I was no longer a virgin, much to the poor chap's chagrin and my embarrassment. He didn't last long either.

Next came a quite significant episode with a 'well-known identity' in harness racing circles. This arose from a chance encounter at one of my new haunts, where I was introduced to someone who would 'look after me and show me a good time'. It was all very exciting as I briefly entered the world of the 'red hots' as horse trotting races were known, albeit on the fringe. I was completely out of my depth, however, and didn't know it.

My new friend was a fatherly type, who I naively believed was in love with me. One weekend he organised for me to fly to Melbourne, where I stayed in a swanky hotel and was escorted by a minder to the Victorian Oaks. At a party after the races, two very glamorous young ladies mysteriously appeared and no-one would tell me who they were or where they came from. Then the bombshell – I found out they were professional escorts and I was terrified of what I might have let myself in for.

After I recovered from that experience, I became emotionally involved in another relationship, but as luck would have it, my new boyfriend turned out to be the first of many cheating men I would encounter, who weaved a tangled web of lies to successfully convince me they were on the singles scene, when in reality they were bored, suburban husbands merely looking for some excitement in their lives. I was not to discover the truth about my first real boyfriend until much further down the track – with the inevitable heartbreak.

During this time I was busily investigating how to get in touch with my family in England and sending off letters to last known whereabouts with the news I had left the Exclusive Brethren. I even went to the GPO in Sydney, looked up the electoral rolls and found the address of my old friends Nora and Tom who I'd heard were living in England.

Fate took a hand in the shape of a wonderful offer made by Qantas Airlines. If you were an Australian citizen under 26 years of age, there was a special deal of a flight to the UK for a very reasonable fare. I had to move fast. I would turn 26 in June – there was not a moment to lose. To obtain an Australian passport the first step was to send away to Somerset House in London for a copy of my original birth certificate. That's when I had to face the reality of my first name in print! Ah well, it didn't matter then, I took dual nationality and my air-ticket was written without question in the name of Joy Nason.

Arrangements for my departure began in earnest. My brother and sisters in England replied in the warmest of terms, welcoming my prospective return with open arms and giving me every encouragement to spread my wings – the sky's the limit I thought. I gave my notice to my understanding boss at The Land Company, packed my bags and set off for the other side of the world. I didn't give any serious thought as to when, or if, I would ever come back.

My then boyfriend must have been relieved at his narrow escape. I had hinted more than once I would change my plans at the drop of a hat with a proposal of marriage, which of course unbeknown to me, he was hardly in a position to make. So I thought I may as well try my hand overseas and take my chances in my old country, where at least I could count on the support of my brother and sisters.

On the 8th of June 1969, two days before my 26th birthday I arrived at London Heathrow Airport, with a motley assortment of luggage and similar emotions to my arrival in Sydney in 1953. Again I faced a fresh start with hope in my heart.

How wonderful to be greeted by my own family – my sister Millie and two of her children, my sister Beryl, my brother John, and his lovely family. Now I could get on with the business of reconnecting with my brother and sisters on an equal footing, after not having seen them for 16 years, and being denied all contact since the Exclusive Brethren separation issue almost a decade ago. The icing on the cake was seeing my old friends Nora and Tom in the arrivals hall. They were happily settled in London, enjoying the expat scene. Now we could put the discomforting circumstances of 1959 behind us and renew our friendship.

At Virginia Waters near London on that balmy English summer's day, the four Nason siblings who, according to our parents and other four siblings, blinded by the teachings of the Exclusive Brethren a world away in Australia, were considered unfit to be associated with. They were now my sole family connection.

While my venture to England turned out to be of relatively short duration, (I was back in Sydney three months later) it was nevertheless a significant turning-point in my life. I stayed with my sister Millie, who lived in Hope Cove, South Devon. Millie was now divorced and had four children. As my oldest sister and 20 years my senior, Millie naturally assumed the role of my surrogate mother. We became very close and I looked on Millie as my long-distance mentor and confidante until she died in October 2004. Millie was well educated, well read and wise in the ways of the world. She had achieved her teaching qualifications after she was freed from the shackles of the religious fundamentalist upbringing which had prevented her from continuing her studies at school.

Millie had put the past behind her and successfully moved on. It was she who encouraged me to question my conviction that it was I who was the sinner and unworthy of the Brethren fellowship – daring me to examine their teachings and view them in a different light. On her recommendation I read George Orwell's *Animal Farm*[8] and this gave me my first insight into the true nature of the sect I had escaped from. Millie sagely nodded when the light bulb switched on in my brain and I exclaimed that *Animal Farm* precisely portrayed the Exclusive Brethren.

Millie had arranged an opportunity for me to work in a marine office in Salcombe, a nearby Devon coastal town, as she was hoping this might be an inducement for me to settle down and make a permanent home in England. While not wanting to appear ungrateful

---

8   George Orwell, 1945, Animal Farm: A Fair Story, Secker and Warburg, London

for Millie's efforts, I was itching to travel and explore the UK, so I threw the job in after only a couple of weeks.

The summer party scene was at its peak in those Devon villages in June of 1969 and no-one embraced it with more enthusiasm than me. I had a wonderful entrée into these circles through my very hip nieces, who were only a few years younger than me, but twice as worldly-wise. They had great fun telling their friends they were going to bring their maiden aunt from Australia along to a party, then watching the reaction when I appeared in my shortest skirts and trendiest outfits. If my sister Millie had any qualms about letting me loose on the locals, she wisely kept quiet and let me have my head.

I started my travels by taking a train to Scotland and doing various coach tours of the Lochs and Highlands, from where I sent postcards to my friends in the Land Company Sydney office, raving about the breathtaking scenery. The highlight of visiting Scotland for me was going to the Land Company's Head Office in George Street, Edinburgh and being wined and dined by the Scottish Chairman of the Board, Mr R I Marshall, and a most eccentric Director, a Dickensian look-alike lawyer Mr T P Spens, who lived in Glasgow. I had to pinch myself that it was really me experiencing this august atmosphere.

I bought a very nifty little red second-hand Morris Cooper S from a Devon car dealer, which I drove hell for leather not only around England but to the Continent and had no trouble selling when I decided to return to Australia in September. The word metamorphosis comes to mind as I recall the transformation in less than 12 months from my previous EB persona to the happy-go-lucky girl zipping in style from here to there without a care in the world.

There was no shortage of boyfriends now. I remember one very swanky youth with an open-tourer MG making sure we were the centre of attention as, with engine revving, we drove through the narrow town-centre streets in Devon at the height of the tourist season. I then decided to visit Ireland, and booked a tour which started in Dublin. The MG youth came in handy by driving me on a whirlwind trip through Wales; on to Chester and Liverpool, where I left him and caught the ferry to Dublin.

My Irish trip was memorable for many reasons, not the least of which was standing on a rain-swept Dublin footpath on 20th July 1969, watching a flickering TV screen in a shop window as the first man landed on the moon. Little did I know then that less than two years later I was to meet Neil Armstrong when I was working as a receptionist at the American National Club in Sydney.

Another unforgettable memory occurred the following day, standing on the same Dublin footpath outside my hotel, suitcase beside me, watching expectantly for the coach to collect me for a 3-day 'Ring of Kerry' tour I had booked from England. A battered, ancient mini-bus came to a creaking halt, and an equally ancient, peculiar little man appeared asking if I was waiting for the Kerry Coach. Yes, I replied, to which he indicated I should step aboard. Much to my consternation the bus was empty, and when I asked him where all the other passengers were, he nonchalantly told me I was the only one as if this was perfectly normal. There was nothing I could do about it at this eleventh hour, so off we went, wending our way through the gorgeous green Irish countryside.

The situation deteriorated drastically when we arrived at a scenic lookout somewhere in Southern Ireland. The weird driver appeared at the bus door ostensibly to help me down the steps for a better look at the view, whereupon he promptly grabbed my hand, pulled it towards his trousers saying: 'Put your hand on it!'; I think I muttered 'Not today thanks', or something equally inane and then sat terrified in the bus making my plans for a hasty exit on arrival at our next destination, which was Killarney.

I found accommodation and decided to hitch-hike to Cork to catch a ferry back to England, to avoid paying for another coach ride and going back to Dublin. It was the weirdest feeling walking to the side of the road, sticking out my arm and holding up my thumb. I never did get any more practice as the first car to appear came screeching to a halt. Luckily I made it to Cork in one piece. It didn't occur to me at the time that hitch-hiking might have landed me in even more hot water than had happened with the coach driver.

14

Travelling Back to Australia

Meanwhile back in England, Millie was working overtime planning a three-week trip around 'the Continent' as we called it then. Millie's friend was to come with us; we were to camp everywhere and take all our own food and cooking equipment. The conveyance for this ambitious venture was to be none other than my trusty little Morris Cooper S. She proved more than capable of the task, never missed a beat the entire journey, but in hindsight, fitting in three adults plus all that baggage must have been a logistical nightmare.

What a fabulous experience this trip around Europe was. The number of countries we visited seemed extraordinary to me. We took the car ferry to Brittany and in France we went to the war graves in Normandy, then toured Paris, Versailles and the Loire Valley. We drove on to Geneva, Liechtenstein, Innsbruck in Austria, Strasbourg, Cortina D'Ampezzo, Lugarno, Lake Como, Venice, Milan, Ravenna, Florence and Pisa. I returned to England happily exhausted with culture overload.

Back in the UK, I went with Millie and her family on various excursions including Lands End and a weekend camping trip on the wild cliffs of the Cornish Coast.

Somehow we managed to see various relatives, although these visits were brief. My sister Beryl and brother John and his wife didn't get much of a look in and no doubt considered I was just a flighty gadabout.

I set off again in my Mini Cooper and took my niece back to university in Canterbury and felt right at home spending an evening with her fascinatingly Bohemian fellow students. I saw Nora and Tom in London, then continued on through England and Scotland, travelling with a very nice young Irish boy I'd met somewhere along the line. I lived for the day and soaked up the heady atmosphere of being foot loose and fancy free. However, I always kept in the back of my mind a piece of sound advice someone gave me before I left Australia: never let your cash get below the cost of your return fare home.

Without my knowing it, a dear kind person at the Land Company Sydney Office kept every one of the postcards I sent from my travels abroad and much to my surprise presented me with them when I returned to Sydney. Looking at them now I see how much I missed Australia, despite my only tangible connection being my friends at work.

Not surprisingly then, when I'd worked my way through my savings and after factoring in the expected proceeds from the sale of my little red car, only the fare back to Australia remained, so I made the decision to return. This must have seemed puzzling to my family in England – why would I choose to go back to a country that held painful memories for me; where I would have no family contact whatsoever; nowhere arranged to live; and only the promise of my employer Mac, the General Manager of The New Zealand and Australian Land Company, that he would keep my position open for me to depend on. I cannot explain my reasoning either, but unseen forces were at work beckoning me back to my adoptive country. I could not escape the fact that Australia did seem like home to me now, despite my years down-under of calling England home like a true Pom.

I made a phone call to my boss in Sydney, reverse charges of course, as Mac knew he would only have three minutes if I was paying. It was wonderful to hear his voice of authority telling the operator to extend each time she called the warning. Mac not only assured me my job as his private secretary was waiting for me, but he also offered to arrange a few nights' accommodation in the city on my arrival. What a rock of stability he was then, and would prove to be for decades until his death in 1998.

So I had no hesitation in disposing of my Morris Cooper and using the last of my money to purchase a ticket on the P&O liner SS *Canberra*, scheduled to leave Southampton on 5th September arriving in Sydney mid October. The itinerary read like a dream, ports of call including Port Everglades Florida, Nassau Bahamas, Panama, Acapulco, Los Angeles, San Francisco, Vancouver, Honolulu, Auckland then Sydney.

There was no time for lingering farewells. I was busy packing every last minute into my remaining days in England, when I should have probably paid more attention to packing my suitcases! A last minute romance meant I'd gone off gallivanting around the countryside once more and I remember screeching to a halt at Millie's house at Hope Cove to collect my gear, making hurried farewells and relying on the boyfriend to get me to the ship on time. The hapless young man (whose name I have completely forgotten, it disappeared into the ether along with all the others) broke speed limits all the way to Southampton, and got me there with only minutes to spare. I completed embarkation formalities and staggered up the gangplank in the nick of time.

Small wonder I don't remember a moment of nostalgia or sense of occasion that it was from this same spot in 1953 I had set out on the momentous journey to my new life in Australia!

What a different journey this 1969 voyage was. From a postcard I wrote to my Sydney office pals dated 8th September, three days into the trip, you can sense my excitement:

'Shipboard life is really great and if the pace keeps up, I'll need a holiday when I get back to Sydney. There is a very happy, lively crowd of young people who are nearly all travelling alone and we have joined up – there is never a dull moment. It is good we got together quickly, as our *next stop, Port Everglades is not until Saturday, so we have to find our entertainment on the ship. I am in a 4-berth cabin, air-conditioned and very smart.'*

There was segregation again – but merely between first class and economy class, no separation of the sexes like in 1953. Goodness knows how I managed it, but the first class demarcation proved no barrier to me anyway – I soon had a boyfriend in the posh end. There was a fancy dress party in economy one night, so I went as a Roman swathed in a bright maroon coloured bed cover. This turned out to be a dead giveaway that I'd been fraternising in first class, as other economy class passengers with the same Roman idea, were merely swathed in nondescript cream coloured coverlets.

My postcards sent to the Land Company Sydney office bring back many happy memories of the various ports of call. Here are some extracts:

PANAMA CANAL:

'We docked at midnight at Cristobal. Just to be in it, I went with 18 others into the town, as the ship was sailing for Balboa Panama at 6 am. I was really scared, it was such a bad place and no white people. There were black policemen on every corner armed with huge rifles. Panama City was mild in comparison. Despite warnings of 'baddies', six of us took a rickety little bus into Panama City. We had a hilarious time and needn't have worried about being attacked.'

ACAPULCO:

'Had a full day in Acapulco on Saturday. We were lucky with the weather, very hot and no rain. There are beautiful hotels in Acapulco, one with 100 rooms and 100 swimming pools. We had a long drive through the hills behind the city, gorgeous views of the Bay.'

LOS ANGELES:

'I am staying on the 11th floor of the Knickerbocker Hotel, and Hollywood looks so enchanting with the many lights. Tomorrow we spend the full day at Disneyland and catch the plane from Los Angeles to San Francisco tomorrow night and rejoin the Canberra there. It is all very exciting.'

'Have had a wonderful day starting with Beverly Hills, then Sunset Boulevard and Sunset Strip. We went to the Universal Studios, riding in an open tram down mock streets and houses. We saw stunt men falling from roof tops, and watched a parrot roll over and curl up his toes when told he'd just been shot. There were instant oceans for shows like McHale's Navy, Lt. Carpenter was there in person and I had my photo taken with him.'

DISNEYLAND:

'I wish you were with me today, you would love Disneyland. Everywhere you look there is something unbelievable to look at. We have been on Mark Twain's steamer boat, a jungle boat, a mono-rail car overlooking Tomorrowland, a tiny boat through 'It's a Small World' – a wonderful display of thousands of animated dolls.'

HONOLULU:

'We had perfect weather for our one day in Honolulu. We went by car right around the Island and I'm now writing this on Waikiki Beach. I've wished I could stay longer at every place I've been. We have 7 days of sea now until Auckland, then Sydney will only be 3 days after that. I'm looking forward to seeing everybody again.'

So I arrived back in Sydney in October 1969, with the golden opportunity to make a completely fresh start – the only link to my previous life being my job. As promised, my boss Mac arranged accommodation for me at the Hotel Metropole near Circular Quay and I started work immediately at NZAL or the Land Company as it was commonly known. The proud old Pastoral Company had been taken over by the stockbrokers Dalgety & Company during 1969 and Mac and I both severed our ties with the organisation only one year later. We had a combined farewell function given by the office staff and left on the same day. I couldn't face working for a new boss under the incoming management after so many years of working for Mac.

I was always to view my 10-year association with the Land Company from 1960 to 1970 with the fondest of memories, as well as the friendships made, it formed the basis of a wonderfully sound secretarial training, which I drew on time and again throughout my subsequent teaching career.

In 1971 I obtained a secretarial position with the Naroo Pastoral subsidiary of British Tobacco, later to become Coca Cola Amatil. I left British Tobacco in 1972 to join the travel industry.

15

Shellcove Road Days

The dawning of the '70s. This was a milestone period in my life, which I fondly think of as the Shellcove Road era. I felt as though the slate had been wiped clean. Maybe the Fort Street School motto *'Faber suæ est quisque Fortunæ'* which translates as: 'you are the architect of your own fortune', might apply to me after all. It was up to me. If I played my cards right, how could I lose?

Around this time I made a conscious decision to conceal my background and previous connection with the EB religion. This subterfuge served me well for the next 20 or more years and was my way of coping with the loss of my family. I had the perfect opportunity to adopt a fresh persona with new flatmates, who knew nothing about me, and were all Ten-Pound Poms. I slotted in, even to the extent of passing myself off as a recently arrived Ten-Pound Pom at parties or with fleeting acquaintances. It was easy to talk about my 6-weeks' voyage from Southampton on the *Canberra* as if it was my first migration to Australia.

I rented an apartment in Colindia Avenue, Neutral Bay, where I shared with Sandy and Fran. At the end of 1970 the three of us moved to Shellcove Road, Neutral Bay where a short time later Sally and Jan moved in to the vacant flat upstairs.

A thrilling thing happened while we were at Colindia Avenue. Fran won a 2GB Radio competition sponsored by Harris Coffee & Teas, the prize being a 10-day holiday for two to Daydream Island in the Barrier Reef. It would have been nice if a boyfriend had materialised for Fran to take along, but I was a handy substitute, filling every minute with fun and excitement.

I met a lovely young man on Daydream, fragile after a recent divorce and licking his wounds while working as a porter on the Island. I may have been just the tonic he needed to lift his spirits and restore his confidence. He looked me up on his first visit to Sydney a year or so later, by which time I was otherwise involved, so I introduced him to one of my workmates. They subsequently married, lived happily ever after and now have 15 grandchildren!

The five of us girls at Neutral Bay, who I call the Shellcove Roaders, forged the strongest and closest of bonds that it was possible to have. I will never forget the Christmas of 1971, which we dubbed 'the Orphans' Christmas Day lunch – the warmth and camaraderie of the occasion so memorable to me, as the last Christmas that I celebrated was in 1952 as a 9-year old with my family in Bristol. Keeping up Christmas had been frowned upon in the Exclusive Brethren since the early 1950s. We were told it was a Pagan festival which should not be recognized. In Sydney in 1971, my 'orphan' friends were separated from their families by the tyranny of distance while my family, although living in the same city, may as well have been on another planet.

The original five Shellcove Roaders all moved on and went our separate ways by the end of 1972, this comparatively short time frame making our subsequent enduring friendship all the more remarkable. I can't imagine my life without their love and support, which they have demonstrated to me unhesitatingly for over 40 years.

Sally played a big part in keeping us together when she instigated her 'Dear Friends Everywhere' annual letter a couple of years after she left Shellcove Road, describing her life and adventurous travels to the four corners of the globe. I have kept every one of her epistles from 1974 to 2014, which is not a bad record. Sandy says our group are truly 'The Golden Girls' – forget the American sitcom of the same name.

Among many fond Shellcove Road memories are the ships parties, which I take full responsibility for starting. My young nephew Stephen was only a teenager in 1970 when he left home in Plymouth, England to join the Merchant Navy as a Cadet. His mother, my sister Millie, worried herself to distraction over his well-being and when she found out his ship, the *Merkara* was to dock in Sydney, obviously Aunty Joy was requisitioned to look after him and show him the sights of Sydney.

The day came, and Stephen informed his senior officer that his aunt would be calling to collect him one afternoon for his shore leave. The ship was strangely quiet as I clambered across the unsteady gang-plank in my mini-skirt and high-heels to be greeted warmly by my nephew. After a while, officers appeared from nowhere, apparently eager to make my acquaintance, and in a master stroke, I gave them an open invitation to attend a Shellcove Road barbecue that very weekend where it would be a pleasure to introduce them to my girlfriends. The subsequent Shellcove Road ships parties tradition lasted for years. A delightful outcome was that Stephen's senior officer on the *Merkara* subsequently married one of the girls he met at these parties. The Aunty Joy story is now firmly part of folklore.

As I became closer to my girlfriends, I couldn't completely hide my past from them, but I was wary of opening the door on the skeletons in the closet. One skeleton that needed dealing with was my first boyfriend, who I still carried a candle for. I decided to track him down and one of the girls came with me. What a shock to discover through a neighbour that he was married with children and had been for years. I was devastated and it took some time to get over that little heartbreak. It would not be the last time my gullibility would get me into all sorts of strife, as my ability to swallow tall tales was, and still is, renowned.

I well remember one Shellcove Road suitor who claimed he was a professional photographer searching for prospective models. Boy, did I fall for that one – I got very excited and spent hours preening myself for futile 'camera shoots'. At least I ended up with a few arty black and white photos to remind me of that little dalliance.

I must have been quite a worry to my friends at times, particularly with my propensity for falling in love at the drop of a hat, and randomly bringing home all sorts of odd bods whom I may well have only met the day before. When I recall how naïve I was to believe some of the fanciful stories concocted to cover up many a Don Juan's actual marital or other status, clearly I was a slow learner.

My persistent dream that the patently elusive marriage proposal would materialise from the latest Mr Right, invariably came crashing down; even genuinely eligible prospects inevitably disappeared over the horizon. Perhaps our circle of acquaintances had more than their fair quota of males suffering from the Big C Commitment phobia. Admittedly it was a two-way street, as there may well have been an equal number of hopeful suitors who summarily received their marching orders if, in the girls' opinion, they didn't come up to scratch.

You don't have to be Einstein to work out the tricky situations the five of us would often find ourselves in at Shellcove Road and the hilarious tales we would share over the washing up. Everyone looked out for each other of course and it was all innocent fun, as perhaps some love-struck swain would be hastily ushered out the back fire-escape if another unexpected visitor had appeared at the front stairs.

It was viewed as sacrilegious not to have at least one party invitation every Saturday night. These invites were mostly secured over Friday night drinks at the Island Trader, where hundreds of Circular Quay office workers like ourselves would congregate and let their hair down at the end of the working week. The days, weeks and months flew by in a heady whirl of work and full-on fun.

For me it was a whole new scenario – life was there to be lived to the max, shaken out and experienced in every facet – no holds barred. My friends, so much more worldly-wise, watched from the wings and would have never let me get in any real danger, but there's no escaping the fact I unwittingly provided my flatmates with a whole new level of entertainment.

In 1989, the Australian Playwright Alex Buzo produced a play called *'Shellcove Road'*. We couldn't let the opportunity pass, and a whole gang of us got together for a reunion, dined at the Marian Street Theatre Restaurant on opening night and took up a block of seats in the front rows. We chatted to Alex after the play – who could resist telling him that the 1970s Shellcove Road girls could have written the script for him – only it might have been too risqué to perform.

16

Joy to the World

The early '70s were busy days indeed. I was stony broke when I returned from overseas at the end of 1969, so I moonlighted as a waitress at the American National Club in Macquarie Street, just around the corner from my day job with the Land Company. Becoming a 'silver service' waitress was a steep learning curve for me. I had to learn fast as I'd indicated in my interview I knew what the term meant (I actually thought they were referring to a canteen of cutlery). Did those slippery green peas make my life a misery on the first night as I grimly clutched the serving spoon and fork in one hand. Mastering chopsticks later in life was a breeze compared to silver-service. I quickly got the hang of things though and as well as waiting on tables, I was soon serving canapés on enormous silver platters at posh functions for the rich, famous and the Who's Who of the Sydney business scene.

On one of these occasions a pleasant, well presented executive trotted out a line that a nice girl like me should be doing better than being a waitress, handed me his business card and told me to contact him if I wanted to learn about the travel industry. It turned out that he was the CEO of Grace Bros Travel and was not trying a 'pick-up trick'. He was genuinely interested in offering me work and the opportunity of a career in the travel industry. So I ended up with three jobs – somehow fitting in Saturday mornings working at the busy Grace Bros Chatswood Travel Agency.

In 1972 I accepted a permanent position with the newly created Tour Wholesale division of Grace Bros Travel – the start of a truly exciting and adventurous time of my life, with loads of travel. My lovely boss, Gerry and his wife Lorna became valued family friends. His premature death from cancer in 1990 was devastating for all of us. His widow Lorna is still one of my closest friends today.

Touring overseas as a Travel Agent meant you were treated to the highest degree of service everywhere you went, the operators bent over backwards to ensure they received glowing reports on the feedback forms. They were heady days. I was entertained royally by a Balinese Prince on this unspoilt island paradise in 1973; had the best accommodation on a cruise to Fiji; upgraded to first class on overseas flights; in other words I experienced travel at a level I could not have afforded myself.

Grace Bros sent me on a Travel Agents' Educational trip to India in October 1972, my report to management headed 'Passage to India', being the first of my Travel Journals. Before submitting our reports of these funded tours to management, some incidents may have been edited, but would form part of a treasured storehouse of memories for many a travel agent.

My favourite story happened on the 'Passage to India' Educational – this trip was an education in more ways than one. The rarefied atmosphere of the Himalayas went to my head, and I became completely besotted with a 'minor princeling' of the ruling Rana family in Nepal. Tourism being the lifeblood of Nepal at that time, the Rana family pulled the strings and our group of travel agents had a right royal welcome. When he came to Australia not long afterwards I took great pleasure in returning the compliment and showing him the Sydney sights. I guess my friends forgave me if I was guilty of showing off a little – it's not every day you get to dine out with royalty – however minor the rank or principality.

In time I was promoted to the American National Club night reception desk after I finished my waitress duties in the restaurant.

This was how I was introduced to Neil Armstrong, the first man on the moon, and also where I fell madly in love with a CEO visiting from the United States. I kept in touch with him for years and still remember him fondly. I would have married him at the drop of a hat, but he was another fish who got away.

Despite the outwardly exciting new life I was enjoying, I could not completely escape the private pain when memories would surface of my previous existence. It was usually something as innocuous as a glimpse of an Exclusive Brethren person in a street; or perhaps snatches of hymn-song when walking near a place of worship, or even the fragrance of lavender, which was my mother's favourite flower. Particular dates on the calendar were always a reminder, such as the New South Wales October long-weekend, which to me will forever represent the annual EB 3-day fellowship meetings at the Sydney Town Hall, rather than the traditional celebrations for the Labour Day holiday.

I especially dreaded unwittingly travelling anywhere near my previous territory, after once finding myself driving along Georges River Road at Croydon Park, when waves of panic swept over me as I grappled with the irrational fear of impending doom. I have never driven down Boyle Street since that fateful day in 1968 when I left my home and I never will. I *Googled* my old address once – it was unrecognisable, the house from whence I departed my former life having been demolished and a smart block of units erected in its place.

I was acutely conscious that, here in Australia, I was totally bereft of any relatives, the only family members I could associate with living 12,000 miles away in England. This was my choice, made with my eyes wide open, but it hurt. On the other hand, it was character building – I was obligated to no one, I would stand or fall by my own hand, I paddled my own canoe. I believe I am no worse off from this strengthening experience – my favourite motto stood by me: 'It's not the hand that counts but how you play the cards that matters'. I had no one to blame but myself for my mistakes – of which there were many.

My personal growth in terms of a true understanding of the nature of the regime I had escaped was slow. The last time I ever saw my brother

Edward and his children was on a train near Ashfield just after I left the EB in 1968. I cowered behind a seat so I could get a glimpse of my loved nieces and nephews without being seen - I felt like an outcast. Once, I saw my brother David and his family walking near Circular Quay and without thinking dashed to say hello. The humiliating rejection as they ignored me and turned away was hard to take. The guilt persisted and it was to be many years before I reached the liberating conclusion it was the EB Cult that was wrong and not me.

I kept my resolve to have no contact with former EBs who had joined breakaway movements. I'm not sure why I made this decision but when I heard that various breakaway groups had formed, it seemed to me these people had not truly moved on from their former lives. I felt the more distance you could put from your past, the more successful the transition would be to a normal life. I had a lucky chance encounter with my friend Rachel, who left the EB shortly after I did, she shared my views and had broken all ties with her former life. We maintained a close friendship from then on.

The tentacles from the EB teachings still reached out and often threatened to overwhelm me. I remember walking into my flat in Neutral Bay one night to hear the song *"Jesus Christ Superstar"*, from the *Hair*[9] musical, blaring from the radio. I leapt to turn it off, terrified God would strike me down for allowing such blasphemy to be broadcast in my home. Taking the Lord's name in vain was high on the list of punishable sins.

Implications of the Rapture still loomed large. I was enjoying some success in forming relationships, and sometimes spending the night together might be expected. If it was a Saturday night, there was no way I would allow a boyfriend to be there on the Sunday morning, or if I was the visitor, I went to great lengths to ensure I was back home in my own bed by the Sabbath. We were told the Rapture would very likely happen at The Lord's Supper held each Sunday morning, and it still haunted me that I might be left behind. Logic soon prevailed on this one, especially when I worked out that with the order of the solar

---

9   Andrew Loyd Webber, 1970, Jesus Christ Superstar, A rock opera

system, Sunday morning happened at different times all over the world, so you couldn't really pinpoint the timing of the Rapture anyway.

Eventually I came to the liberating conclusion that along with many other bigoted teachings, I could consign the Rapture fable to the scrapheap. A pivotal moment for me was when I saw a postcard from the USA depicting the Los Angeles freeway with car crashes all over the place and planes falling from the sky because the drivers/pilots had been Raptured away to heaven. The absurdity of this situation was a factor in my enlightenment and I now marvel how intelligent people can believe such rubbish.

Around 1970 I heard there was another major schism in the ranks of the Exclusive Brethren overseas. It defies belief that the leaders of the Australian branch of the Brethren were so powerful that the rank and file members were intimidated into throwing unopened letters into the bin if the handwriting could be identified and the sender was known to be unsympathetic to the cause of the then World Leader, James Taylor Jnr. This achieved the desired result of the Australian flock being kept in ignorance of the indisputable evidence that JTJnr was indeed a hopeless alcoholic, a womaniser, and gatherings he conducted often descended into blasphemous tirades and drunken outbursts.

The evidence is irrefutable because all Brethren meetings were tape recorded, proceedings transcribed and can be accessed online today if anyone cares to do so. One particular occasion in Aberdeen, Scotland in 1970, just months before JTJnr died, was the last straw for many faithful followers. The scandal hit the press, but this made no difference to the complete cover up by JTJnr's dedicated henchmen, particularly in Sydney. The Aberdeen fall-out was to have far-reaching ramifications for my family. Somehow my father learned the truth, and he would not be silenced. It took the EB a few years, but in the end he was excommunicated for his temerity.

Among the many accounts of the Aberdeen incident, highly recommended is a publication by Norman Adams "*Goodbye Beloved Brethren*", Impulse Books, Aberdeen, 1972[10].

10 Norman Adams "Goodbye Beloved Brethren" Impulse Books Aberdeen, 1972

17

A New Life

In Shellcove Road in 1970 there was one particular personage who entered my life who would not be fobbed off. His name was Norman and he was to become the father of my only child, Anthony. I spent the next 20 years or so in a highly colourful, chequered relationship with Norman – even including marriage later down the track. I met Norman on a blind date arranged through a friend at British Tobacco in 1970. She and I were the envy of the office as this invitation was for a posh dinner for four at Kings Cross, and included an after-dinner show in the Silver Spade Room at The Chevron Hotel.

On this first date I did not exactly view Norman as the man of my dreams, not the least reason being that he was nearly 15 years older than me and I didn't think he was suitable. I firmly and politely declined his invitation to go out with him again.

You had to hand him a prize for persistence however. He devised a scheme which he called 'points on the board'. He went to enormous lengths to get 'points on the board' with me, including hosting dinner parties at venues such as the Neutral Bay Music Hall, to which he regularly invited my friends just to please me. He discovered my interest in fast cars – so he bought a fancy, red Jaguar. He was generous to a fault, highly intelligent but totally eccentric.

Norman must have twigged that my sheltered upbringing meant I was way behind the eight- ball in many of the ways of the world, in particular social graces, so he offered to pay for me to do a June Dally Watkins Deportment and Grooming course. June Dally-Watkins established Australia's first school of personal and professional development (initially for ladies) in 1950 and it was considered the height of social kudos to be a JDW graduate.

I had no hesitation in accepting Norman's largesse and I just loved the course. It gave me the confidence boost I sorely needed to feel I was part of the social scene and not an ignoramus who could unwittingly be an embarrassment to my friends.

Ultimately Norman's persistence paid off. I left Shellcove Road and we moved in together, renting a small harbour-side apartment. When I first met Norman he was separated from his wife and living in temporary accommodation. It was quite a shock when he told me straightaway he had seven children, ranging in age from 10 to early 20s. No wonder my friends viewed my liaison with him with a degree of scepticism and concern, despite the fact he sort of "grew on you" and everyone became very fond of him.

Norman's cause was definitely enhanced when he introduced me to his siblings and their families and I was made welcome in their homes, experiencing again the family life that I had missed. I'll never forget visiting Norman's brother and wife for the first time, suddenly realising that here I was communing with Catholics - the ultimate irony after having the evils of Roman Catholicism drummed into me my entire life. It was obvious to me what a warm, loving family they were - here was a prime example of the erroneous beliefs held by the Exclusive Brethren.

Over the ensuing years, I was to become particularly close to members of Norman's family, most of whom were of Catholic persuasion. Many times I had occasion to recall the EBs bigoted view of other religions, in particular the Catholic faith. Norman's extended family were devout Catholics and displayed true qualities of Christianity and compassion - attributes the EB were incapable of expressing.

There is one enduring truth for which I am forever indebted to Norman. He introduced me to the world of learning, encouraged me to further my studies and set me on a path which not only led to a university education but formed the foundation of a long and rewarding career in the TAFE system. The restrictive Brethren shackles of ignorance fell away and the theory of achieving upward mobility through education proved true for me – I have Norman to thank for this.

I loved my first experience at being a housewife (well, my idea of a housewife!), and found the whole scenario exciting, but unfortunately our relationship was destined to be rocky from the outset. Norman could not shake off his own religious upbringing, despite being a truly lapsed Catholic and an avowed socialist. Guilt overwhelmed him; he returned to his wife and tried to pick up the pieces of his broken marriage. I didn't let the grass grow under my feet either, and cast around trying to find a more suitable partner, but to no avail.

As it happened, Norman's first attempt to make a go of things in his old domain was short-lived – so we resumed our relationship, he moved to where I was living in Cammeray and almost immediately I became pregnant. While the pregnancy was totally unplanned, I was overjoyed, and naively assumed Norman would make an honest woman of me before I became a mother in 1974. This was not to be, and while Norman welcomed his eighth child into this world with genuine affection, as a former Catholic, he simply could not bring himself to put his estranged spouse through the shameful process of divorce, even though he and I were now living together as man and wife.

Somehow I kept the joyous news of my pregnancy a secret for some months. By the end of 1973 my condition was barely noticeable, and I well remember my surprise when the CEO of Grace Bros Travel, asked me straight out if I was pregnant. I categorically denied it, making some vague excuse about putting on weight lately. I didn't want to jeopardise my chances of a forthcoming free trip, as in those days there may have been issues over my suitability as a Tour Escort in my 'delicate condition'. So I got the nod to be Leader on a 10-day escorted group tour to Bali and I loved it. I'm sure no one on the tour had any idea I was pregnant and it made not the slightest difference in the discharge of my responsibilities.

After this trip I had no reason to hide my pregnancy, so I happily gave notice and left Grace Bros Travel just six weeks before I was due to give birth. There was no such thing as maternity leave in those days. I went on a short holiday with Norman's sister-in-law to visit her family on the north coast of NSW. I was especially fond of this family who were non-judgemental and kindness itself to me.

No one had any inkling that this was to be only days before Anthony was born. Major flooding occurred while we were on the north coast and train services were cancelled, so I flew back to Sydney. I believe the flight in a small aircraft brought on premature labour the day after I arrived home. Norman drove me to North Shore Hospital where the reception desk staff thought I had arrived for visiting hours as you could hardly tell I was pregnant, let alone about to give birth.

It turned out to be a painfully protracted 36-hour labour with no epidural and a forceps delivery. When the crucial moment came in the afternoon of Saturday 23rd March, 1974, true to form, Norman was outside betting on the races. After they showed me my son, who weighed in at less than 5 lbs, I overheard the nurses in the delivery room discussing the identification tag they were preparing before whisking him away into a humidicrib. Because I was unmarried and had not decided on a first name, they wanted to write 'Baby Nason' on the label.

Through a bleary haze, I perceived a whiff of shame attached to this name tag, and even though I was totally exhausted, I summoned the strength to speak out and put an end to that idea. I wanted my son to proudly face the world from day one and both Norman and I had never considered anything other than our child would take his surname.

There seems to be a common thread that names are of paramount importance to me. I have never willingly relinquished my own surname and few would guess the reason why. It is because I wanted to uphold my family name in the outside world, to show that there could a 'normal' Nason, other than the barmy lot inside the Exclusive Brethren.

Nothing in this world ever came close to the feeling of delight when I held my baby for the first time. Whatever the future brings, as every new mother can attest, that moment is locked in your heart forever. The innocent new life you have been part of creating has your unconditional love – while this love might be sorely tested when reality bites, as far as I can tell, it lasts a lifetime.

I had continued to keep my parents informed of any change to my address details, but these contacts were perfunctory and only resulted in raw memories surfacing. I made several futile attempts to contact my brothers and sisters, only to have the phone hung up in my ear as soon as my voice was recognised.

One phone call I made to my mother stands out above the rest. It was March 1974, a few days after the birth of my son Anthony. I missed my mother then more than I believed possible and wanted to let her know about her new grandson. She silently listened to my news, miraculously did not hang up the phone immediately, but said: 'He will be a great comfort to you', then the connection was cut. How could I ever forget those few precious words?

Both of us knew that a visit was out of the question – my mother would never entertain such a scandalous notion of allowing her excommunicated daughter to darken her doorstep. It wasn't worth enduring the pain of rejection to suggest it.

18

My Father's Excommunication

As I always made sure my parents had my contact details, this proved fortuitous for my father. One day in 1974 he phoned me in a panic to tell me he had been withdrawn from the Exclusive Brethren. Someone had arrived in a car to collect my mother, but Dad called the Police and they had intervened temporarily. The Police informed Dad that if my mother wished to leave of her own accord there was not a thing anyone could do to prevent it.

Nothing, certainly not 50 years of marriage to my father, could stand in the way of my mother's staunch belief in the infallibility of the Exclusive Brethren teachings. However sorrowful it must have been to her, at the age of 74 she would have gathered a few necessary possessions, made her own phone call, presumably to a taxi company, left her family home in Ashfield where she and my father were then living, and made the fateful journey to her eldest son Donald's house at Kellyville.

My mother would never have considered the alternative – that is, exclude herself from the Exclusive Brethren in order to stay with her husband. To her, the Brethren's wishes were her command, in fact God's command – she had never believed otherwise.

So commenced the final tragic saga in my father's life, in which I became necessarily involved as he had no one else to turn to. Since that day in 1974, I have often puzzled over the actual circumstances of my father's excommunication from the Exclusive Brethren as he never discussed it with me. It was the harshest penalty possible for him, resulting as it did in the loss of his wife, who was the only person he truly cared about in this world.

In 2011, while doing research for this memoir, I wrote to my sister asking for confirmation of the facts surrounding my father's case at that time. I was fairly sure my sister would reply. Since the mid-2000s, the media spotlight has often focused on the cruel practices of the Exclusive Brethren, and has had the desired effect of forcing a softening in some of their rules. My sister had already written a letter to me in conciliatory terms, acknowledging some of the wrongs she perceived I had suffered.

In the letter to my sister I said I felt it was important for me to know the truth about our Dad's excommunication as it had bothered me for years. She responded promptly and her reply speaks volumes in its sincerity and simplicity. My heart aches as I quote my sister's words, decipher the 'Brethren-speak' and visualise the situation:

'Dad was against the leadership, at that time this was Mr Symington universally and Mr John Hales in Sydney, with a carry-over of resentment against Mr James Taylor Jnr who died in October 1970. I think the problem with Dad was that in his natural character, he found it very hard to accept anybody's guidance, particularly if it went against his natural inclinations. Don't you remember how he would gaily ignore parking restrictions, dismissing traffic police with a wave of his hand? You weren't even born until just before the War was over, but I clearly remember how Dad hated conforming to the blackouts. At the point of crisis in about April 1974, Mr John Hales had oversight in what was done in reluctantly withdrawing from Dad, although he did not personally serve him privately, but appealed to him in the meetings, but to no avail.'

My Dad had the courage of his convictions, spoke out against this particularly cruel and vindictive Cult leader, James Harvey Symington (1913-1987) who 'reigned' from 1970 to 1987. Dad paid the ultimate price of losing his beloved wife to the system. He never recovered and died 10 years later, a broken man. I'm proud of my father and dare to think I may have inherited some of his guts and determination.

While my sister's letter made me grieve for the lost years and family history we could have shared, I smiled as I instantly recalled an incident when travelling with my father not many years after we arrived in Australia. We were driving to Melbourne when near the township of Euroa, my father was pulled over by a patrol vehicle and booked for speeding. The constable asked Dad if he had anything to say and Dad muttered gruffly 'Least said, soonest mended with you Police'. 'I beg your pardon?' said the startled officer, while we sat silently quaking, knowing our father's short fuse. Dad repeated loudly 'I said "least said soonest mended with you Police"'. The officer, sensing he was dealing with a tough customer, finished writing the ticket and retreated without another word.

The sad fact is, when my father was excommunicated in 1974, it would not have been necessary for him to turn to me, an outsider, if any of the Brethren had shown him even an ounce of compassion. How well I remember in the early days of his exile, taking him a prepared dinner one Sunday. As he opened his gate to let me in, a carload of EBs drove by. Not a word was said, but we both knew Dad would never be let back in the EB now because he had been seen with me, and I was an exile from the Church. I did whatever I could to ease the burden of grief Dad carried in his remaining years, but I'm sure I fell short. I took my young son Anthony to see his grandfather as often as I could, bringing some joy into his lonely existence.

Dad made several unsuccessful attempts to return to the Brethren, but his pleas fell on deaf ears, even to the extent of his being sent a solicitor's letter on behalf of the Brethren warning him against trying to contact my mother by phone or letter. My father's mission in life was to open the way for his wife to return to him.

My Dad was a shattered man, but even well into his 70s he showed the backbone he was made of with his courageous attempts to pick up the pieces of his life and start again. The Lands Title history below shows how many times he sold up, moved to England then came back again, in his fruitless search for peace. The records make interesting reading, starting in 1955 when only a little over two years after my father's arrival in Australia in 1952, his work ethic was rewarded with the purchase of his first home.

Property purchases by J E Nason:

1955 to 1959	19 Croydon Avenue, Croydon
1960 to 1970	44 Boyle Street, Croydon Park
1970 to 1975	11 Yeo Avenue, Ashfield (First return to England following his excommunication from the EB)
1976 to 1977	Batten Crescent, Ermington (Second return to England)
1978 to 1979	Shaftesbury Road, West Ryde (Third return to England)
1980 to 1983	Kendall Street, Ermington

His last move in 1983 was beyond his control. Dad was suffering from dementia and I had no choice but to arrange for his move into the Aeolus Nursing Home at Ryde, where he passed away on 13th March 1984.

19

Married Life

Meanwhile, back in Cammeray when Anthony was about 3 months old, I became restless and realised I was not cut out for life as a house-bound parent. My first priority was suitable day care for my baby, and I found a lovely young mother, a former nurse, looking for extra cash in hand. A block or so away, the 3M Company advertised for a secretary. Everything fell into place and I went back to full-time work.

On the home front however, nothing was falling into place. Norman's business was in dire straits and I found his random attempts to be reconciled with his wife very unsettling. To add to my woes, as so often happens in these domestic situations, some of Norman's children felt I was responsible for the breakup of their parents' marriage. It was all a mess.

I qualified for government assisted child-care, so at the end of the year, I booked Anthony into a long-day care centre at Crows Nest. At the same time Grace Bros Travel told me they had a vacancy for a consultant at their Chatswood agency. This was fabulous news, as I had loved my work in the travel industry. I accepted the job and at the beginning of 1975, I started at Chatswood as a front-line senior consultant.

Towards the end of 1975, Grace Bros gave me a bonus of a return air flight to London which I could use on my annual leave. These tickets were highly sought after as they did not involve any associated tourist work or reporting to management – it was simply a freebie. My sister-in-law kindly offered to look after 18-month old Anthony to enable me to go to the UK for a two-week break.

Off I went, and what a chain of events was set in train (train being the operative word!) I had arranged to go straight to Cornwall to visit my sister Millie, so after arriving at Heathrow I caught the shuttle to Reading, for the rail connection to Plymouth. In the same carriage was one Phillip P, a friendly fellow, deeply tanned, returning from Bahrain to his home in Cornwall. By the time the train arrived in Plymouth where we both disembarked, the scene was set for a holiday romance.

Ah, it should have remained a holiday affair, but I was ensnared, hook, line and sinker. My recollections of this trip are at best hazy, but I do remember meeting Phillip's mother, who lived in an imposing stone house overlooking the ocean in a remote Cornish village. I was a bundle of nerves as I was put through the third degree. The bar was high – I had to prepare the roast beef Sunday lunch. Funny how little things stick in your mind – I forgot to clarify the fat for the Yorkshire pudding, so I clearly failed the test! My vague responses to her questions regarding my background didn't help either. The class system was alive and well in that quarter of the world and I was left with the distinct impression I didn't measure up as a suitable prospect for her son.

On our last evening together, after he had driven me to Heathrow airport for my return flight to Sydney, Phillip proposed over a romantic, candle-lit dinner. At last, here was my first true marriage proposal – my heart ruled my head, rationality went out the window, and I accepted.

Phillip styled himself as 'Captain', even signing his name as 'Captain P'. I had visions of him in charge of ocean-going liners, whereas in reality he was a tugboat captain in Bahrain. He was the smoothest talker I've ever come across, and even my complicated domestic situation back in Sydney wasn't an issue as far as Phillip was concerned. I had the long Qantas flight home to mull over the tricky question of how to disentangle myself from my relationship with Norman. I reasoned that we weren't actually married and I had no guarantee that he wouldn't eventually patch up his marriage, so in fact it would be better for all concerned if I was off the scene.

The next couple of months went by in a whirl. You can imagine the scenario. Norman was less than impressed, so I had all that emotional mine-field to deal with, as well as packing my entire possessions to ship to England, arrange a long-distance wedding and maintain a cool, calm appearance for the sake of my young son Anthony, the innocent bystander in all this.

My friends sure had more than enough material for dinner party conversations. There were many well-meaning hints dropped as to whether I'd taken leave of my senses to fly off to the other side of the world to marry someone I'd met merely days ago on a train. I took no notice whatsoever. Once my mind was made up, it was all systems go.

Early in 1976 I departed with Anthony, leaving my crated belongings with shipping agents to be dispatched at a later date. I arrived in England in February and got cold feet in more ways than one. The winter weather was diabolical, Phillip had arranged a flat for me somewhere in Cornwall, and I truly felt my nose was frostbitten simply walking from one room to another.

Our wedding was supposed to take place almost immediately, but I cried off at the last minute. I can't remember what excuse I gave; I probably said I needed more time to think. No-one thought to let Phillip's family overseas know it was all off and it was so embarrassing to receive all these congratulatory telegrams when Phillip was trying to come to terms with being let down. As a compromise, I agreed to try and make a go of things in Bahrain, where he was to return to work, thinking at least the weather there might be better.

It was all a debacle, but I was able to stop my belongings leaving Australia and arranged to have them stored until I knew what I was doing. My few weeks in Bahrain is best forgotten, and I returned to

Sydney, chastened, but none of my friends even dreamed of saying 'I told you so'. Even Norman excelled himself and showed one of the better quirks of his nature by kindly arranging for me to house share at Pymble with a girl he knew who was a divorcee with a young child Anthony's age. She and I became firm friends.

Sorry to say the Captain P saga was not to end here. Phillip got it into his head that if he came to Australia, he could sort out any problems in our relationship. He duly arrived and smooth-talked me into getting married. I had been fortunate enough to get a great job at Ku-ring-gai Municipal Council, conveniently close to both my home and a child-care centre. Phillip thought he could easily get work.

After the embarrassment of the last minute cancellation of my wedding in England, I played it safe with my friends and invited them to a party to meet Phillip, vaguely hinting that it might turn out to be a wedding – most of them got quite a shock when they got there. What I've put my long-suffering friends through over the years!

Norman's brother and his wife were absolutely marvellous. To all intents and purposes they were the only family I had so I asked them to be witnesses at the wedding, held al fresco in the garden at Pymble. Phillip's family overseas must have decided once bitten twice shy if the absence of any congratulatory telegrams from them on the day was anything to go by.

If any of my friends predicated that my first marriage would end in disaster, they were right. Phillip couldn't get work, he didn't even qualify as a ferry captain in Sydney and he soon ran out of money. His flaws became apparent to me thick and fast. After a couple of months, Phillip decided he would return to his job in Bahrain, the idea being he would regroup, earn enough to be in a better position to provide for his new wife and step-son and come up with Plan B. I couldn't believe how relieved I was when he left.

I got on with life as best I could, picking up from where I'd left off. I was fortunate to have the unquestioned support of my friends and Norman's family. The grim reality that I had no family of my own to call upon was not lost on anyone.

I loved my job as Secretary to the Chief Engineer of Ku-ring-gai Municipal Council, Gordon, and now having a young child to consider, benefited from the slower pace of being a public servant compared to the hectic whirl of the travel industry. The inner workings of local government was a revelation to me in more ways than one. For instance, there was nothing slow about certain colleagues who fancied themselves as Casanovas and viewed me as a prime target for their attentions.

I often seemed to find myself in tricky situations at various workplaces where the last thing I wanted was to give the impression that my raison d'être was to add a bit of spice to some Tom, Dick or Harry's dull life. If I unwittingly sent out the wrong signals, I blame Gullible Girlie for this. I remember being astounded when someone invited me for drinks after work once and remarked that I must have been expecting him to ask me out on a date. When pressed to explain, the interested party replied defensively it was the way I looked at him. Huh? That was a wake-up call – I was hardly aware of his existence. I learned pretty fast to be more careful not only who I smiled at, but how!

That being said, the machinations of working relationships between colleagues in the office world of the 1970s were a far cry from today. Now unwanted sexual advances receive the deserved punishment. But back then, you simply rebuffed overtures you didn't fancy, kept out of the perpetrator's way and thought no more about it. If the feelings were mutual however, there was many an opportunity for a fine romance.

I believe this lent a certain intrigue and sparkle to your working life and I don't regret any of my harmless office flirtations. I seldom took offence and saw no reason to knock back the occasional invitation to be wined, dined or whatever if I so wished.

One of my fellow Council workers at Ku-ring-gai, who I shall call Neill, had shown more than a passing interest in me, and over lunch in the canteen one day, I blurted out my marital troubles. Neill took the wind out of my sails by suggesting I could get a divorce. Far out I thought – I've only been married three months! The seemingly outrageous idea took hold, I needed no convincing I had made a terrible mistake, so I composed a carefully worded telegram to Phillip telling him our marriage was all over and indicated he needn't bother coming back. I naively thought problem solved.

I should have known better, as within days I received an urgent telegram from Bahrain advising me that my husband was returning to Sydney with all speed to be reunited with his wife and 'son' – you can imagine my reaction. Within weeks the dreaded moment arrived, and at work one day, Phillip appeared at the Engineer's counter, face contorted with rage. He demanded the keys to 'our' car, saying he wanted to borrow it temporarily and would return it. The car was mine of course, but for all I knew it was possible Phillip had used our marriage certificate to add his name to the registration papers, and I thought it prudent to hand over the keys.

My heart was in my mouth as I thought of my little son down the road at the child care centre, but I had warned them trouble was brewing. As Phillip turned on his heels and stormed off, I rushed to the nearest phone and fortunately there was time for the child care centre manager to conceal Anthony somewhere out of harm's way.

The ensuing weeks were a nightmare, including several raging rows at reconciliation meetings I agreed to attend with Phillip. Neill leapt at the opportunity to provide a safe haven for me at his house, drove me to work, took Anthony to child care and generally looked after me. Somehow I got through this terrible time, full of apprehension as to what each day might bring.

One day, after Phillip had not returned my car at an arranged time, I got a flash of intuition, walked into the local travel agent's office, where the consultant was known to me, and asked her if she had seen Phillip recently. The consultant's face was a picture as she breathlessly told me Phillip had purchased an air ticket and that very day had departed Sydney for London.

Being fully aware of Phillip's impecunious state, I realised immediately that he must have sold my car, but that didn't stop me walking back to the Council offices in a happy dream. I felt as though I was walking on air – Phillip had gone from my life forever.

I reckoned having my car sold from under my very nose was a small price to pay. I'd lost my car for the cost of two tickets – his to London – mine to freedom.

Unsurprisingly, I got rid of every shred of evidence that Phillip had been part of my life. I systematically tore up photographs of our time together, including our quite charming garden wedding. I know I wore a beautiful white dress because at the time I wanted everything to be correct for my first marriage, right down to virginal white - but I needed no photos to remind me of the occasion.

I have absolutely no memory of my first husband's face, nor was I emotionally scarred in the least by this episode. I was extremely embarrassed at my stupidity though, and this was one skeleton in the closet I intended to shut the door on forever. My family and friends knew better than to discuss Phillip, and life returned to normal.

As soon as the statutory two years of separation was up and never having heard from Phillip since his 'midnight flit' in 1976, I lodged notice of divorce. This was crucial as far as I was concerned especially since it had been pointed out to me that in legal parlance, my young son Anthony could be deemed 'a child of the marriage'. My solicitor advised me to retain the services of a barrister as Captain P had not acknowledged receipt of the divorce papers posted to his last known address in Bahrain, causing a tricky situation which needed a Judge's ruling.

I'll never forget my trepidation as I waited to be summonsed before His Honour in the Family Court. When the case was called, I trotted in meekly behind the barrister and when I was seated I made sure to look carefully around the courtroom to see if by any remote chance Philip had decided to turn up after all – but my fears were groundless.

The barrister presented the case; the Judge quizzed him regarding possible reasons for non-response to the service of divorce papers, then asked me for my version of events. The Judge listened as I earnestly recounted my story, doubtless with mounting incredulity, then with a withering glance from under bushy eyebrows, posed the question as to what had possessed me to accept a marriage proposal from someone who I had met mere days previously on a train trip. When I replied in all sincerity that I thought if only I could get married everything would be all right, a 'titter ran round the court'!

I was granted a divorce and walked away a free woman. The barrister heartily congratulated me on my performance for His Honour, which really miffed me – performance indeed, I'd never been more serious; there wasn't a shred of acting on my part. With lesson learned (hopefully!), I pressed on with life.

A postscript to this happened nearly 20 years later, on a night out with friends at a local restaurant, where I had taken my former Pymble house-mate who was visiting from Queensland. She innocently reminisced about my marriage to Captain P all those years ago, having no idea she was revealing one of my best kept secrets. You could have heard a pin drop as my new group of friends sat in stunned silence digesting this news. Well, the cat was well and truly out of the bag, I had no option but to own up, and everyone had a huge laugh at my expense – who could blame them.

20

A New Start

Once the coast was clear after Phillip's departure in 1976, I took stock of my situation. At least I had the stability of my job at Ku-ring-gai Council, which gave me confidence as well as time and space to consider my next move - how best to play my hand of cards.

It didn't take me long to come to the conclusion there was no future in a relationship with Neill, my Council colleague who had been so kind to me during the whole sorry saga. At the same time I decided I should give Anthony the opportunity to get to know his real father.

Norman was renting a small office at Eastwood railway station, where he had started a new business from scratch. Evidently nothing could be salvaged from the ashes of his old company. So he established a coaching college, which he still personally ran well into his 80s. Norman had legendary mathematical abilities and was a charismatic character.

The catalyst for me came one day when Norman phoned me asking me to bring him some soap, apparently he was dossing down at his office and there must have been a shower on the premises. Typical Norman - he was absolutely hopeless looking after himself. I crossed the road at Eastwood station, holding Anthony by one hand, soap in the other - knowing in my heart that Norman needed me and Anthony needed his father. Recalling this incident, I was reminded of my first trip to China in 2002 to visit Anthony after he had moved there to start work – a cryptic line in an email he sent before I left read: 'Please bring razor-blades'. Like father, like son I mused.

Norman and I both realised there was no point wasting time in recriminations, so we leased a flat nearby, and started life once more as a family unit. This is when my life and career took off in a totally different direction. Norman knew I had a chip on my shoulder at my lack of school qualifications and packed me off to an educational psychologist to prove I was capable of undertaking higher studies. Some seeds of hope had therefore been sown when Norman's brother, who was a teacher with TAFE, came up with the idea that I should consider teaching with TAFE. Even so, the notion seemed nothing short of preposterous. Me – the Fort Street failure – how could I dream of being a teacher?

I am forever indebted to Norman's brother and his wife who convinced me to give it a try, pointing out that TAFE was truly 'second-chance' education and as long as you could prove your skills in your trade, TAFE would take care of the rest. They told me about a bridging course at Ultimo college for prospective Secretarial Studies teachers, which I attended in the second semester of 1977 in preparation for the Stage IV Shorthand and Typewriting courses the next year.

I faced strong opposition from the Secretarial Studies staff when I enrolled in both the Shorthand as well as the Typewriting Instructor's courses in 1978. They told me no one ever undertook these certificates simultaneously and made dire predictions of failure. They didn't count on my determination to prove people wrong once my mind was made up, and I graduated at the end of 1978 with the two precious pieces of paper granting me an entrée into the world of Education.

The relatively low-pressure Ku-ring-gai Council job proved a blessing, enabling me to cope with work, study and an intense homework regime – plus caring for a young child and his father. Housework has never been my long suit and fortunately for me in Norman's world, the fact that he may have been living in total chaos simply would not have registered.

Little did I know at the time, but I was to combine full time work and part time study continuously for the next 10 years. My new career provided me with all the challenges and rewards I could ever hope for, including the motivation to move up the TAFE promotional ladder. To have any chance, you had to constantly upgrade your qualifications and you learned to keep a sharp eye out for courses to complete which would 'look good on your CV'. It was like a treadmill but the sweet sense of success and the joy of learning is an addictive mix and I didn't want to get off. Not only that, but I had a point to prove and when you work for an educational institution, studying is part of the scene.

The visionary words of the keynote speaker at my first graduation ceremony: *'Don't rest on your laurels - learning is a lifelong experience'* were pretty spot on. Many years later when I decided my career aspirations had gone as far as they were going, I happily left further formal studies off my agenda, knowing I could genuinely look back with no regrets.

After the TAFE 1978 exam results were announced, I had to face the hurdle of an interview with Miss Joan Fielding, the Head of the Department of Secretarial Studies, a reincarnation of Miss Lilian Whiteoak, the formidable Headmistress at Fort Street High. Miss Fielding ruled the Department with a rod of iron - it meant the kiss of death for your career if you didn't measure up to her stringent standards. I passed muster and was offered a full time teaching position in the next year's intake, provided I was prepared to comply with the Department's mandatory country service policy. There were plenty of aspiring teachers, who even after putting so much effort into completing the Instructor's courses, had to be content with part time work in the Sydney Metropolitan area if it was impossible for them to relocate to country NSW.

Fate was to play a part at this juncture, as I initially knocked back this highly prized job offer - with good reason. Things were more settled on the home front since Norman and I had set up shop again, and I longed to have another child. During the last term of classes, to my delight I discovered I was pregnant. In reality, I only went through the motions of the TAFE interview, as the prospect of coping with both a new job at an unknown location and a new baby later in the year was too daunting.

1979 was to be a huge year for me. In January, tragedy struck. A miscarriage threatened, and being over three months' pregnant, I was told to go by ambulance directly to North Shore Hospital Emergency. The baby could not be saved, and I'll never forget the coldly clinical manner of the ward nurse as she collected my expelled foetus in a bed-pan. I was in excruciating pain and extreme distress, but all she said was: 'You have aborted'. No word of sympathy, no indication of the sex of the baby which I believe it may have been possible to determine at that stage. I was kept in hospital for a week because of the massive blood loss and ensuing infection.

After being discharged, I returned home, devastated and depressed with all my hopes dashed. Suddenly an inspirational thought occurred to me - there was light at the end of the tunnel - I could now accept the teaching position with TAFE after all. I urgently arranged an appointment with the Head of Department to tell her I had changed my mind. I didn't divulge the real reason, saying something vague about it was OK for me to do country service now. Miss Fielding tut-tutted away as she signed the forms to formally reverse my rejection letter, but nevertheless told me to report for duty on 1st February 1979 at Tighes Hill Technical College, Newcastle. This location was considered practically Metropolitan and was chosen because of TAFE's Teacher Training arrangements with Newcastle College of Advanced Education (CAE). However you always had the threat hanging over your head of being sent to Boggabilla or some other remote location at the end of the two year period.

Norman gave his unquestioned support to my taking the job, entailing as it would travelling by train to Newcastle every Sunday night, returning to Sydney each Friday and taking Anthony with me. One of the conditions of accepting the position was agreeing to undertake the 2-year Teacher Training program at Newcastle CAE, and as far as Norman was concerned, furthering one's education was of paramount importance.

21

My Career with TAFE Begins

I handed in my notice to Ku-ring-gai Municipal Council and became NSW State Government employee No 7946264 – you never forget your name, rank and serial number. As I write this, I feel incredibly privileged that 35 years later, I am still counted amongst the ranks of TAFE employees, admittedly part-time and having pulled back a gear or two since reaching the official retirement age of 55 in 1998.

In 1979, there was absolutely no question of wriggling out of country service on compassionate grounds, such as having a young child about to start school along with a household in Sydney depending on you, to say nothing of the recent miscarriage ordeal. At this time I was also conscious of the responsibility I now had regarding my father. He was approaching 80 and, while still capable of caring for himself, the trauma of the forced separation from his wife was taking a physical and emotional toll on him.

Also during 1979, in his disturbed state, my father again sold up in Sydney and moved to England in one further effort to settle. It was to be the last time he made this long, sad journey, and he returned to Sydney in 1980. By then his funds were so depleted, he uncharacteristically had to seek my financial help to purchase a modest property in Ermington. Dad continued his futile campaign to be reunited with my mother and I could only watch helplessly from the wings.

Any attempts I made to contact my family to take up his cause, met with a stony wall of silence. I braced myself each time I made a phone call to them, but it never ceased to upset me, when my pleas for help on Dad's behalf not only fell on deaf ears, but the conversation would be rudely terminated mid-sentence when they recognised my voice.

The worst incident of all for my father, the one which finally broke his spirit, was when he received a letter from a solicitor, couched in legalese, warning him from making any approaches to his wife, either by letter, in person, or phone call otherwise divorce proceedings could follow. I believe many such letters were instigated by the EB hierarchy at the time. My father showed it to me in disbelief. I knew as well as he did that all he ever wanted was to be heard, to put his side of the story, to be allowed to speak to my mother however briefly. To be denied this opportunity was despicable, cruel and heartless in the extreme - perpetrated by so-called Christians.

In a heart-felt letter from my sister some years after Dad died, she told me how grieved she was to have returned a letter unopened that she received from my father around this time. My sister said how could she know what he wanted to say if she didn't open the letter to read the contents? That would be obvious to any rational person, but to the brainwashed multitudes of the EB faithful, opening a letter from an 'opposer of the position' was strictly forbidden and it was a brave person indeed who would defy this ruling. This is another example of a ruling that has now been relaxed - too late for my father.

Not long after I had started in Newcastle in 1979 I took my five-year old son Anthony and attempted to see my mother where she was living with my eldest brother Donald at Kellyville on the outskirts of Sydney. I wanted to make absolutely sure she was not being held in my brother's house against her wishes. I needed to hear from her lips that her refusal to acknowledge my father's endeavours to contact her was of her own free will. This episode ranks among the most distressing incidents I have ever been through, and one that will haunt me for the rest of my life. It is far too painful for me to put into fresh words now, but my account of it was aired in the 2006 ABC TV *Four-Corners* program, *'Separate Lives'*. An extract from this interview follows:

'Interviewer QUENTIN MCDERMOTT:

Renewed faith, though, doesn't dull the memories or the pain. After her father was excommunicated, Joy Nason took her son to see her mother, to check that she was OK, and was where she wanted to be.

JOY NASON

I found out she was staying with one of my brothers, and I was determined to find out for myself that this is what she wanted to do. But I was afraid of trespassing, so I rang the police station in the locality where my brother was living, and I said, "What rights do I have to see my mother?" They said I had every right to be told by my mother herself that she was where she wanted to be.

My son was four or five years of age and I took him with me, and I found the house, I'd obviously never been there before. I knocked on the door and knew I had the right address because my sister-in-law opened the door, recognised me and immediately closed the door. So I said I wanted to see my mother, and she of course wouldn't let me see her. So I then said that the police had told me that my mother must be able to say, from her own free will, that that's where she was staying and she wanted to be there.

My mother eventually came to the door, and I was probably fairly hysterical by this stage, and I said, "I just want to know that you're okay, that you want to be here". She said, yes, she was okay, she wanted to be there. I said, "But I want to see you", and she was behind a closed door. I just couldn't bear it. I couldn't bear that I was so close and couldn't see her. And I suddenly remembered, they always have a scripture to go by. They always have something, and it's the door, the closed door. You weren't allowed to let an ex-member through an open door, and I suddenly saw there was a flyscreen and the door, and I said, "Mum, if you open the door, there'll still be a closed door".

She took the bait and opened the door, and all the words of condemnation of the Brethren that I was going to hurl at her just went. I just looked at her and I said, "I love you, Mum". To my amazement she mouthed, "I know", silently, and then said, "Go and get right with God" out loud, so that the people in the house would not know. I've never forgotten it, and I turned and went and took my son.'

There was no chance of breaking down the physical and psychological barriers behind which the EB Cult sheltered – I knew my mother was lost to me forever.

I maintained my resolve to dissociate myself from my past connection with the Exclusive Brethren. I deliberately avoided being drawn into discussions that might lead to people discovering my background. There was simply no need to mention it, especially not to my new colleagues at Newcastle. They probably thought I was crazy enough anyway, without having the added stigma of once belonging to a Cult.

While this stance was liberating to me in many ways and undoubtedly aided my successful transition to being part of normal society, it prevented me from baring my soul or sharing the pain of such incidents as happened with my mother. Norman knew what I was going through of course, and one or two close friends, but I preferred to keep my feelings to myself – for better or worse.

The years 1979 and 1980 represented a huge learning curve for me, with many milestones. My first day of teaching was terrifying. As I walked into the classroom with legs like jelly, churning stomach and dry mouth, my 'Good morning everyone' was just a croak. Then I realised it too was the first day for all those upturned faces staring at me – they were probably as nervous as I was. I'm happy to report things improved after that.

I couldn't get over the experience of true job satisfaction, resulting from simply being the conduit through which such a diverse array of TAFE students could achieve their goals – it was a great feeling. I considered myself incredibly lucky: from secretary to teacher was a significant increase in salary, plus excellent working conditions, and all the paid school vacations. Provided I was prepared to work hard and study hard, prospects for my future career were definitely bright. Not everyone shared my enthusiasm. Many people in my Teacher Training group at Newcastle CAE in 1979 had actually dropped in salary to become teachers, and some also found the study load arduous. I couldn't understand why they chose a career in TAFE in the first place and I never did get a straight answer.

It wasn't all beer and skittles though. There were some rough patches and hurdles to negotiate in my first term. My top priority of finding suitable accommodation for myself and 5-year old son proved a nightmare. I tried several rented rooms over the weeks, even being reduced to sleeping on someone's couch at one stage. My colleagues were most concerned at the unsettling effect this was having on me, coupled with the strain of the weekly train commute from Sydney, the added pressure of a new job, intense study load and Anthony starting school at Tighes Hill, Newcastle, at the same time.

Finally, a young man with a roomy house put an advertisement for a flat-mate on the Newcastle CAE notice-board. It was in a convenient location and when I met Ken, taking Anthony along with me, he raised no objections to having a child on the premises. It is a measure of the strain I must have been under after the weeks of turmoil and virtually living out of a suitcase, when Ken said it was OK to move in, I was so relieved that much to my embarrassment I sat down and burst into tears. Anthony asked Ken why Mummy was crying; he said he had no idea but he was going to make a cup of tea. I pulled myself together smartly, drank the tea gratefully and finalised arrangements. It was great to settle down and relax a little and I stayed here until Ken moved on at the end of the year. Things improved even more when I brought my car up from Sydney and took to leaving it in the Broadmeadow Station car park each weekend.

My young landlord Ken was from a large family with whom I became friends, they were outdoor sporty types and I have fond memories of joining them on excursions, such as an exhilarating weekend camping in Barrington Tops and shooting the rapids in canoes down the fast-flowing Barrington River. It didn't happen often of course, there not being a whole lot of opportunity to take a weekend off.

At the beginning of 1980, after moving out of Ken's home, I heard about a teacher in the new year's intake who was looking to house share. She and I teamed up and found a lovely house nearby, where Anthony and I stayed happily the whole year, commuting most weekends to Sydney. I threw myself into my work and studies and did the additional CAE units required to be granted a Diploma of Teaching at the end of the two-year TAFE Teacher Training course.

At the end of the 1980 academic year, the TAFE School of Secretarial Studies was agog with the news that country service had been abolished. You could have heard the cheering for miles, as you no longer had the threat of Boggabilla hanging over your head. You simply had to fill in a transfer form and in all probability, you would get the college of your choice. I listed Ultimo in Sydney as my number one priority – and got it! I could hardly believe my good fortune. My family and friends often jokingly refer to me as 'Lucky Joy', and they're not far wrong.

Norman had recently relocated his coaching college to an office near Wynyard, and moved to a tiny apartment in the city. Getting a transfer to Ultimo College was beyond my wildest dreams. I found out there was a little primary school at Millers Point which only had about 12 pupils all up that Anthony could attend. It happened to be the oldest continuously operating Catholic school in Sydney and Sister Joseph, the Nun who ran the school had an excellent reputation as an educator. I decided to put my religious prejudices aside for the sake of convenience! My optimism for the future knew no bounds.

Perhaps the most significant event of 1980 was an unexpected phone call from Norman one day towards the end of the year suggesting that we should get married. Even though I knew he had finally instigated divorce proceedings, I nearly fell over. I had grown accustomed to the status quo with Norman. I agreed it was probably a good idea and we picked a date in May 1981 when his divorce became absolute.

In the meantime, to celebrate my graduation and surviving the first two years of teaching, with all the attendant highs and lows, I booked a two-week holiday at the end of the year for Anthony and myself to go to the USA. The itinerary included Disneyland, Universal Studios, Las Vegas, the Grand Canyon, a coach tour along the Pacific Coast through Monterey to San Francisco, Alcatraz and finally Yosemite National Park. It was fabulous and just perfect for a 6-year old boy.

We returned in time to spend Christmas with Norman. As was a tradition in those years, we joined his brother and their family at South West Rocks and enjoyed a wonderful old-fashioned fun-filled beach holiday. To this day I fondly remember those carefree holidays at South West Rocks.

22

Kirribilli Days

1981 dawned with Anthony and me joining Norman in his apartment and experiencing the heart of city living. On the one hand it was exciting, we considered the Sydney Botanic Gardens our back yard and made the most of every entertainment you could wish for on the door step. Practicalities had to be considered however and we only stayed a few months. Anthony's bed was a sleeping bag underneath a fold-up table in the minuscule apartment, so we probably did well to last that long. I started to look around for flats to rent in Kirribilli – Norman's condition on moving being that I must find somewhere to live the shortest distance from Sydney CBD as possible.

Anthony started school at St Brigid's at Millers Point and had a wonderful year there – Sister Joseph proved to be the dedicated, caring educator we had heard so much about. His after-school care was at the Abraham Mott Hall in The Rocks, where he mixed it with all walks of life. The Millers Point community spirit was so strong, the lady at the local laundromat offered to look after Anthony before school and see him safely across the road when the bell rang.

A red letter day for me was at the end of January when I signed on for duty at the Secretarial Studies department, Ultimo campus – over the moon that I was now a fully-fledged permanent teacher with a city posting. I'll never forget the staff meeting on the first day, looking around at all the new faces and wondering who I would be sharing a staff room with.

Good Karma ruled that day, as the three lovely girls allocated to a four-desk office with me, Susan, Barbara and Kate are still among my closest friends today. We soon moved to a larger office, which we shared with many interesting colleagues over the years. Kate's good friend Maureen was one, and in 2011 we all had a wonderful weekend away to celebrate 30 years of friendship, shared highs and lows, hundreds of lunches and bottles of champagne, since that far off January day.

The next red-letter day for me was in May, 1981 when Norman and I were married at the Sydney Registry Office. Norman's brother and his wife, were our witnesses. If they were remembering the last time they were witnesses at a wedding of mine, they would have been far too polite to mention it!

Our reception for a small group of family and friends was held at the Woolloomooloo Woolshed, and everything went off without a hitch. Entertaining speeches have always been a legendary feature at this family's functions and our wedding was no exception. One of the guests who gave a speech was Jack (Basher) Birney, a 'colourful Sydney identity'. Jack was a criminal barrister later turned politician.

They say there's no such thing as coincidence, but while writing this manuscript I was searching on an unrelated issue, when my name leapt out at me from an Internet posting I had not seen before. The reference was in a book *Exposé: Scandals, Stars and Scoops* written by the former Sydney journalist, Toni McRae and published in 2011. Toni was at one time married to Jack Birney. I remember Toni so well and thought she was the most sophisticated, worldly-wise person I had ever met. I completely lost touch with her after she and Basher were divorced and was amazed to see Norman and me mentioned in her memoirs.

I recall at the time Norman told her about my background, and in 1974 when my son Anthony was a few months old, Toni implored me to let her write an article for the Sydney Sun newspaper. She envisaged a front-page splash with a picture of Anthony and the sensationalised heading: *'This is the baby the grandmother will never see'*. I was terrified and adamant in my refusal - imagine how the EB would gloat if the story led to the discovery that I had a child out of wedlock. Thanks, but no thanks, Toni!

Marriage to Norman seemed to bring with it a new level of contentment. To say he had a steadying influence on me might be stretching the imagination, nevertheless I was happy with life and glad that at last there seemed a sense of purpose in our relationship. It took a while to get settled after we went to Kirribilli, moving to three different flats in the first 18 months. Then in 1983 we found an apartment with stunning views right on the waterfront at Kirribilli wharf, where we were to stay until I moved out in 1991. All this accommodation was rented of course.

Norman's eccentricities were not affected by his marriage to me, in fact they may well have attained new heights. With him you never knew what to expect. There was never a dull moment. I have often had occasion to reminisce with friends who fondly recall the crazy Kirribilli days, particularly the dynamic dinner parties and barbecues in the communal front garden at the water's edge.

Norman always worked seven days a week, which placed some restrictions on family outings or social activities and I learned to live with that. He was a gregarious person and liked nothing better than a party, so I was delighted when he organised a function for 45 guests at the Pitt Club for my 40th birthday in 1983. It meant a lot to me to invite family and friends to a big party, something I'd always wanted to do and it went a long way towards softening the blow of turning 40.

My friend Mac was there and Basher of course and another colourful lawyer friend of Norman's, one Bruce Miles. He and his wife Lillian were kindness itself to me. Bruce died in 2002 and his obituary in the Sydney Morning Herald was headed *'A Lifelong Campaign for the Voiceless'*. The Governor, Marie Bashir, made a special visit to Bruce's home to bestow on him the Medal of the Order of Australia. He passed away the next day.

Meanwhile, Norman's coaching business was going well, and I was to benefit hugely from associations nurtured through it. He had a penchant for bringing home various acquaintances he might have met during the course of his day's work. They often stayed with us for days to weeks, every one of them were interesting characters and while often impecunious, were enriching to our bohemian existence. We referred to them as our 'minders'. Norman literally put these people at our beck and call for any range of 'duties' it was possible to imagine. They loved it, we loved it, and Norman would have rewarded them handsomely for their services. Most of them remained friends of his for life.

Anthony went to Milsons Point Primary in 1982 and was never short of an after-school carer to accompany him on an amazing variety of activities Norman dreamed up for him – some (such as ballet) more short lived than others. I had no objections to having all this extra assistance on tap, and best of all it was a learning experience for everyone. One of the 'minders' assisted Norman to start a Bridge Club in the city (so I learned to play Bridge), another taught Anthony to play golf (so I took up golf), another was employed by Norman as a tutor in French and Mandarin (Anthony learned Chinese – I didn't but should have). Yet another was always on hand for odd jobs and to rustle up an evening meal for whatever number of guests might unexpectedly turn up with my husband.

One of the people Norman befriended was a dour Scottish gentleman, Alex, who had moved to Sydney after retiring from the British Air Force in Hong Kong. He was living in a flat in Coogee at the time and was another minder who played a significant role in our lives. He came to us on an almost daily basis for years and we looked on him as an especially close friend. I considered him a surrogate grandfather for Anthony.

A most hilarious tale concerning Alex was when Norman told him to take Anthony to the Art Gallery where there was a Picasso exhibition on. Alex and Ant returned almost immediately, and when questioned as to what happened, Alex replied: *'I'm not wasting money taking him to see that roobish'*, whereupon Norman promptly instructed him to go straight back to see the exhibition regardless of the cost!

For years we had semi-permanent lodgers who were former pupils of Norman's and as well, he was forever bringing home students for extra study. Overflow classes from his tutoring were often held in our apartment. Norman made it his mission to utilise every last inch of space in the apartment – the lounge room was divided into two by a makeshift curtain, a bay-window seat was converted into a bed with a nifty arrangement of fold up legs, double-bunks were installed in the spare rooms.

Once, when I was away Norman even transformed our bedroom into a potential classroom by getting a foldaway contraption installed whereby the double bed became a cupboard when not being used. When you retired for the night, you never knew who you were going to step over in the morning. Every couple of years we would get the door-locks changed because he had lost count of who he had given spare keys to.

Material possessions meant nothing to Norman, and just as well I was under no illusion that marrying him would mean financial stability or security. His generosity knew no bounds, and many a student received hours of free tuition if their parents could not afford to pay. He used to devise all sorts of 'barter' schemes to cover these costs, one of the more outlandish being a boat, which he thought Anthony might learn to sail in the harbour. From memory it was only launched once, right into the path of an oncoming ferry with alarming blasts of its horn. It would have been a brave person to try that again, so the boat was left to gather dust in the storeroom.

Anyone who ever stayed at Kirribilli will remember the cry of *'ferry's at Kurraba'* as a look-out was posted at the front window to report on the progress of the commuter ferry to Circular Quay. Students and 'minders' would appear from all directions, fly out of the door and down the steps to the Kirribilli wharf. This life may have been unconventional to say the least, but our visiting students' parents cared only about results, and they got this in spades. Norman had a unique gift for inspiring students to lift their game and reach their full potential. The result? Hundreds of students' lives were changed for the better and Norman lives on in their memories.

I recently came across a copy of a letter I sent during the '80s to a friend in Queensland. Reading it instantly transported me back to the Kirribilli days. A line or two sums up a typical Sunday at that time:

> 'I had a late night last night and Norman has just gone to work. The front two rooms are set up for a Maths and English class, so I am writing this before the hordes get here. DuHua arrives at 9 am for Ant's Chinese lesson (in his room), Steve P stayed overnight and is studying in Rod's room, so we have a full house you might say. After I finish this letter I'm going to close my door and have a sleep.'

I am particularly indebted to Mark, who set up Norman's Bridge club. Mark ranks among the more colourful characters of the Kirribilli days; he was an intellectual, a Labor Party stalwart and a big influence in our lives. We operated in the milieu of education, so Norman was keen for me to progress with part-time studies. First I enrolled in a two-year Bachelor's Degree at Sydney CAE, then a four-year Master's Degree in Education at Sydney University.

Mark became my study-buddy. Instead of assignments being an arduous, hard slog after work and at weekends, I looked forward to getting stuck into the next subject and enjoyed the intense debate Mark would generate over various topics in the courses. In 1984 I graduated with a B.Ed. then in 1988, my M.Ed. Mark played no small part in this success.

23

Shadows from the Past

The shadows of my former life could never be entirely dismissed.

In my early days at Kirribilli, I heard some disturbing news regarding my own sister Janet in the Exclusive Brethren. To the casual observer, the cruelties of the EB sect in the 1970s and 1980s beggared belief. The EB hierarchy introduced a system known as 'Shutting Up', a preliminary stage to either full excommunication or restoration to Brethren privileges. The terror of being 'Shut Up' was used by the hierarchy as a means of total subjugation of the rank and file, with the poor and weak amongst the flock inevitably being singled out. To be 'Shut Up' meant total exclusion from every facet of EB life – and that included family life. For instance, a husband and wife 'Shut Up' together were forbidden sexual relations and any children still in the house were not permitted to share a meal with their parents, plates of food would be left for them outside their rooms.

The following story concerning my sister Janet and her husband is correct in every detail – but in writing it I am only too aware that to any normal person it must rate in the realms of fantasy. They were 'Shut Up' in March or April 1980 on the flimsiest of reasons. Her husband had accompanied an EB brother on a 'priestly visit' to a member who was currently 'under investigation'. The EB hierarchy decided this was inappropriate so he was 'Shut Up'. At the time they had five children, ranging in age from five to 15. Yes, Janet was 'Shut Up' with her husband, while all their children were sent to various Brethren homes. This extraordinary situation continued intermittently for nearly three years – I believe occasionally some of the children were permitted to return home for short periods.

What happened to my sister's family was not an isolated instance – many such cases have been documented and verified.

I heard through the grapevine about these events in 1982 and made my first phone call for many years to my sister Janet, as I was so shocked. I knew that never in her entire life had my sister aspired to anything but to be a good Brethren person and to enjoy a quiet family life. I recognised my sister's voice when she answered the call and I quickly told her what I'd heard. She did not reply but handed the phone to her husband who shouted repeatedly – *'OUR CHILDREN HAVE NOT BEEN TAKEN FROM US'*, then terminated the call.

Clearly their children had been taken from them. Such is the power of a Cult. My sister and her husband knew only too well that to have any chance of 'Restoration' they would have *requested* their children be removed and the children themselves would have parroted the words *'we want to go and stay with other Brethren while our parents are shut up'*. Therefore my poor brainwashed sister and her husband in some convoluted way felt they could truthfully say their children had not been taken from them.

There was a resolution to the crisis around 1983 when the eldest son, Nelson, who was also in a 'Shut Up' situation at the family home, decided to leave. He moved in with a caring Christian family in his home town which allowed his parents to be 'restored'. He was never to return to the EB. At Nelson's wedding a few years ago, I was privileged to meet the kind benefactors who gave safe haven to my nephew and thanked them on our family's behalf.

Around this time two of my brother's sons also left the EB of their own accord. They located me and I was delighted to see them. The next nephew to escape was Michael, the 6-week old baby in a bassinet shown to me when I made the break in 1968. Michael turned up on my doorstep in 1984, having obtained my address from his cousins.

My nephew was only 16 and looked so vulnerable. I was terribly concerned for his well-being and begged him to consider returning home until he was more mature and better prepared to handle the long hard road that is a consequence of separation from your family and the only life you have ever known. He played his cards beautifully, returned to his home town, was given shelter by a High School Counsellor, completed his School Certificate, then returned to Sydney when he secured an apprenticeship. Norman was particularly compassionate to this newly liberated nephew of mine. He became a mentor to him and actively encouraged his further education.

My sister's daughter, who was born after I left the EB, eventually escaped in the year 2000. Two more nephews, sons of another brother, have also since made the break. At the time of writing, six nephews and one niece have followed in my footsteps and decided the movement is not for them. But ten other nephews and nieces, plus their spouses, and 50 great-nephews and nieces (none of whom I have ever seen) remain behind closed doors in the Exclusive Brethren. I have a large, lost family in Australia. When my eldest brother Donald passed away some years ago in the EB, the news reached me several months after the event. However, it meant nothing to me. It was as though I was hearing about the death of a total stranger.

Meanwhile, the final tragic scenes of my father's life were being played out in suburban Ermington. His funds had drastically dwindled with his moves from one side of the world to the other in his disturbed state of mind following his excommunication from the EB. He traversed the oceans and returned to Australia for the last time in 1980. With my assistance, he purchased a house, once again in Ermington. His preferred location was no coincidence as the EB Headquarters were not more than a stone's throw away. I am convinced my father reasoned that to live close to the seat of power would enhance his chances of my mother returning to him. The daily reminders, as he would have observed the comings and goings of the church gatherings, can only have added to his grief.

I saw him as often as I could, but for all the temporary lifting of his spirits my visits occasioned, he never recovered from the heartbreak of his enforced separation from my mother. In 1983 Dad showed alarming signs of dementia, and I had to make the agonising decision to admit him to the Aeolus Nursing Home at Ryde.

Despite his declining health, he was stubborn to the last, meaning I had to resort to subterfuge to execute the move. I let him think he was going to a temporary convalescent situation. I felt like a traitor. My father took some time to settle into his new surroundings and he even escaped once. I'll never forget the late night phone call from the nursing home and the ensuing drama until the police located him miles away in a phone box – trying to call my mother of course. Dad remained at the Aeolus Home until he passed away in March 1984. By that time the entire staff had become very fond of him.

The circumstances surrounding my father's death are harrowing for me to go through again. I made several attempts to proof-read this section, but my nightmares returned in earnest. As I felt it was vital to include this story, which highlights the extremely cruel practices of the Exclusive Brethren at that time, I finally enlisted the help of a friend to edit it. The verbatim account I wrote to my family in England follows.

Copy of letter dated 14th March 1984 sent to my brother and sisters in England

After I wrote to you on Friday telling you about Dad's stroke, I visited him on each of the next two days, and could see very little change in him. I was sure he recognised me and when I said I was going, he waved his hand quite strongly. On the Sunday I told him I would have to go to work next day but that I would ring to see how he was, and he raised his eyebrows, I think to indicate he understood what I was saying.

He often used to say to me 'Now don't you do anything to jeopardise that good job of yours on my account!'; so I was hoping he would understand I couldn't come to see him every day. I rang on the Monday and the Matron said there was no change. I don't finish work on Mondays until 5.30 and that evening I had to attend the Annual General Meeting of Anthony's School P & C. of which I am Vice-President, so I couldn't get out to see Dad.

The next morning, Tuesday 13th, they called me off class at about 11.00 am with an urgent message from the Matron and she informed me Dad had passed away peacefully about 15 minutes ago. The Matron said he had been just the same, wanting to get out of bed so they propped him up in his chair and he reached out for his little red-checked cap he always wore and put it on his head himself. The nurses teased him and said his cap didn't go with his pyjamas and he gave a smile. He then nodded off to sleep in his chair and when they looked in a few minutes later, he was peacefully breathing his last.

Norman and I went straight out to the Home (which is about half an hour's drive from where we live), and he was laid out and he did look so peaceful. The Nurse that was so fond of him had put his Bible on his chest. I'm glad she did because the day he had the stroke last week, he was trying to reach for something, and the Nurse held out all his things for him from his bedside table, and she discovered it was his bible he wanted. When she gave it to him, he just held it and became very peaceful.

I had decided to ring David with the news about Dad's stroke, as I just couldn't face ringing Donald as they had refused to listen to me so many times before, and when I gave David the news and asked if he would get a message through to Mother he said I would have to ring a certain person in Sydney – (one of their Elders I think) and he gave me a phone number. I stressed to David how crucial it was and how Dad had continually asked for Mum but he would not comment.

I then thought about what the Matron had said about Dad with his Bible, and rang David back. However, he had left for work and his wife answered the phone, and immediately said she wouldn't talk to me. She said she wasn't related to me (!) and did not wish to speak to me. I quickly said the few words I'd prepared and ended by saying how sad it all was, and she replied: 'What is sad is how Dad treated his wife and family right from when they were married and he couldn't call himself a Christian after treating his family the way he did' and she then hung up in my ear.

That upset me so much that when Dad did pass away a week later, I told the Matron I couldn't possibly face any more phone calls, so she undertook to get a message through. Donald had rung the Home the day after Dad had the stroke, so they had got the message - but they didn't come to see him. Mum must know that Dad has passed away as there were certain details for the death registration form which I couldn't supply, so the Matron said she'd ask Donald when she rang to give them the news.

The Matron later rang me to say that Donald had rung back with the information (such as Dad's mother's maiden name, Dad's father's name, date and place of Dad's marriage, etc, which by the way was 60 years last September), which surely only Mother would have known and she must have been told why they wanted the information. The Matron actually told me later that the chilling response she received from the family on phoning to advise them of my father's death were the stark words: 'You've done your duty. Good-bye!' before the phone call was terminated.

I've told the Funeral Directors that if they bring Mum to see Dad at the funeral home that is OK, but that under no circumstances are they to interfere with the funeral arrangements. I'm dreading them turning up tomorrow but I very much doubt if they will.

I will never forgive any of them for not allowing Dad to contact Mum this past seven or eight years since they excommunicated him for doing no wrong but quarrelling with their doctrine. Especially I will never forgive them for not allowing them to make their peace with each other before he died. As the Matron said it wasn't much to ask and they could have at least gone through the motions to grant Dad his dying wish.

Of course we had plenty of unhappy times at home, but Dad worked hard all his life to provide for us as we were growing up and I'll never forget Mum telling me that he used to work so hard it used to break her heart to see him, especially during the Depression. As far as I can recall the major part of all the rows at home were over Dad's constant quarrels with the Brethren. If it hadn't been for the Brethren's influence and interference, I venture to say Dad, and life at home, would have been quite different.

Even taking account of Dad's failings, etc anyone with an ounce of compassion would have felt for him in the torment of mind he has had these last few years. I'm sure he's paid a heavy price for any wrongs he may have done, and I must say I never thought of any of his wrongs as I went out there week by week and saw his anguish as he asked for any news of Mum. He had no right to end his days the way he did. He should have had the care and companionship of his life-long friends and family. Anyway, the Matron and nurses at the Home were wonderful to him and told me they really got to love him. I have sent them a flower arrangement with thanks for all they'd done for him.

Of course he also had a few people from a 'breakaway' movement who often visited him, and it was Dad's wish that if he hadn't got back with Mum when he died, that they bury him, so I've arranged for his friends from the breakaway movement to conduct a short service at the chapel of the funeral home tomorrow.

I've got a photo of Mum taken about 20 years ago that Dad always had on his table when he lived alone at Ermington, and which I kept when he went into the Home for fear that constantly looking at it might upset him, and I'm going to put it in his Bible before they seal the coffin tomorrow - he wasn't granted a sight of her before he died, so at least he'll have a photo of her with him.

I'm enclosing a copy of the Death Notice I put in the Sydney papers, and feel it best expressed the situation, out of respect for Dad and us four who had compassion for him. I've arranged for the flowers to be on the coffin from you, as you asked on the telephone.

Naturally, the Matron feels very strongly about the way Dad was treated but thank goodness I was able to do the right thing by Dad in caring for him, to save the family's name, and I used to tell the Matron that Mum couldn't help it because Mum had been brainwashed to believe that what she was doing was right.

Of course Norman and his family will be with me tomorrow, and I am so thankful for their support, and there are some other friends of mine who will be going, which helps me feel a lot better about the situation. I'll continue this letter after the funeral tomorrow, to let you know how everything went.

Thursday 15 March
(Before the funeral)

I lay awake last night thinking about Mum a lot, and this morning I mustered up the courage to ring Mum myself, so that I would know for sure that she knew all about it and to try and set my mind at rest. I'm so glad I did as although Doris answered the phone, she did get Mum and Mum and I had a long conversation. Although it was so sad, it was such a relief to be able to tell her personally about Dad's last few days and to know that she understood how I felt and she said she was thinking and praying for me.

Mum particularly stressed she couldn't have visited Dad because of the situation and I told her I knew she couldn't help it because it was her beliefs, and she said it was a relief to know I understood. I think she got a lot of comfort from believing that God worked with Dad at the end, and if in her mind that is what matters, I don't begrudge her that.

I said to her I was dreading them interfering at the funeral today, and she said: 'Oh no, we won't be there because we couldn't get complete control'. It has been known for the Exclusives to try and take a body from a funeral parlour, and the funeral home where Dad is knew all about that sort of thing before I mentioned it to them, and they assured me they were aware of the situation and that as far as they were concerned I was in complete control as I was the one who had notified them of the death and had made the arrangements with them. So I went to the funeral in a much more peaceful state of mind.

While I was on the phone to Mum I asked her if anyone would let me know if ever anything happened to her as she is 84 this year – Dad would have been 83 – Mum said 'Oh, yes of course'. I said, but Mum I've understood that they won't (which is correct by the way from stories I've heard and I've been dreading for years hearing about Mum's death after the event), and mum said 'I'll tell them to tell you'. But I can't believe they'd have the decency to respect her wishes.

(After the funeral)

The funeral itself went off very well. Norman and I and my friend Rachel (who left the Exclusives 15 years ago like me) stood at the door to welcome the people. We'd dressed in our best and applied tasteful make-up as Rachel said to me before the funeral. 'We must never let 'them" think we've gone downhill!' I wore a pure silk lemon blouse and a green suede skirt – green was Dad's favourite colour.

A lot of Norman's family came, although they didn't know Dad personally, as you know he wouldn't accept them in the past, but they came for my sake as I think they knew I was dreading Dad being buried without mourners there. As well as the few old people who had been so good to him since he was in the home, and quite a few others from different 'breakaway-movements'. I wanted anyone to come who had known Dad in the past, regardless of which group they were attached to.

So there was quite a good gathering there, about 40 in all, and although I have nothing in common with these people, I was glad to see them and could vaguely remember them from the past, and for Dad's sake it was good they were there. Thank goodness no-one from the exclusives showed their face. I put the photo of Mum on Dad's chest and kissed him goodbye from all of us, then they sealed the coffin.

Your flowers looked beautiful and some of my friends had sent flowers, including some beautiful arrangements to my place. Rachel's card read: 'In fond memory and warm respect of a man who had the courage of his convictions. Peace – Rachel'. Norman has always said how he's always admired Dad because he was such a 'tough old fellow'. He was always saying how tough Dad was to have stood up to the bashing he'd had. I took Ant to the funeral, but I didn't let him see Dad before they sealed the coffin, as I think it's best for him to remember his Grandpa as he was.

The service was just what Dad would have wanted, – hymns, prayers and Bible reading etc and affectionate words about Dad. While all those 'breakaway' people looked so odd to me and still have so many shackles from the past, Dad would have been proud they were there.

At the grave when they finally lowered the coffin, I looked down and managed to whisper 'Bye bye Dad' as I'd always said when I was leaving him, and I was comforted to know he'd really had the best that could have been done for him at the end. The weather was gloriously sunny, with a beautiful, gentle breeze blowing.

I'm buying 'In Appreciation' cards today to send to all who were there, and also to a very kind neighbour of mine who came in while we were out at the funeral, made the place spotless and prepared a wonderful spread for those who came back with me after. It was a lovely gesture, done out of kindness and completely unasked. And to think 'they' used to make us believe there was no loving kindness out there in the world!

By the way, I forgot to mention earlier, that it is quite likely the Exclusives may have come after we left the graveside to conduct their own service. They quite often do this, and if they did I would be glad for Mum's sake.

I think I should mention that Dad's faith and courage never wavered right to the end. Not only physically in that he vigorously brushed aside all my attempts to make him use a stick even when he became unsteady on his feet, and in the few days after the stroke he still made the nurses understand that he wanted to get out of bed and sit in his chair – but spiritually he clung to his beliefs.

If I happened to go on a Sunday instead of my usual Saturday, and would offer to send Ant round to the shop to get Dad an ice-cream like I would on Saturdays, Dad would say: 'Its Sunday isn't it? I don't want you buying anything on a Sunday!' (or actually Lord's Day he called it). And of course I always respected his beliefs and also never wore my slacks or jeans or any make-up when I visited him. I'm glad now that I did that for his sake, even though at the time if often used to be a nuisance changing into a skirt or rubbing lipstick off in the car! And to think he never joined in with any of the activities of the Home and never went near the TV. room or on any of their outings, even though I wished he would.

I remember persuading him to walk round to a nearby hall for the home's Christmas 'do' because everyone was going, but no amount of persuasion could get him to go inside, so I had to bring him back. He was separate because that was what he believed in, and for the last year or so he couldn't even get out to the group's meetings, but just sat alone on the patio or in his room day in day out, his only thoughts or lucid words being his wish to be reconciled with Mum. It pains my heart that according to them he was not worthy of reconciliation, yet never once did they go near the home, or phone, so how could they know that his soul was steadfast to the end. My only comfort is that he knew I cared and I continually told him Mum would have come if she could but that there was no way she could have got there.

Also a plaque for the grave has to be arranged. Do you want anything particular on the plaque? I have a Bible that Mum gave to Dad in 1939 with an inscription in it from her of a verse, the words of which might be suitable to use on the plaque. The inscription in Mum's handwriting in Dad's Bible reads:

'As the Father has loved me, I also have loved you: abide in my love. John 15.9'

So ends Dad's story as written by me at the time to my brothers and sisters in England who were not in the Exclusive Brethren.

In 1984, the year my father died, the forced estrangement from my mother weighed heavily on my mind. One of Mum's mantras when I was growing up was 'Let not the sun set on your wrath'. In other words don't end the day with unfinished business – sound advice indeed. I decided I would attempt to see her once more, whatever it took, to make my peace with my mother. I was questioned about this incident on the ABC TV *Four Corners* program in 2006.

I knew of a sympathetic EB Elder in the locality where my mother resided at my brother's house. I contacted him with a carefully worded request, couched in 'Brethren-speak' that I needed to put some spiritual matters right with my mother and suggesting he act as an intermediary on my behalf in arranging an interview. This approach worked and a date was negotiated with my brother Donald, provided I agreed to the meeting taking place under certain conditions, such as various Elders and others being present. I was prepared to agree to anything to see my mother.

My son Anthony was by then 10 years old, and his only previous memory of visiting his grandmother was the disastrous occasion five years before when I had almost collapsed with grief. There was no way I was going to leave him behind this time, as I particularly wanted him to see his grandmother under more favourable circumstances.

My mind was in tumult as I drove to the address I'd been given where my brother lived in Kellyville, but the overwhelming emotion was one of happiness at the prospect of seeing my mother again. I'll never forget walking through that house, seemingly surrounded by faces from the past, as they led me towards where my 83-year old mother was sitting in an easy chair waiting for me. I introduced Anthony to his grandmother and she said a few kind words to him, then I told him to wait for me outside. Initially I hoped the Elders would be flexible with the terms of the meeting and at least have the decency to grant me a few moments alone with my mother – but it was soon obvious they had no intention of moving so much as an inch.

In the end nothing spoilt the occasion for me. Everyone in the room seemed to fade from my vision as I grasped my mother's hands in mine and looked her straight in the eyes, saying how much I loved and missed her. I felt she and I were alone in our own space. I knew my mother well enough to realise she would have always felt a degree of responsibility over my defection from the EB in 1968 – it was in her nature to blame herself for anything that went wrong. I wanted to free her from this burden of guilt and was determined to assure her she was in no way at fault. I told her from the bottom of my heart how sorry I was to have caused her so much suffering by straying from the one true path that she believed in - and I meant it.

I loved my mother so much, to make my peace with her this side of the grave was vital to me. I believe I achieved this at that moment and I felt a sense of victory over the EB as I drove away. Even though this was the last time I ever saw or spoke to my mother, I knew in my heart the EB could never break the bond between us.

24

More Travels Abroad

At the end of 1984 after much planning, I took Anthony overseas for the six-week TAFE vacation. Anthony was 10 and it was not lost on me that at the same age, I was travelling in the other direction - by migrant ship. No such hardship now I thought as we buckled into our Qantas seats for the outward bound leg on 6th December. Our itinerary included Greece, Egypt, the UK, France, Canton and Hong Kong before returning to Sydney on 14th January 1985. I kept a diary for this trip and don't know how we fitted so much into this holiday - makes me tired reading it again after all these years.

This Yuletide of 1984 in the UK was the first Christmas celebration with any of my family since 1952 when I was 9 years old. The four Nason siblings, outcasts from the rest of our family, made the most of this rare time together. Anthony and I enjoyed a traditional English Christmas Day lunch at a Country Club in Downderry, Cornwall, with my brother John and his wife and my sisters Beryl and Millie. We even got a mention in the social pages of the local rag: *'Joy and Anthony swapped the 84 degree Fahrenheit climate of Sydney, Australia, to brave the chilly temperatures of South-East Cornwall'* - a newsworthy item in this tiny village.

On this same holiday, I made a pilgrimage to my childhood home in Uplands Road, Fishponds, Bristol. Thirty-two years after I left as a young child on the brink of a new life, I found my old home, walked up the path and knocked on the door. The kindly householder welcomed my sister Millie, Anthony and me in to have a look around. It was incredibly emotional, the passage of time not diminishing the painful memories. Millie, who had left that same house before I was born, embraced me and we wept in each other's arms. Anthony and the householder simply looked on in bemusement.

The next half of the 1980s can only be described as living in the fast lane, burning the candle at both ends, progressing through life's journey at a rate of knots. My home, work, social and study life combined to ensure each day passed in a whirl. In hindsight, I believe an inner urge was compelling me to make up for lost time. I wanted to prove to the outside world that I wasn't a second-class citizen, to throw off forever my perceived stigma of working-class origins and religious fundamentalism.

My old boss, Mac, remained a constant friend and enjoyed taking me on various lovely outings whenever time permitted, and this went a long way to improving my self-esteem.

My friendship with the Shellcove Road 'Golden Girls' remained as strong as ever and we enjoyed some riotous occasions when we got together.

From 1986 to 1988 I completed a Masters of Education degree at Sydney University. While it involved a huge amount of work, I loved every minute of it. It was a different view of the world entirely, totally unrelated to my previous TAFE-based vocational studies. I thrived on the broadening experience. I remember the graduation ceremony so well. Like a proud father, Mac accompanied me to the Great Hall to watch as my degree was conferred by the Chancellor, Sir Hermann Black.

Doing the MEd was essential to climb up the rungs of the TAFE ladder. It paid off and in 1987, I became a Head Teacher, my first posting being to Liverpool College for six months, then Ultimo for two years and North Sydney for two and a half years. I was promoted to Senior Head Teacher in 1992. The learning curve was steep as well as the increased responsibility and work load, but I was happy and knew that switching to a job in the education field was the best career decision I ever made.

To celebrate completing my Masters, I took Anthony on another overseas holiday. We were away almost two months from 7th December to 30th January 1989. A novel component of this trip was that we were accompanied by two teenage students, Belinda and Julie, from Norman's coaching college. The trip was a reward from their parents for excellent HSC results and it was assumed I would be their chaperone. Just as well I didn't sign anything – it was a case of 'all care but no responsibility taken'.

Something you can bet on though: it was one holiday both Belinda and Julie will never forget. I remember overhearing a phone call on Christmas day in England between Julie and her mother in Australia with Julie declaring: 'I'm making up for every single time I've ever been deprived in my entire life'. She was just 17 and I imagine her mother shuddered.

Our itinerary started off with Athens and the Greek Islands. For our three nights on Mykonos, the Hotel Leto was the only tourist hotel open. It was mid-winter and it seemed as though we were the only people visiting Mykonos. The locals took us into their hearts and homes and made our stay very special.

When we got to England, Belinda and Julie escaped my care for some sightseeing of their own, while Anthony and I did a whirlwind tour of various friends and relatives in England. We visited London, Dorset, Somerset, Worcester, Stratford on Avon, Coventry and Birmingham, being treated like royalty everywhere. The girls went to Scotland for a few days and I'm sure they behaved impeccably. They met up with us again to spend Christmas with my sister Millie in Cornwall.

We saw the New Year in at Hastings and Rye, then on 1st January 1989 went by Hovercraft from Dover to Calais. We toured Paris, including an unforgettable night at the Moulin Rouge for a family-friendly cabaret where I could take Anthony even though he was only 14. We then hopped on the TGV for the south of France and spent a fortnight in Nice in a stunning apartment on the Promenade des Anglais overlooking the ocean. My teenage companions ensured every day brought a new adventure. On a day trip to Monaco, Belinda and Julie were most put out, when they were barred from entering the Monte Carlo casino where proof of age was demanded. They vowed to return to Monte Carlo when they reached the required age of 21.

Norman had arranged French classes for Anthony in Nice. He was put in a homestay with a French family nearby and attended a local language school each weekday. Anthony still has a good command of French, which I'm sure can be attributed to this immersion course. I don't think he was too happy at the time however!

Then we set off for Rome, Naples and Pompeii, with a final stopover in Singapore before arriving in Sydney at the end of January. I started back at work the next day, convincing myself that jet-lag was simply mind over matter.

A pattern was emerging in my life where Norman did not participate in significant events, holiday arrangements or family outings. He was immersed almost literally 24/7 in his own coaching college world and I forged on regardless. If either of us noticed we were increasingly operating as independent units, we would not have remarked on it, accepting it as a normality.

25

Endings

Fearful of being left behind in the technology race, during 1989 I completed the TAFE Word Processing Instructor's course. The writing had been on the wall since the early 1980s for typewriters (electronic or otherwise). I seemed to be forever doing various computer related workshops. The Word Processing Instructor's certificate was necessary so these skills were formally recognised. You had to resign yourself to acquiring all the qualifications deemed necessary for success, so I also undertook a two-year Graduate Diploma in Computer Education with UTS Sydney in 1990 and 1991. If you weren't competitive in the information technology revolution, you didn't get a look in on the promotions list. The study treadmill was hard at work!

I had achieved so much, yet I was restless and discontented. My take on my domestic state of affairs by 1990 is that I had 'moved on' or could it have been 'the grass is always greener on the other side'. Whatever the reason, there was no denying I was 'over' my marital situation with my husband Norman.

For quite some time Norman had developed the embarrassing habit of announcing to all and sundry that I would leave him, when at that stage I had no intention of doing so. This was possibly a defence mechanism for him, or he may have sincerely believed this would eventuate. Norman had been incredibly supportive and non-judgemental throughout the rocky road of our twenty years together and apart. I always credited him with putting me on the path to education – in my eyes he had in effect *'raised me from the dunghill and set me among princes',* to quote a line from the Bible (Prophet Samuel 2:8). I considered it would be shallow in the extreme to come to a parting of the ways – and besides, Anthony, now 16, was devastated whenever talk of a separation was mooted.

However, as Norman prophesied, eventually my feelings of dissatisfaction overwhelmed me. I weighed up the consequences, considered the ramifications, and opted to take my chances on my own once more.

Life with Norman had always been day to day. Most of my friends and family declared they wouldn't last a day in the seemingly haphazard existence at Kirribilli. It was easy to use this as my reason for moving on – who could blame me? However in moments of clarity, I knew it was deeper than that. The truth hit home when one of my friends expressed surprise that I was leaving Norman and said perceptively: *'But I thought you liked this crazy life'.*

Yes, I did, but the inescapable fact was Norman had always been a father figure to me in every sense of the word and, as I developed in my emotional state and achieved academic and career success, I didn't need this representation any more. Freud would have had a field day. I had reached a point where I internalised Norman as my father and to continue in a relationship as husband and wife was to continue living a lie.

Early in 1991, I found a furnished room in a house-share nearby at North Sydney and made plans to move. The financial arrangements for running the household at Kirribilli had always been whoever had the cash when the bills came in paid them. It worked for us, but this cavalier attitude towards managing money ensured there was never anything put aside for a rainy day. When the time came to go I didn't have the ready cash for the bond, and typical of Norman's open attitude, he paid it for me. With a sense of *déjà vu*, I packed my personal possessions and drove away to a new life.

Renting a room meant I had to leave Anthony behind. Even though he was 16, this was the toughest decision of all for me. A major concern was that Anthony was in his HSC year, however I reassured myself that as his father was operating a successful HSC coaching business, he would be OK. I rationalised that when I departed Kirribilli, my son was in the best situation possible under the circumstances. The household at that time consisted of four people – Norman and Anthony plus a more or less permanent 'minder' and one of Norman's very sensible sons.

However, they only lasted a matter of weeks after my departure before the apartment was disbanded. Norman moved to a boarding house, Anthony was sent to live with one of his older half-brothers and the 'minder' and Norman's other son also departed. I found this news disturbing and was most concerned at the unsettling effect it might have on Anthony in his final year at High School.

This was one instance when I was glad to be proved wrong. In 1991, Anthony made the coveted walk on to the stage at his High School. He had achieved a Highly Commended award in the Sydney Morning Herald writing competition. To qualify for an Assembly Award in the competitive milieu that was North Sydney Boys selective school was no mean feat – he might have left it until his final year – but he got there. Despite my fears, Anthony achieved a respectable HSC score and the following year I was again so proud of him when he received a commendation certificate in the 1992 Stanton Library Young Writers Awards.

Anthony was bitterly disappointed when I moved out and wanted to come and live with me. As all I could afford was a room in a share-house with other women, this was out of the question. My love for Anthony was unconditional. From the moment he was born, my son had meant more to me than anything in this world. I had no control over the forced separation from my parents, which doubled my determination to never let anything come between me and my own flesh and blood.

At this new cross-road in my life, however, there was no alternative but to go it alone. I resolved I would make it up to Anthony in the years to come. Anthony's half-brother and his wife were kindness itself to Anthony during this tough period in his life, and have continued to be a support to him, as have Norman's other children.

In this same year, another chapter in my life closed. Skimming through my account of my father's last days in 1984, the following paragraph leaps out at me:

'While I was on the phone to Mum I asked her if anyone would let me know if ever anything happened to her as she is 84 this year – Dad would have been 83 – Mum said 'Oh, yes of course'. I said, but Mum I've understood that they won't (from stories I've heard I'd been dreading for years hearing about Mum's death after the event), and mum said "I'll tell them to tell you". But I can't believe they'd have the decency to respect her wishes.'

What I predicted came true - I was not informed when my mother passed away. One day early in August 1991, I was visiting a friend when I received a message that my sister Millie in England was trying to contact me urgently. I got through to her late that night and she started off the conversation with words of comfort and condolence. To her horror she immediately realised I had no idea what she was talking about. Someone in the family had told her our mother had passed away the previous day and she wanted to show her support for me.

In the twisted minds of the Exclusive Brethren, my older siblings in England were not rated as high on the sinners scale as me. They had left the movement long before the 1959 separation issue and were deemed less responsible for their actions. I had been formally excommunicated from the EB fellowship in 1968 in the full knowledge that I would be from henceforth considered an outcast, an untouchable, unworthy of any communication. Hence my sister in England was advised of my mother's demise, not me.

I now faced the daunting prospect of attempting to discover whatever details I could about my mother's death and burial arrangements. However the EB could have no control over what happened that very night. I was sleeping fitfully when I became aware of a presence in my room. I opened my eyes to see my mother walking towards me, her arms outstretched in greeting, the old familiar smile lighting up her face. As I leapt out of bed to embrace her, she said *'Everything's OK'*, then disappeared from view. My heart was filled with joy at this visitation. Freed from the mortal chains that had bound her for so long, her spirit reached out to me, giving me the comfort and strength I sorely needed.

Never again have I argued that a supernatural experience is impossible.

The following day I made the dreaded calls to my family in the Exclusive Brethren to find out about my mother's death and to ask about her funeral. Obviously I had no recent contact details for any of my siblings, which greatly complicated the task of finding their correct phone numbers. When I tracked down my first two brothers, they refused to give me any information. Somehow I established that my mother had definitely been living with my brother in Wagga Wagga. I rang the number I had been given for him and will never forget his words. 'Do you have a particular interest in this matter?' was his chilling response after I had identified myself. I gave up – to continue the conversation was to continue the torment.

It took me until the next day, when after fruitless calls to various firms of undertakers in the Wagga Wagga area, I rang the local Cemetery Office, to find that yes, indeed, one Hilda Stonall Nason was to be buried in the cemetery that very afternoon. There was no way an excommunicated person would be permitted to attend a funeral service in an EB meeting room in any case, but some were known to take the brave step and go to the graveside for the burial of a family member. The heartlessly inconsiderate way bereaved outsiders were treated on these occasions was typical of the EB *modus operandi* at that time, so in hindsight it was just as well it was too late for me to get from Sydney to Wagga Wagga in time.

Instead, I made my own symbolic journey to the little island off Balmoral Beach in Mosman. It was one of my favourite spots and not crowded on a weekday. I stood there in solitude on the rocky outcrop, recalling my childhood outings with my mother and how much she loved the sea. I mourned our lost relationship. I took no flowers to cast on the waters – flowers for funerals were not part of my mother's belief system. I focused on the waves rolling in below, knowing at that very moment, a group of hardened religious fundamentalists were lowering my mother into her final resting place. I took comfort that our bond had not been broken – her spirit having transcended earthly restrictions and given me peace.

Some weeks later, I made the pilgrimage to my mother's grave in the Wagga Wagga Cemetery to pay my respects. The inscription on her simple headstone read: *'With Christ which is very much better'*. My mother would have approved of that – neither would I dispute it.

Photos Part 3

Left to Right: John, Beryl, Joy and Mildred – London 8 June 1969

Land's End 1969

Anthony and Grandfather J E Nason, Ashfield, 1974

MEd graduation ceremony, Sydney University 1988 with Sir Hermann Black, Chancellor

PART 4
1992 to 2013 . . . .
and beyond

26

All Things New

1992 – A new year, a new boyfriend, a new house, a new job, a new image. Like a new broom, I swept away my old life.

I had met a charming man through my job and threw myself into this new relationship with great gusto, enjoying the thrill of being with someone my own age who had an active social life and was not tied to working seven days a week. I must have been smitten, because after wearing my hair long all my life, he persuaded me to chop it off. He also introduced me to the wonderful world of skiing, and best of all, had no objection to me taking the wheel of his super-fast sports car.

It was all great fun while it lasted. The relationship was ruined by my boyfriend's jealous streak verging on paranoia. I put up with it for too long and the last straw came towards the end of 1993. He was of Italian descent, very excitable and prone to over-exuberance. One weekend after a breakthrough in a knotty computer problem we were solving together, in his exhilaration he leapt up, grabbed hold of me and literally swept me off my feet. Days later when I showed him the clear imprint of his thumb bruised on my breast-bone, he went into a fit of rage accusing me of infidelity. As I had eyes for him alone, this latest insult was unforgivable – so that was the end of that.

In February 1992 I achieved my dream of buying my own home. It was a cute studio apartment in Lane Cove and I'll never forget the feeling of becoming a home owner for the first time. When the deal was done and I collected my keys, I felt as though I was walking on air. The purchase was made possible through the NSW Superannuation Board. In the nick of time I was able to borrow 95% of the mortgage before the Board closed this generous housing loan scheme forever. Lucky Joy! I pulled all stops out and made up the missing 5% by selling my car and putting the rest on my credit card. I didn't care how close I was sailing to the wind – the house was mine.

The studio was too small for Anthony to live with me, so he continued to stay at his brother's house. But at least I had a foot on the bottom rung of the home-owner's ladder.

I lived there less than two years. In November 1993 I sold the property, making a handsome profit. Bank lending rates were at an all time low, enabling me to buy a 2-bedroom apartment in West Street, North Sydney. At last, Anthony could come and live with me again – it meant so much to both of us.

Another dream came true in 1992 – I was appointed Senior Head Teacher in TAFE's Administration Studies department at Ultimo campus. To me this was a plum position, as the section was recognised as a leader in the State. The department was split into four divisions, each under the charge of a Senior Head assisted by a Head Teacher. A quote from my CV at the time paints the picture:

'The Section runs 900 program hours weekly with 4 SHTs and 4 HTs. My division is responsible for both Administration Studies and Information Technology courses, totalling 230 weekly program hours, with 30 classes and 450 students. I have front line management of 35 part time teachers, five full time teachers and one Head Teacher. Each semester, two groups of full-time International fee-paying Information Technology students are also my responsibility.'

I held this position until my retirement from full-time teaching in 1998. The years went by in the blink of an eye – why wouldn't they with the gruelling pace you had to work to keep your Division running smoothly. I loved it however and wouldn't have swapped places with anyone. There was never a dull moment and challenging opportunities continually came along to try yourself out in various Project Officer roles or temporarily act in more senior management positions.

My favourite of all was running the Basic Methods of Instruction (BMI) program, a compulsory short course for TAFE part-time teachers, held each Saturday over four weekends. BMI was extremely rewarding and I lost count of how many courses I presented from 1989 to 1995. It was a no-frills program designed to give staff who were highly trained in their vocational field but without teaching qualifications, the nuts and bolts of the art and craft of teaching – and it worked. To this day, I see people who stop me and fondly recall how the BMI program saved them from certain disaster in the classroom.

By 1993 I had been separated from Norman for two years. It didn't bother me one way or another about getting a divorce, but I was not surprised when Norman asked me if I had any objections. He had met a lovely Asian lady, Catherine, the year before and wanted to formalise their relationship. She and I had become firm friends – we still are. Our friendship may have raised some eyebrows, but she made an enormous difference to both Norman and Anthony when she came into their lives and I will be forever grateful to her for this. Catherine was a victim of Chairman Mao's Cultural Revolution and her life story would make gripping reading.

Norman and I decided on a do-it-yourself divorce. After all, Anthony was over 18 years of age and we had no property settlement to consider. All we had to do was fill out some forms, go to the Divorce Court, pay $300 and Bob's your Uncle. I turned up at the appointed hour, cheque for my half in my hot little hand. I should have known never to take anything for granted with Norman – when I asked him where his $150 was, he responded as only he could. *'I'm not paying for this'* he said in his gruff, gravelly voice, *'if you don't write out another cheque for $150 we're not getting divorced'.* That he was the one who wanted the divorce was a minor detail. I wrote out the second cheque.

Why did I weep that morning when it was all over and the clerk took the divorce papers away to be filed? Wasn't I relieved to have moved on, proved I could be a successful person in my own right, free once more to do as I pleased? Norman said soothing words over a cup of coffee, but I was full of sadness, thinking of the 20 years of Bohemian chaos with him, pondering if I could have played my hand of cards more cleverly. Always ready to move forward however, any feelings of regret or guilt I had probably didn't last long.

It was through Norman's new wife that Anthony's life-changing connection with China commenced. He first of all spent three months in Beijing in 1993, working at a Language Institute. In 2002 he was to move more or less permanently to China. Norman gave a party for Anthony's 19th birthday in 1993 which was a most convivial occasion, with Catherine and I the best of friends.

Another milestone in June 1993: turning 50! I decided to throw a party and planning it went a long way towards fending off a severe case of depression I developed about reaching the dreaded 5 zero. It turned out to be one of the best nights of my life, worth every minute of all the planning. My photo-album of the occasion is full of precious memories. My four nephews who, up to that time, were the only other members of my family to have left the Exclusive Brethren also attended the party. It was very special having them there.

On the night, two of my former Shellcove Road housemates, Sally and Fran, who by then had lived in Western Australia for many years, turned up as a total surprise, which was a highlight of the occasion. I was overcome with emotion when Sally, Fran, Sandy and Jan presented me with a wonderful, artistic caricature, taken from old photos, depicting the five of us at Shellcove Road in the '70s, surrounded by vignettes representing various episodes from those halcyon days more than 20 years before.

Twenty-eight of us continued my 50th birthday celebrations the same weekend at a Yulefest event in Katoomba in the Blue Mountains – it was an unforgettable occasion.

27

Losing in Love

1994 - the year I lost my heart. Katherine Hepburn once described her feelings on meeting Spencer Tracey as akin to being hit over the head with a sledgehammer. I felt exactly the same when I met Des. I was on Cloud Nine, as though my whole life had been moving towards this point. The myriad times I thought I'd fallen in love previously, paled into insignificance compared with the emotion I felt for Des. I was convinced he was the only one in the world for me and went to extraordinary lengths to keep the romance alive. My friends despaired of my 'obsession' as they termed it - I don't know how they put up with me.

After a couple of years, I had to admit defeat and face the cold, hard fact that Des was just 'not that into me', to quote a popular saying. Want to know about unrequited love? Ask me! It was a new and totally demoralising experience to be in the position of the 'Dumpee' not the 'Dumper'. I suppose it was character building but I didn't view it as such at the time. I locked this episode away into a tiny corner of my heart and threw away the key, determined never to let it happen again.

A sense of humour is a great quality to get you through the vicissitudes of life and usually you don't have to look far to see the funny side of things. In 1994, when Norman's niece got married,

I was invited to the wedding in the School Chapel of Monte Saint Angelo, North Sydney. I arrived with Norman's wife, Catherine, and we took our seats in a pew directly behind Norman's brother and his wife. She and her husband were childhood sweethearts and I envied their long and happy marriage.

My ex-brother-in-law may well have been taken aback to see Catherine and me sitting happily together, and I was far from the only former partner present. Any potential awkwardness was dispelled when he turned around and said to me in a stage whisper – 'Well, here I am with my two brothers and five of their six wives'! It was a tonic – no use getting precious about failed relationships I decided.

The following year Anthony turned 21. Anthony's half-brother and his wife kindly offered their home for the occasion – the whole extended family clan was there to celebrate Anthony's coming of age. It was a memorable night and another classic example of the inclusiveness of my former family.

My dear friend Mac was never far from the scene, and we continued to enjoy many happy times together. In 1995 my girlfriend, Fran flew from Perth to join the *Endeavour* as a crew member. The Sydney to New Zealand leg was *Endeavour's* maiden international voyage. Fran proudly showed Mac and me around her beloved ship, which she had been closely connected with since it was launched in Fremantle in 1993. Fran's book, *Wind in my Wings*[11] published in 2008 is a fascinating account of how she fulfilled her dream of running away to sea, albeit in later life.

In 1997 I got itchy feet again and decided it would do me the world of good to have another overseas holiday. It was hard to believe it had been so long since my last trip in 1988. So much had happened in the intervening years, not the least being the responsibility of a mortgage, so it was not surprising that going overseas hadn't figured in my calculations.

My good friend, Susan, and I planned a holiday to the United States together. Susan knew the trip would be a strain on my finances

---

11 Fran Taylor, 2008, Wind in my Wings: Running Away to Sea in the 20th Century, Albatross Press, South Perth

- to put it mildly. Typically, once I'd made up my mind to go, being a bit short of ready cash wasn't going to stop me. Scarlet O'Hara was a role model of mine - I'd worry about that tomorrow.

Out of the blue, Susan, bless her heart, discreetly pressed a very generous cheque in my hand just before our departure, so I wouldn't have the embarrassment of declining any little luxuries that might tempt us while we were travelling. What a friend! Yes, it did make a difference sipping cocktails without a worry in the world in the Rainbow Room on the 65th floor of the Rockefeller Centre in New York and other exotic experiences.

We left Sydney on 1st October and spent three weeks in the USA and Canada, before I went on to visit my relatives in England. I got back to Sydney on 12th November. There were many highlights in the USA and Canada - the stunning fall colours in Vermont, the elegant city of Boston, the French flavour of Montreal. But best of all for me was New York. It was such a thrilling city, I couldn't imagine why I hadn't considered travelling there before.

Not long after my return, my dear friend Mac who had always been such an influential figure in my life, passed away early in 1998. Mac had kept his faith in me throughout my final turbulent years with the Exclusive Brethren and my stints of leave from the Land Company. I'm sure his steady influence meant more to me than I ever realised at the time. He became one of my closest friends, a mentor and benefactor, then in turn I looked after him in his latter years. Mac had a great career, including War Service. He joined the Army at the outbreak of World War II, and as a member of the 2/4th Infantry Battalion, he was on active service from 1939 to 1945. Mac was mentioned in Dispatches and finished the War with the rank of Lieutenant.

In the '70s, I probably would have married Mac if he'd have asked me. Back then, I was acutely aware that none of my holiday, shipboard or office romances had developed into long-term prospects and I seemed destined to be left on the shelf. Mac disclosed to me years later he regretted not proposing to me, partly because of his conservatism and the shock it would cause his family. I can understand his dilemma - I wasn't exactly 'establishment' and was

30 years Mac's junior to boot. I drew a poignant parallel between Mac and the introverted butler Stevens, in Kazuo Ishiguro's insightful book *The Remains of the Day*[12].

In the period before Mac's death, I spent untold hours unravelling the diabolical mess his financial affairs had descended into. I discovered almost by chance that having lost all interest in his share portfolio, Mac had secreted thousands of unopened envelopes in his house. For years, he had taken to paying for essential services in cash and was headed for disaster, particularly as far as rates and taxes were concerned.

I'll never forget when I eventually persuaded Mac to let me take charge, I made many trips, filling the back seat and boot of my car with colossal piles of documents that I had found hidden throughout his house in such bizarre places as the back of food cupboards and in clothing drawers.

It was a nightmare – but I am proud to say I persevered until every last cent was accounted for and recorded. This involved mountains of correspondence, not only returning hundreds of cheques for re-issue, but delving into the murky world of Unclaimed Monies and pursuing paper trails for missing funds, both within Australia and overseas. A spreadsheet I prepared in 1997 about a year before Mac died, shows the recovered funds represented more than 100,000 mainly blue-chip shares, spread over a portfolio with 14 major institutions.

Quite a staggering clean-up job really, considering that apart from some invaluable help from trusted friends in the initial opening and sorting envelopes stage, I completed the project on my own in what spare time I had at nights and weekends.

In getting Mac's affairs sorted out, not only did the Executors of Mac's estate, the Perpetual Trustee, have a lot to thank me for, but so did Mac's family. I was never introduced to them and when I met some of his relatives at the Funeral Directors the day after Mac passed away, they could not disguise their profound astonishment that a person they had virtually never heard of was in charge of organising his funeral and was obviously grief-stricken.

---

12 Kazuo Ishiguro, 1990, The Remains of the day, Vintage International

The previous day had been a long one. Mac was ill in a Nursing Home and I had taken a weekend break to visit friends in Melbourne. Mac was in good spirits when I left and I assured him I would not be away long. I had only been in Melbourne a day, when the dreaded call came that Mac had lapsed into unconsciousness. I went straight to the airport and got the first plane home. Mac did not recover consciousness and passed away in the early hours. I held Mac's hand as I sat at his bedside, listening to his labored breathing, the silent hours only broken by occasional checks from nursing staff. A poignant time indeed to reflect on what might have been. If Mac sensed my presence, I hope he found comfort that I was with him as he departed this life.

Mac's family were completely unaware we had kept in touch since leaving Dalgety's in 1970 and that he had appointed me his Power of Attorney. Mac entrusted his entire financial affairs to me, including asking for my assistance in re-writing his will. This was a situation which required total integrity and I felt an awesome responsibility on my shoulders. Mac was a stickler for convention and he wanted to be satisfied his affairs were in order and would stand up to the scrutiny of his family after his death. During his lifetime, Mac had been generous to a fault with me, had bailed me out of financial difficulties on more than one occasion, but I always viewed my relationship with Mac as one of true friendship, not for material gain.

My time with the Land Company and my friendship with Mac meant a lot to me and in 2009, 40 years after the Dalgety takeover, I was proud to pay tribute to Mac at a nostalgic Land Company reunion. I quote in part from The Land newspaper article written by reporter Peter Austin covering this reunion.

'Sixty former Land Company Station and Head Office staff enjoyed the memorable occasion held at Port Stephens, NSW. In its heyday, NZAL owned more than 50 station properties, running 1.6 million sheep and 100,000 head of cattle, with annual wool production of 25,000 bales.

Among non-Station staff present was Joy Nason, well known to all as the former secretary (and later personal carer) of the Company's last General Manager, Mac, who died in 1998. In an emotional speech, Ms Nason paid tribute to her former boss (who rose through the company's ranks, starting as a jackaroo on "Weilmoringle") and his amazing knowledge of his vast domain. Joy said Mac knew – by name at least – every paddock of every property under his control, and precious little took place on any of the stations that escaped his eagle eye'.

28

Winning in Love

In a twist of fate, my ex-husband Norman and his wife Catherine ended up living in an apartment directly below mine in North Sydney for some years. How it happened was this. Catherine called me one day and said she had decided to live on her own. She was about to move into a boarding house and wanted to let me know. I did not want to interfere in her domestic circumstances, but I was determined to prevent Catherine ending up in a sleazy hostel somewhere – she was too decent a person for this.

Anthony had recently moved out to set up house for the first time with his girlfriend – they had my unquestioned support and I thought it would be a marvellous experience for them both. As I had a spare room, I offered Catherine the option of moving in with me, which she accepted. We got on famously.

More surprises were in store. Later on, Norman and Catherine got back together and needed somewhere to live. Tenants had just vacated the apartment below. Being Secretary of the Body Corporate, I pulled some strings with the agent and hey presto – Norman and Catherine moved in downstairs. Shades of the Bohemian Kirribilli days, but the general consensus was it was all very civilised and far from the arrangement presenting any problems, we enjoyed being close neighbours.

I imagine this scenario once again raised eyebrows among my friends who had probably quite decided life for Joy would never really be normal. In fact I remember a dire prediction from a friend at the time that I would never find a suitable partner while my ex-husband was living downstairs.

Around this time I came to the conclusion that I was not cut out to live alone despite being perfectly capable of doing so. I accepted that I needed a partner to share my life with. It was harder to accept the fact that inexplicably, suitable suitors seemed suddenly thin on the ground!

There was nothing for it but to tread the path of dating agencies. I signed up with a highly respected company which at least gave me the confidence I would be protected from any nasty experiences. However, the day I walked through their discreet front office for my first appointment was one of the lowest points in my life. Me, the good-time party person, the girl who was used to 'knocking 'em back', reduced to putting herself on the market like a common commodity! How wrong I was to feel depressed – that decision turned out to be one of the wisest I had made in my entire life.

You had to fill out a veritable swag of documents to build up your profile and present the best picture of yourself to prospective partners. This included signing a form declaring you were telling the truth, the whole truth and nothing but the truth. Nevertheless I was left in no doubt that ladies over a certain age had a less than favourable chance of finding a suitable partner than those under a certain age – so I immediately became five years younger. You didn't have to produce your birth certificate, so I was saved the embarrassment of revealing my real DOB as well as my first given name!

I also decided there was no need to mention more than one previous marriage. After all a marriage which lasted less than three months didn't really count. There was one section on the profile however where I had no compunction about being completely frank. It asked you to sum up what you wanted in an ideal partner. That was easy, I only had one condition: it had to be someone who was prepared to become a member of the Sydney Swans AFL football club immediately!

They say you have to kiss a lot of frogs before you meet a handsome prince, and nothing was truer throughout the term of my contract with the Agency. Apologies to any gentlemen who may be reading this of course. Early in 1998, in the nick of time before my contract expired and with one more profile to go - my knight in shining armour appeared in the form of Peter.

By our second date, I realised Pete was the perfect partner for me - we seemed made for each other. I remember taking great care so everything was in apple pie order for his first visit to my house. I noticed on my bookshelves my 50th birthday album which presented a glamorous pictorial account of people in my life and thought I would show it to him. Then I realised - horrors - the actual date of said party was writ large on the inside front cover. Out came the white-out, year obliterated, but the touch up job was obvious, so the album had to be hidden.

When I subsequently felt secure enough to reveal my true age and showed Pete the album, he thought my subterfuge was hilarious rather than questioning my dubious honesty. He also graciously overlooked the little sin of omission about my number of marriages.

That Peter did not suffer from the commitment phobia afflicting a large percentage of the eligible male population in my age bracket became clear from the outset - I was never in doubt as to his readiness to make a total commitment to a relationship with me. Over a wine or three at our first weekend away, our bond firmed as we divulged we each had a curious given name we'd prefer not be made public.

In June, I made the big decision to retire from TAFE, having ticked the 55-year age of retirement box when I joined the NSW Public Service in 1979. 55 had seemed ancient to me at 35, but now I was grateful. I knew I could count on part-time work in the colleges - which I am still enjoying to this day.

My retirement dinner in June 1998 is one of my fondest memories - I couldn't believe how full of love that room was. Sixty of my colleagues attended, and every one of them was a friend to me. I was so happy to bring my new partner, Pete, and my son Anthony to share the occasion. Anthony had been well known to many of the TAFE staff from his earliest school days – he had started school when I started work at TAFE in 1979. My colleagues had watched his progress with great interest, and marvelled that Anthony had come through all the ups and downs of the intervening years seemingly unscathed.

There were lots of humorous speeches and activities on the night – TAFE retirement dinners are legendary in that regard. My 2nd in charge at the time, Barbara, gave a speech. Afterwards she gave me a copy of her notes, saying I might like to keep it in my memorabilia. I found it when I was writing this section. Reading it brought tears to my eyes so I've included it below:

JOY'S FAREWELL

The very first day I started working for Joy I got there bright and early ... and hung about a bit ... and then Joy rushed in! and said, Now we've got to go and pick up these student application forms; we'll have to go on the bus because you can't possibly park, so here's a Travel Ten for you, and I've got one as well. So we went on the bus, to this enormous apartment block somewhere down behind the QVB, and there was a bit of a hiccup while we tried to get the doorman to let us in. Is this where you live? I asked. Good heavens no, said Joy - my ex husband!!

And so I learned at the outset, that Joy's life is very ... complicated.

We got the boxes of application forms, and struggled back onto the bus, and managed somehow to get back to Building W - and so I also learned that for Joy, nothing is too much trouble.

In particular, nothing was ever too much trouble when it came to students. Everyone here knows that Joy bent over backwards, she would take no end of time and trouble, when it came to anything that was in the interests of students. You always knew that that was the core, the focus of everything she was doing.

And nothing was too much trouble when it came to staff. She is so warm, so approachable, to all her staff - very fair, and very supportive . And her generosity is boundless.

Joy is the best boss I've ever had. But even using the word "boss" seems an anomaly. She was more of a guide, counsellor and friend. Even now, if I have a problem to deal with, I'll sometimes stop and think, Now how would Joy handle this ...

Joy has always been a person who would energise and inspire. And she's still doing it! Earlier this year, she walked into the room and announced, I've put on six kilos, I'll have to just go on a diet and lose it. Everyone looked sceptical and said, Oh yeah, that's what we'd all like. Some time later, someone asked, Oh how's that weight loss programme going, Joy. Joy beamed - Lost it! she said.

So Joy, you're still inspiring us....

Life with Joy was a mixture of energy, laughter, hard work, and being inspired, as well as the sense of working with a good friend.

Joy, we're going to miss you terribly....

Thank you Barbara!

Before the year was out I had moved in with Pete at Pennant Hills, paving the way for Anthony to move back to my flat at North Sydney with his girlfriend. Everyone was happy.

Pete was an incurable romantic, and proposed to me in an idyllic beach setting at our favourite holiday destination on the North Coast of NSW. That stopped me in my tracks. I had made up my mind to stop at marriage No 2, and was perfectly content having found such a caring partner to share my life with.

However, Pete was persuasive and even met my challenge of coming up with a unique wedding venue outside of Australia. No way would I entertain the idea of getting married in Sydney – I couldn't bear the thought of putting my friends through that again. Out of the blue Pete suggested Gretna Green, having thought of the idea from reading Ken Follett's *Eye of the Needle*[13] which describes the mad dash of the deadly secret agent across the border from England to Scotland.

I couldn't dispute it would be unique, so I agreed on condition that we tell not a soul of our plans. After all, that would be in keeping with the historic Gretna tradition of elopement, where it all started in the 1750s to cater for lovers who wanted to tie the knot in face of strong opposition from wrathful parents south of the border.

We carried it off and in August 1999 had the perfect romantic wedding at Gretna Green to coincide with Pete's planned business trip to the UK and Europe. We cleverly disguised the itinerary so it showed us attending the Military Tattoo in Edinburgh – no need to include our little excursion to Gretna the previous day!

As far as I was concerned, it was the best thing we ever did and I had enormous pleasure telling everyone after the event and causing a stir. Our families were delighted with our news and no doubt my friends were mightily relieved at the prospect that I might settle down at long last.

---

13 Ken Follett, 1978, Eye of the Needle, Penguin

Being fans of Ken Follett and as we had him to thank for the idea for our wedding venue, in 2010 Pete and I went to a literary luncheon in Sydney for Ken's latest publication *'The Fall of Giants'*. In speeches at the lunch, it was revealed Ken grew up in the Exclusive Brethren in the UK. I was amazed. When it was my turn in the queue for him to sign his book, I said to Ken: 'I was in the EB too'. He gave me a look of complete understanding and replied: 'You know all about it then'. What a success he has made of his life after such an inauspicious beginning.

29

Apron Strings Untied

In 2001, I was over the moon when Pete agreed we should pool our finances and move nearer the city. To sell up at Pennant Hills was a sacrifice for Pete, meaning as it did a major down-size in space just to placate my longing to get back to city living. I felt like a fish out of water in the suburbs and will always be grateful to Pete for making this decision. I was not the only one affected by our move from North Sydney. My beloved cat, Foggy, a prize-winning Australian Mist pedigreed pussy, was decidedly put out when he was uprooted and moved to a suburban house and garden. The advertising slogan for the breed was 'Bred for the Great Indoors' – a perfect sales pitch for a city unit-dweller like me. I lost no time purchasing Foggy at great expense from a Cat Show where he'd been entered as a Best-of-Breed kitten.

Foggy had never been allowed outside my unit, so knew nothing other than indoor living. The first time Foggy felt grass under his feet was a comical sight, as he picked up one paw after another and shook it vigorously as though to get rid of this strange sensation. Worse yet for Foggy, he had to share his life with Pete's two cats, mere moggies, who had prior claim on the territory. They barely tolerated each other until the end of their days. Foggy and I went through a lot together in his 14-years. He even made an appearance on National TV in the 2006 ABC Four Corners program about the Exclusive Brethren.

It was with a sense of satisfaction that I was able to meet Pete half-way in purchasing the property we found at Neutral Bay, not that Pete could have cared less if this hadn't been possible for me. I've come a long way from Fishponds, Bristol, I thought! It was another monkey off my back, my parents would have been proud that I had achieved so much and it was another step along the path of proving the EB's dire predictions of failure wrong.

There was a downside to this however, and that was I had to sell my flat at West Street, where Anthony was living happily with his girlfriend. To say this was traumatic for Anthony is an understatement, and who could blame him. To soften the blow and appease my feelings of guilt, I offered to help Anthony with alternative accommodation. I had no say in how Ant controlled his finances; he was 27 and would not have appreciated his mother meddling in his affairs. At the time, Anthony had just started a fledgling business and as a temporary measure, he decided the best course of action was for him to stay with Norman and Catherine, who had recently moved back to an apartment in the city.

Despite their cramped conditions, Norman and Catherine had no objection to Anthony and his girlfriend living with them - in keeping with the Kirribilli tradition. The upshot of all this was that Norman felt I had 'sold the roof over Anthony's head'. Norman then made one of his irreversible decisions that I would henceforth be persona non grata in his life which saddened me, as I much preferred it when he and I were friends.

To Catherine's great credit, Norman's change of heart towards me has never made the slightest difference to our friendship. I've lost count of how many times I've sought her wise counsel – Catherine's inscrutable wisdom has often stood me in good stead. Maybe it's because of the loss of my own family but for years, I relied on the support of members of Norman's family over various issues. In 2003, my former sister-in-law died, I missed her deeply. Since then,

Catherine and my other former sister-in-law, have stepped up to fill the void. They have never felt anything other than family to me.

Fate was taking a hand in Anthony's life and he did not stay long with his father. Through Catherine's network, he took up the offer of a teaching job in Changsha, China, leaving Sydney in 2002. While I was unutterably sad to see him go, I knew it was in Anthony's best interests. The apron strings were being cut, a chapter in my life was closing, but a door was opening for Anthony.

Who could know in 2002 that Anthony's departure would lead to what I call my 'China connection' with many visits to this incredible country, including Anthony's marriage and the most priceless joy of all – a new life – my precious grandson Justin born in Changsha in 2005.

The seven China travelogues I wrote (unpublished) from 2002 to 2008 give a fly-on-the-wall description of my forays deep into the heart of rural China. I felt privileged to gain an insight into the traditional community way of life of the Chinese farming family which my son had married into.

In 2009, I decided it high time to organise a get-together for all the Nason family who had left the Exclusive Brethren. I recalled the moment in the year 2000 when my niece had written the 'off-the-cuff' family tree for me after her escape from the EB, and my incredulous reaction to the news that there were more than 50 other family members living in Australia that I had never seen, nor was I ever likely to. I dreamed of a reunion of us all, regardless of the 'Ins' or 'Outs' – imagining how many there would be.

Realism set in of course; we would never be together as a family. So I thought why not have a gathering of my nieces and nephews and their partners who were no longer members of the EB. Some had not seen each other for many years, some had never met before. I dubbed the occasion 'Hug-a-Cuz', and it was held in Melbourne. I was delighted at the attendance; there were 21 of us present. It meant a lot to me to show support for those of my family who, like myself, have had so many obstacles to overcome in their transition to a normal life.

30

My Nemesis

At this juncture in my evolution from outcast and misfit to accepted member of society, how did I view my former nemesis – the Exclusive Brethren church? On the odd occasion when I saw any of the EB, I felt sorry for them – as they once had felt sorry for me. I might come across a group of EB, say at an airport, or see individual members in the street. They were instantly recognisable to me despite not going to their gatherings for nearly 40 years. They resemble the Amish in appearance and when seen in public, the women in particular attract curious looks with their unfashionable clothes, hair-style and scarves.

I felt they could have no possible influence on anyone outside their cloistered circle. To me they were non-entities, a light-weight, nutty, fringe group, not worthy of a second glance. Yes, I had come the full distance along the pathway from their dominance of my every thought, action, word or deed. I had moved beyond their ignorant, bigoted and narrow lives.

This is where the story of my life's journey could have reached a satisfactory conclusion, the final chapter neatly rounded off. I had thrown off any vestige of my former existence and I was content with the person I had become. This is the point where the past could be put behind me forever.

However, in 2000 I heard about a website entirely devoted to matters concerning the Exclusive Brethren. The first time I visited this site was a pivotal moment for me. My initial reaction being – who could possibly care? I was wrong. A great many people did care. Their horrifying histories were revealed in stark detail on this site. They were my soul brothers and sisters from another life, their stories were my stories.

My first posting on the site in December 2000 shows my cautious approach to revealing myself, fearing I may be opening old wounds, to say nothing of a Pandora's box:

> 'Congratulations on a most informative website on the Exclusive Brethren. It has taken me much soul searching to even access the website, let alone write this contribution. I have always attributed my successful transition to "life after the EBs" to the fact that I made a considered decision when I left the sect in 1968 to completely dissociate myself with my former life – and this has worked for me. To contribute to an EB website seems inconsistent with that decision. However, I have several relatives who have left the EB over this last 30 years, some of whose names appear on the EB website, and I would like to show my support and respect for them.'[14]

At first glance, the website appeared to be no more than a place for former Exclusive Brethren to bare their souls, pour out their grievances and seek comfort from like-minded people. Further research revealed much more.

I will never forget my incredulity at discovering that far from being an innocuous group of uninfluential religious fundamentalist God-botherers, who went about their business, hidden from the outside world, the EB were, in actuality, wielding dangerous levels of influence in business and political spheres. The EB now had power, they had money, they had clout and they were manipulating Industry and Government decision-making to feather the nests of the EB hierarchy and at the same time, to silence criticism.

---

14 Joy Nason 2000, www.Peebs.net posting December 2000

I was shaken to the core – how could this be happening? I reasoned that if intelligent people knew the truth about this crazy cult, justice would prevail. How wrong I was. I had carried the personal scars of hurt for over 30 years – but had always believed it was up to the individual to play out their hand of cards, to bury the past and not use an accident of birth as a crutch to seek sympathy from outsiders. Now inescapably, staring me in the face from those web pages was a cause that needed solidarity of action if the Exclusive Brethren were ever to be scrutinised in the light of day.

It was impossible to put the lid back on Pandora's box – my personal crusade was about to begin. Firstly though, I had to take stock of my own belief systems. It was not enough to feel passionate about righting wrongs on behalf of thousands of wounded individuals; I needed to be clear and rational about what was motivating me and the stance I took.

The Peebs.net website was weighted with postings from former EB members who still clung tenaciously to their Christian faith. I was not one of them. I had long ago accepted that the Christian belief system was not for me. Would my views be welcome on a site where the majority were resting their case on the Almighty to deliver justice?

I was comfortable with the Secular Humanist label I had adopted; I carry the creed with me as a daily reminder of what I strive for. It is worth noting here:

> 'Secular Humanism is a way of thinking and living that aims to bring out the best in people, so that all people can have the best in life. Secular humanists reject supernatural and authoritarian beliefs. They affirm that we must take responsibility for own lives and the communities and world in which we live. Secular humanism emphasised reason and scientific inquiry, individual freedom and responsibility, human values and compassion and the need for tolerance and cooperation.'[15]

---

15 The Council for Secular Humanism, quoted http://www.pluralism.org/resources/tradition/atheism.php 2014

It was a further step, a further evolution in my development away from the Exclusive Brethren, to acknowledge that they were a cult. Up until 2000, I had stopped short of attaching this label to them. I now have no such qualms.

The breakthrough for me was researching various authors on cult studies, and finding this definition by Robert Jay Lifton. Lifton is an American psychiatrist and author born 1926, chiefly known for his studies of the psychological causes and effects of war and political violence and for his theory of thought reform. Lifton's book, published in 1961 was a study of coercive techniques that he labelled thought reform or 'brainwashing' though he preferred the former term. Others have labelled it also as 'mind control'.

CULTS CAN BE IDENTIFIED BY THREE CHARACTERISTICS:

A charismatic leader who increasingly becomes an object of worship as the general principles that may have originally sustained the group lose their power;

A process called coercive persuasion or thought reform;

Economic, sexual, and other exploitation of group members by the leader and the ruling coterie.

Lifton describes in detail eight methods which he says are used to change people's minds without their agreement:

Milieu Control
The control of information and communication

Mystical Manipulation
The manipulation of experiences that appear spontaneous but in fact, were planned and orchestrated.

Demand for Purity
The world is viewed as black and white and the members are constantly exhorted to conform to the ideology of the group and strive for perfection.

Confession
Sins, as defined by the group, are to be confessed either to a personal monitor or publicly to the group.

Sacred Science
The group's doctrine or ideology is considered to be the ultimate Truth, beyond all questioning or dispute.

Loading the Language
The group interprets or uses words and phrases in new ways so that often the outside world does not understand.

Doctrine over person
The member's personal experiences are subordinated to the sacred science and any contrary experiences must be denied or reinterpreted to fit the ideology of the group.

Dispensing of existence
The group has the prerogative to decide who has the right to exist and who does not.'[16]

I ticked every box as applying to the Exclusive Brethren. No one with experience or knowledge of the workings of the EB could deny any of the above criteria. Once the EB were shown for what they are, a cult, I felt sure the general public, governments, etc. would see through the guises they portrayed to protect themselves and bring the EB to account.

---

16 Robert Jay Lifton, 1961, Thought Reform and the Psychology of Totalism, Norton, New York

I found an Australian publication: *'Cults - Too Good to be True'* by Raphael Aron[17], an informative and disturbing guide to cults, their nature and their hold over their followers. It meant a lot to me to read this text published by a complete 'outsider' which had many references to the Exclusive Brethren. I recommended this book in a posting on the Peebs.net website. Too many former EB laboured under the delusion that the EB were somehow different or special. I wanted this myth to be dispelled. It is very helpful to see the EBs in their true light, i.e. just another cult among many as demonstrated in Raphael Aron's book.

In 2001 I responded to a request by Jill Mytton, a senior lecturer in Psychology at the University of East London to participate in a survey on the Trauma in Adulthood of former EB members. She continues to work on vital research into the mental health of ex members of the EB. Jill's research was further evidence that the EB could no longer continue to fly beneath the radar. The spotlight of the outside world was slowly but surely being turned directly on them.

I later had the pleasure of meeting Jill. In 2009, we both experienced an extraordinary wave of emotion on seeing a website posting of scanned text from 1952. My sister Beryl in her 'Memories of Bristol' wrote about 'The Searchings', an activity to occupy little Brethren children on Sunday afternoons. Someone in England had kept a copy of one of these booklets, and there in print under the heading 'Diligent Gleaners Under 10', was my name right alongside Jill Mytton's. Neither Jill nor I had ever given another thought to our diligent bible readings. That 57 years later, such powerful memories were evoked, is testament to how impressionable children can be in their formative years.

I had a similar experience with powerful emotions on a trip to Europe in 2005. On my way from Plymouth to visit my sister in Worcester, I had to change trains at Bristol Temple Meads Station. I was completely unprepared for the intensity of emotion I felt, when stepping down on to the platform, I immediately realised I was

---

17 Raphael Aron, 1999, Cults: too good to be true, Harper Collins Publishers

standing in the exact spot where I had waved goodbye to my father at the start of his journey to find a new life in Australia in 1952. It was here that as an insensitive 9-year old I had questioned why my mother was crying as she sat in the very tearoom on this platform, which looked remarkably unchanged to me since I last saw it 53 years ago.

After I settled into my seat on the British Rail service to Worcester, I started to reflect on the subsequent heartbreak caused to our family by the Exclusive Brethren. I guess it's no wonder I lost the struggle with my emotions, ending up in floods of tears as more Stations out of Bristol became painful reminders of the various journeys my father made in his later years in his futile search for peace when his life was destroyed by the EB. I recovered my equilibrium by the time I reached Worcester, so thankful to be greeted warmly by my sister and cousin, who like myself, had long ago escaped the shackles of this fundamentalist religious order.

31

Activism

In 2004, I heard about a book – Ngaire Thomas's bench-mark publication *Behind Closed Doors*[18]. Reading Ngaire's book was a turning point for me – it seemed incredible that someone had the courage to commit their experiences in the Brethren to print. Her story was now in the public arena. I contacted Ngaire and discovered the EB were under investigation. Ngaire was born one day after me in 1943 – we had a lot in common.

I knew I had to stand up and be counted. The story must be told, whatever the cost. As the Irish philosopher Edmund Burke said: 'evil will flourish when good men fear to speak'. Secular Humanist or not, the former EB community needed the help of every person who was prepared to speak out. There was a successful campaign to bring the secretive and questionable practices of the EB to public attention, with the EB becoming the target of media scrutiny. In July 2006, the Sydney journalist, David Marr, wrote an expose on the Exclusive Brethren called '*Hidden Prophets*'. An extract from this article in the Sydney Morning Herald follows:

---

18 Ngaire Thomas, 2004, Behind Closed Doors, Random House New Zealand

'WITH an iron hand, West Ryde businessman Bruce D. Hales rules his world church. To his 40,000 followers in the Exclusive Brethren, this prosperous supplier of office equipment in the Sydney suburbs is known as the Elect Vessel, the Lord's Representative on Earth, the Great Man, the Paul of Our Day, Minister of the Lord in Recovery and Mr Bruce.

For 175 years the sect has counted among its strange proscriptions – no public entertainment, no novels, no eating with outsiders, no university, no membership of other organisations of any kind, no shorts ("God has no pleasure in the legs of a man"), no party walls shared with non-Brethren, no films, no radio, no television and no mobile phones – an absolute ban on worldly politics.

Brethren members have never voted. Since they came together in Dublin in 1829 to live their pure life, they have believed it is God's prerogative and His alone to choose governments, as laid down in Romans chapter 13 verse 1: "The powers that be are ordained of God". That rule held until the 2004 re-election campaign of John Howard where Brethren – never acknowledging their sect – advertised, leafleted and campaigned on behalf of the Prime Minister.

Within weeks of campaigning for Howard, Brethren were offering covert but well-funded support for George Bush. Intervention in Canada and New Zealand followed. Earlier this year, the Brethren campaigned hard against the Greens in Tasmania. The strategy involved billboards attacking the Greens, towed through Hobart's streets by men wearing party masks of freaks and ghouls. The message on the billboards was: "Dangerous Extreme".

They cover their tracks. The name of the sect is never mentioned. Their political demands are a seamless mix of business breaks and hard-line Christian morality. Under Hales, the Exclusive Brethren have become a new player in the right-wing politics of the world. And they have lots and lots and lots of money.'

The Sydney Morning Herald (3 July 2006) published four responses to David Marr's article in their Letters to the Editor. My letter was one of them:

> 'David Marr's article "Hidden Prophets" reveals a sinister side to the secretive sect the Exclusive Brethren. That this group receives Government funding to perpetuate their doctrine should cause decent citizens of Australia the greatest concern. The Greens' Bob Brown is to be commended in his call for a Senate enquiry into their operations. I speak with first-hand knowledge, as I escaped the Brethren's clutches nearly 40 years ago – my freedom coming at the price of being cut off from my family forever. Joy Nason, Neutral Bay.'

Through Ngaire Thomas, I learned that the ABC TV Four Corners investigative unit was planning a documentary on the Exclusive Brethren, which was to screen in September 2006. I contacted them and they asked me to submit my story for their perusal. They replied almost immediately with the request for me to appear on the program.

The chips were down. Thirty-eight years of life on the outside. Thirty-eight years of consciously distancing myself publicly from anything that might associate me with my former life within the Cult. Thirty-eight years after passing myself off as a Ten-pound Pom, embarrassed and afraid of the stigma I perceived would attach to me if I told the truth about my past. The letter to the SMH a few weeks before was my first public acknowledgement of my link with the Exclusive Brethren. The ABC TV program would be a 'coming out' on a grand scale. Was I prepared for it?

I had to consider the implications that appearing on national TV would have on my family. My husband Peter was deeply concerned about my 'crusade' obsession and the effect it was having on my health. Pete had barely heard of the Exclusive Brethren before he met me - and now this. That he would support me was never in doubt, both he and my son knew how much it meant to me for the truth to be told. 'Go for it' they said.

A serendipitous moment happened the week before the interview. I was at rehearsals with the Beethoven Choir which I had joined a few years previously. I spoke to the choir Chairman and he announced that the choir might be interested in watching next week's ABC Four Corners program as Joy, one of the members, would be in it but was not prepared to divulge what is was about.

After weekly rehearsals, I always travelled home with Sophie, a lady I had met at the choir. This night Sophie grilled me about my mysterious announcement on the way home. We had never exchanged surnames, so when I told her it was an investigation into an obscure religious sect that she may never have heard of, she pressed me for more information. On hearing the words 'Exclusive Brethren', she shrieked, told me her surname and we realised immediately we had known each other as children 40 years ago in the church. Sophie had endured unspeakable hurt at the hands of the Exclusive Brethren. She and her family were to be the subject of an entire chapter only two years later in Michael Bachelard's seminal book *'Behind the Exclusive Brethren'*.

When I arrived at choir practice after the documentary went to air, the Choir rose to their feet as one and applauded. Many rushed to embrace me. Such was the powerful effect of that program.

The program, *'Separate Lives'* screened on Monday, 25 September, 2006. Never again have I heard the ABC TV Four Corners theme music without being transported back to that momentous night. The last two paragraphs quoted from the program transcript will suffice to demonstrate its impact:

ABC REPORTER QUENTIN MCDERMOTT

Renewed faith, though, doesn't dull the memories or the pain. After her father was excommunicated, Joy Nason took her son to see her mother, to check that she was OK, and was where she wanted to be.

JOY NASON, EX-MEMBER, EXCLUSIVE BRETHREN

She was behind a closed door. I just couldn't bear it. I couldn't bear that I was so close... and couldn't see her, and I suddenly remembered they always have a scripture to go by, they always have something, and it's the door, the closed door. You weren't allowed to let an ex-member through an open door. And I suddenly saw there was a flyscreen and the door, and I said, "Mum, if you open the door, there'll still be a closed door." And she took the bait and opened the door, and all the words of condemnation of the Brethren that I was going to hurl at her just went. I just looked and I said, "I love you, Mum." And to my amazement she mouthed... she mouthed "I know" silently, and then said, "Go and get right with God" out loud... so that the people in the house would not know. I've never forgotten it, and I turned and went and took my son.

SELWYN WALLACE, EX-MEMBER, EXCLUSIVE BRETHREN

These people claim to represent Christianity in its purest form, but you look at the history stretching back 30 or 40 years, and it's just carnage - broken families, broken lives. Children that don't know their parents. Brothers and sisters that haven't seen each other for 20, 30 years, and it's all over the world. And that's one reason why I'm speaking today. The carnage must stop. And if we don't speak out, the wheels of pain will just keep turning.

The vindication for me appearing on national TV manifested itself in a curious way. Following the documentary, I was inundated with messages of support from all and sundry. The most significant factor was the reaction of work colleagues and neighbours who knew nothing of my background. Everyone expressed incredulity that I had once been associated with such a cult. Proof positive that I had made a successful transition to life after the Exclusive Brethren.

I felt the double stigma I was born with - of poverty and religious fundamentalism - had been dispatched to the scrap-heap.

A few days after the program was screened, I wrote the following letter to the Rt Hon John Howard, then Prime Minister of Australia.

'Dear Mr Howard

On Monday 25 September 2006 I appeared on ABC Four Corners in the documentary about the Exclusive Brethren. Have you watched that program Mr Howard? Did it reach your heart?

I hope your words reported in the Sydney Morning Herald (28/9/2006) 'The Prime Minister defended the movement saying: "Its beliefs should be respected and not vilified", were uttered before you knew the full facts about this group.

Come next election the voting public will know that the Exclusive Brethren, far from being (in the words of your Treasurer Peter Costello): "essentially no different to mainstream churches and therefore entitled to the same tax exemptions and other breaks" – are essentially a cult. Do you want to be viewed as a cult sympathizer Mr Howard?

Joy Nason, Neutral Bay.'

I duly received the following reply from the Department of the Prime Minister and Cabinet, signed by the Assistant Secretary of the Awards and Culture Branch:

Dear M/s Nason

Thank you for your letter to the Prime Minister regarding the Exclusive Brethren. I have been asked to reply on the Prime Minister's behalf.

Australia is home to many faiths, encompassing all the world's major religions, and the Australian Government is committed to ensuring that all Australians respect the principle of freedom of religion. Australians

*are free to choose their religion and are able to express and practise their
religion and their beliefs, without intimidation and without interference,
as long as those practices are within the framework of Australian law.*

Thank you for taking the time to raise your views on this matter."

Some months later, when The Greens' leader, Senator Bob Brown, called for a Government enquiry into the Exclusive Brethren, I again wrote to Prime Minister Howard expressing support for such an enquiry. The reply I received was identical, word for word, to the first response from the Prime Minister's curiously named 'Awards and Culture Branch'. Clearly, correspondence from the public on religious issues is treated with a standard reply. No attempt is made to convey that your concerns are taken seriously.

There was no going back now – I had put my hand to the plough. At the end of the year, the Melbourne Age published a letter from me. They entitled it *'Christians of another ilk'*:

*'The day after Christmas was a most appropriate time to publish a
further damning article on the Exclusive Brethren ("Brethren chief tells
child to disown dad", The Age, 26/12). This sect claims to uphold
Christian values, but no sect member would have exchanged gifts,
attended church services on December 25 to commemorate Christ's birth
or even have enjoyed traditional turkey with Christmas trimmings. It
bans any association with Christmas celebrations, branding even
Christmas church services as pagan.*

*Michael Bachelard's report, that the Exclusive Brethren have ignored
conditions imposed by the Family Court, is yet another example of how
they believe themselves to be above the law and that they operate outside
the norms of our society.*

*After the ABC Four Corners documentary Separate Lives in September
exposed the sinister side of this sect, our Prime Minister defended the
movement, saying: "Its beliefs should be respected and not vilified." He*

*was backed up by the Treasurer, who said "the Exclusive Brethren are
essentially no different to mainstream churches and therefore entitled to
the same tax exemptions and other breaks".*

*Think again, Mr Howard and Mr Costello, when you are carving up
large sections of the educational funding pie to subsidise dozens of schools
around Australia operated by this secretive and hypocritical movement.*

Joy Nason, Neutral Bay, NSW.'

I continued to write to politicians only to receive the customary
meaningless responses. On New Year's Day 2007 the Sydney
Morning Herald published my letter in response to a further article
alleging an EB cover up of assaults on girls (*SMH December 30,
2006*). The news archives of the Wikipeebia.com website, mentioned
earlier, contains many examples of media items on the Exclusive
Brethren from around the world.

In the first week of the 2007 Australian Federal Election campaign,
I was contacted by Channel Nine's *A Current Affair* (ACA) program
with a request for an interview. It went to air on 16 October. A short
quote from the interview follows:

Tracy Grimshaw *(ACA Presenter)*

It's Australia's most secretive cult, the Exclusive Brethren. And
in recent months we've brought you many stories on this
religious group, with claims of cover-ups involving sexual assault
and bitter family separations. Now the focus is on the Exclusive
Brethren's political donations, and strong links to the Prime
Minister.

Joy Nason

I have written to Mr Howard and asked him if he really knew the
facts about the Exclusive Brethren, would he still say that they are
decent law abiding citizens? Because I believe that the Australian

people wouldn't want a Prime Minister who gives favours to an extremist cult that breaks up families. They say they don't break up families. They say it's sin that breaks up families. But believe me, the Exclusive Brethren do break up families.

Tracy Grimshaw

Ben Fordham reporting. And today we sent Joy's details to the Prime Minister's office in the hope of arranging a meeting. We'll let you know the outcome.'

I didn't wait for an answer from Mr Howard. Instead I joined the well-known community activist group 'GetUp!' as I was angry at the strong support the EB attracted from the government of John Howard. Together with my friend Sophie, we tramped for miles around the streets of the Bennelong electorate, dropping 'GetUp'! leaflets urging the public to think carefully before casting their vote. They did. How sweet it was to help unseat the Prime Minister in his own electorate.

In Michael Bachelard's book *Behind the Exclusive Brethren*, he describes how Sophie confronted John Howard face to face while he was on the campaign trail in 2007:

> 'I grabbed his hand in both of mine and said, "Mr Howard, I'm Sophie, and I'm a former member of the Exclusive Brethren, and I feel utterly and totally betrayed by you. There are thousands of us who have lost our families". He just kept saying, "I'm sorry, I'm sorry". He heard though. At least I got the message through.'[19]

We were so proud of Sophie.

In 2008, a fellow activist, Peter Flinn, prepared and coordinated a submission to the then Prime Minister, Kevin Rudd in an attempt to persuade the Government to instigate a public inquiry into the

19 Michael Bachelard, 2008, Behind the Exclusive Brethren, Scribe Melbourne

questionable practices of the Exclusive Brethren. Peter was a former EB who, with many others, had put up his hand to be counted in the campaign to bring the EB to account, in particular the damage inflicted on families. Feelings were running high in the ex-Exclusive Brethren community at the time, as traumatised victims of this cruel regime took the courageous step of going public with their stories.

Just as I had felt in the year 2000 when I first discovered the extraordinary power of the Exclusive Brethren and the influence they wielded both in business and political circles, I again believed if the truth was presented to the highest levels of Government, then justice would prevail and an Inquiry into the EB would be deemed justified. Peter's submission was powerfully expressed, strongly worded, with no lack of evidence to support the serious allegations. I had high hopes that a favourable response would be received from the Prime Minister.

Peter reminded Mr Rudd of his concern expressed when in Opposition about the controversial political and financial activities of the Exclusive Brethren, and of the damage they have inflicted on families. Peter thanked the Prime Minister for his then public statement that year, when Mr Rudd said: "I believe this is an extremist cult and sect. I also believe they break up families." Many ex-members around the world would attest to just how true this is.

To add credibility to the submission and to demonstrate that the negative impact of the Exclusive Brethren was not contained to Australia but is in fact world-wide, a selection of "life stories", some of them horrific, written by people from a variety of countries and walks of life was included. An explanatory note sent with the stories makes poignant reading, and gives an insight into the trauma experienced by so many whose fate it was to be born into the Exclusive Brethren:

'All of these experiences have been prepared individually by the respective authors. They have agreed to tell their stories especially for this submission to the Prime Minister. Many of the stories tell of extremely painful events, and are provided on the understanding that the names of the authors are kept confidential. Many of the people involved still have close family

212 | JOY and SORROW

members within the Exclusive Brethren, and are anxious that no harm will come to them as a result of the information being provided. We have given the authors an undertaking that their stories will not be used for any other purpose by us without their express permission.

Several other ex-members would have liked to provide their stories as well, but they fear the consequences for their loved ones still inside the Brethren system. In one case, tentative contact with family members has been secretly re-established after some years. If this particular story were told, and word of it somehow reaches the Brethren, that long-sought contact would immediately cease, with fear and anxiety caused to the "captives", who are elderly.

In addition to the above names, several others have indicated that they strongly support the submission but are not willing to have their names listed, for fear of further intimidation to themselves or members of their families still with the Exclusive Brethren. This, we believe, sends another powerful message about this cult.'

I agreed for my story to be one of the 13 submitted to the Prime Minister. As the names of the authors were confidential, I have never known the identity of the other 12 people. Somehow I managed to condense my story to one page. It is copied below:

My Story
Joy Nason, NSW, Australia 2008

I was born in Bristol, England in 1943, the youngest of 8 children. Our family were all Exclusive Brethren (EB). We moved to Sydney in 1953 and attended the Ashfield EB meeting. I left the sect aged 25 in 1968. The trauma of leaving my home and parents has remained with me to this day – I am still deeply hurt that for 40 years the EB rules have prevented me from having normal contact with any family or friends still in the Brethren.

The following are some very painful personal experiences that illustrate the evil nature of the EB doctrine of separation introduced after 1960 and still in practice today.

The EB excommunicated my father when he was in his late 70s. My father had committed no sin, other than disagreeing with the EB leadership. They forced my mother to leave him and go and live with one of my siblings. My father's heart was literally broken, and he tried continuously until his death to get back into the EB and be re-united with his wife. I took on the responsibility of his care, and he ended his life in a nursing home, and died of a stroke, a broken-hearted old man of 82. He grieved daily and any attempts at contact were rebuffed. The EB even sent a horrible solicitor's letter to him warning him not to attempt to contact his wife, as he had written her several letters and may also have tried to call her by phone.

In 1980 I attempted to see my mother to find out if she was willingly living apart from my father. The trauma of this visit, where I was denied access and could only speak to my mother through a closed door was vividly exposed in the ABC TV Four Corners Documentary "Separate Lives" in September 2006. When my father died in 1983 the Nursing Home tried to contact my mother at my brother's home, and when the Matron told them my father had died, my brother replied "You've done your duty" and hung up the phone.

When my mother died in 1991 at aged 91, I found this out only through a secondary source. I rang each of my brothers and sisters to try and confirm this information and they all hung up the phone when I identified myself, one brother saying before he hung up "what interest do you have in this matter?" My mother had died the day before! I attempted to find out where the funeral was being held, which was almost impossible because the EB now have their own undertaking licences for the sole purpose of carrying out burials in unseemly haste to prevent excommunicated family members from attending. I discovered by contacting several cemeteries that my mother's burial was to take place in Wagga Wagga within hours – too late for me to get there from Sydney.

I am putting in writing some of the bare facts about a cruel and heartless sect, and the pain they have caused just one person; multiply this by thousands and you have some idea of the monstrousness of their operations.

End of Joy's story.

The reply to the submission, from Mr Rudd's Chief-of-Staff, contained mixed messages. It was not surprising that no support was forthcoming for a public inquiry, as understandably there was concern among Parliamentarians that the fundamental right to freedom of religion in a free and democratic society must be protected - which is not in question. However, the Prime Minister stood by the views he expressed earlier about the Exclusive Brethren, and also referred to the Government's determination to undertake electoral reform, especially in relation to transparency surrounding political donations. He agreed that religious observance should not be regarded as a shield behind which breaches of the law can be hidden.

Much remains to be done in ensuring an appropriate balance between religious freedom and other equally important basic human rights, many of which have been brazenly flouted by the Exclusive Brethren over many years.

The EB continued to hit the headlines in 2009. They are homophobic and their treatment of a young gay man, Craig Hoyle, from New Zealand is typical of the EB modus operandi. Craig is now a good friend of mine and is happy for me to include this potted version of events which he sent me.

All references to Exclusive Brethren persons in the following account have been made public in various Media outlets:

'Leaving the Exclusive Brethren was traumatic. I came out as gay to the priests at the age of eighteen, and they spent several months trying to help me "change" around the end of 2007. In December of that year, I had an interview with the Man of God, Bruce Hales (world leader of the EB). He told me never to accept myself for what I was, and to always fight against myself. He referred me to Roger Kirkpatrick (a doctor within the EB) with a view to my being placed on medication to "cure" my homosexuality. Kirkpatrick told me that homosexuality was "constitutional", and that there was nothing I could do to change it. I simply had to hold out faith that maybe one day God in his infinite wisdom, would see fit to change my sexuality. In the meantime, I was instructed to suppress my feelings – the expectation was that I would marry a woman and start a family like everyone else.

This was too much to bear. I ran away the following week, but was tracked down by the church. They persuaded me to return, and I was sent to live in Sydney. (The home of Bruce Hales.) While I was in Sydney, Bruce Hales once more referred me to an EB doctor. This doctor, Mark Craddock, placed me on hormonal suppressant to reduce my sexual urges. He also told me that he was experimenting with different drugs on another young gay person within the EB.

I returned to New Zealand in April 2008. I was sent back to Australia in August and returned after six weeks. At that point I began making plans to leave. In March, 2009 I told the priests I was leaving the EB, and for several months the church tried every means possible to persuade me to change my mind. Their various methods included threats of damnation, offers of bribery, and relentless brow-beating. I was excommunicated in May after I came out as gay to my siblings. My parents threw me out.

I went public with my story in December 2009. It was published across a wide range of media, including television, print and online. Today Tonight picked up on the story in Australia in February 2010, and I spent several days filming with them. During this process, we filmed outside the main EB meeting hall in Ermington. We were subsequently chased by sect

members, and after several hours were forced to seek refuge in the central
city police station. Arrests were made and in October 2010 sect member
Lionel Laming was found guilty in court of 'stalking and intimidation.'

The Exclusive Brethren's handling of Craig's case spectacularly
backfired on them. Craig himself has made a successful transition to a
new life after the EB. He is now firmly established in a Media career.

On 25th June 2009, an extraordinary decision was handed
down by the Family Court of Australia, which prompted national
outrage and wide media coverage. The Court ruling was that an
excommunicated Exclusive Brethren father was denied all access to
his children in the EB Church.

Former EB community activists moved into action as it was felt
the EB contravened basic human rights, particularly in relation to
children. I pondered what avenues could be used to bring the EB to
account and discussed it with my husband Pete. He came up with the
idea of enlisting the support of the high profile human rights lawyer,
Geoffrey Robertson. This seemed a brilliant strategy, which resulted
in a submission which Peter Flinn and I compiled and sent to Mr
Robertson regarding the 2009 Family Court ruling. A quote from
this submission follows:

'This long-running case, the outcome of which was a father being
refused all access to his children, is one of many heart-rending examples
over the last fifty years where the Brethren have forced families apart,
pouring thousands of dollars into legal action to ensure that the
children involved in such cases remained in the sect's clutches.

We believe the recent Family Court judgment is particularly disturbing,
and constitutes a serious violation of human rights. We are in the
process of seeking advice on how to persuade the Government and the
judiciary that such a judgment should never happen again.

When Australian Prime Minister, Kevin Rudd was in Opposition, he
described the Exclusive Brethren as "a damaging cult", which "breaks up

families". We know only too well how true that is, and we believe that it is now time for him to back up those words with action. Otherwise, the Brethren will see this judgment as a vindication, and will continue to tear families apart as they have done for decades.

The Brethren always maintain that they comply with Family Court judgments, in cases where the ex-member parent is allowed access rights. However, in reality, they will obstruct access at every turn, appealing court decisions and continuing vexatious litigation until the ex-member finally gives up the battle, financially or emotionally broken, or both.

Mr Robertson, if there is any advice you can provide us on this appalling situation, we would be most grateful.'

The great man however, did not reply - he had bigger fish to fry. Yet another example of voices in the wilderness going unheard.

In 2009, I discovered CIFS - the Cult Information and Family Support group incorporated in Queensland. Their inaugural National Conference was held in Brisbane in February 2010. It was a watershed moment for me to be present at a convention attended by escapees from more than 60 cults, to show solidarity and support.

There were many high profile presenters at the 2010 CIFS Conference, including Senator Nick Xenophon, who is well known for his activism in exposing cults such as the Church of Scientology and the Exclusive Brethren. His commitment to this cause, along with other Senators including Bob Brown of The Greens Party, continues.

As a direct result of considerable media exposure, the Exclusive Brethren modified their practices and abandoned many of their former inhumane policies. For instance, 'Shutting Up' and excommunication is now quite rare. A heartening change has also been that families are now not punished for contacting 'outside' relatives. I believe this is solely because of the public scrutiny the EB were subjected to as a result of the truth being told.

I decided to find out if it was possible for me to see my own family again and met with mixed success. I contacted one of my brothers to ask if I could meet him. I had been told he now had a connection with his son and family who are not in the EB fellowship and regularly takes his disabled grandson to the EB gatherings. This information gave me hope that my brother might treat me sympathetically.

When I spoke to him on the phone, he stated that I am viewed as being opposed to the EB teachings because of my public stance on the issues. Obviously he was referring to the ABC TV *Four Corners* EB documentary. My brother told me if I retracted my statements and publicly apologised for criticising the EB 'position', only then might he reconsider my request to see him.

On the other hand another of my siblings displayed great courtesy when I contacted the family. I was in the area and they invited me into their house and offered refreshments. I declined on principal when it became obvious they would not share the food with me. They offered to accompany me to the cemetery where our mother was buried and even went so far in most conciliatory terms to express their regret that at the time of my mother's death I was treated so callously.

I was left in no doubt that I must not expect to receive any official apology from the EB hierarchy and I departed with the distinct impression that this member of my family had shown great courage in speaking to me in this manner. It meant a lot to me to have this face to face contact after so many decades of separation. I had no hesitation in telling them how much I appreciated our meeting and hearing their sympathetic words.

In 2011 pressure continued to be exerted on the Exclusive Brethren in the media, e.g.

Exclusive Brethren parents claim 'Tax lurk of biblical proportions' Michael Bachelard The Age March 25, 2011. Extract:

Parents in the Exclusive Brethren avoid paying tax on the bulk of their children's school fees in an arrangement that would be illegal if sought by other Australian parents. Independent senator Nick Xenophon has called for a tax office investigation into the arrangement which he said looked "at first blush like a tax lurk of biblical proportions".

When most parents pay school fees, they are paying it from income which has already been taxed. If they sought to avoid tax by paying it via tax-deductable donations, or through a family trust, they could be prosecuted for tax evasion.

But figures released on the MySchool website show the Exclusive Brethren, a radically separatist Christian sect with about 15,000 members in Australia, gets around this law. The website reveals that, at their Victorian school, Glenvale, 54 per cent of the income is tax-free because it is paid by parents through distributions from family trusts as well as donations. Because a school is a tax-free entity, Brethren families who arrange their business in this way do not need to pay tax on that money.

The pattern is replicated at the six Exclusive Brethren schools around Australia. In 2009, the sect raised $32.4 million in tax-free money to send its 2537 students to school. This dwarfs the tax-free component of any other private school in Australia, and acts as a de facto second government subsidy to Exclusive Brethren schools. At other comparable small Christian schools, tax-free payments by parents make up between about 1 and 4 per cent of income.

Senator Xenophon said the tax office "needs to tell Australian taxpayers whether this sort of arrangement is sanctioned. If what the Exclusive Brethren is doing is more broadly applied it could cause a multi-billion dollar hole in tax revenue," he said.'

In recent years, the Exclusive Brethren have hired a company of 'spin doctors', Jackson Wells of Sydney. Now when there is adverse media publicity, Jackson Wells speak as EB spokespersons and provide press releases. This has worked wonders for the EB in enabling them to fly beneath the radar, or if caught out, the expertise of Jackson Wells ensures they come up looking squeaky clean. It begs the question – why does a so-called 'inoffensive group of decent God-fearing Christians' need the services of professional spin doctors?

I am confident that through the tireless efforts of organisations such as CIFS and CAASA (Cult Awareness And Support Australia); scrutiny by the media airing concerns of the general public; activism of empathetic Politicians; the power of social media – the silent voices of those still trapped in Cults will be heard. There will be justice for all.

32

Finishing Business

My journey of healing moved to its inevitable conclusion without my ever knowing it. In particular, the therapeutic benefits of writing the story of my life cannot be underestimated.

In January 2011, while idly reading the *Sydney Morning Herald* 'Summer' supplement, an article by Peter FitzSimons the celebrated author and columnist, caught my eye. I had often been encouraged by friends to write my life story but I was not convinced it would be of interest. Peter's message for budding writers seemed aimed at me: 'Find your voice and listen to it. Don't ever say your subject is boring, that only means you're boring'. Spurred into action, I spent every spare moment from then on putting my memoir together – it practically took over my life. Daily routines, activities and work commitments seemed intrusive, but I stuck with it until I'd finished writing my story.

At the end of the year, I attended a workshop at the University of Sydney, facilitated by Dr Bernadette Brennan, Senior Lecturer, Department of English. The program was called 'The Narrative and Healing', with a writers' panel of prominent Australian authors and poets including Helen Garner (Joe Cinque's Consolation, The Spare Room); Brenda Walker (Reading by Moonlight: How Books Saved a

Life); Judith Beveridge and Carolyn Rickett (Poetry and Healing: The New Leaves Project).

Over round table discussions at this workshop, a light bulb switched on in my head. It dawned on me that I not only felt a new sense of calm, but I couldn't even recall the last time I had experienced my terrifying nightmares. I excitedly blurted out this revelation to the panel facilitators who smiled and nodded knowingly. That's the whole point they said – the power of healing through narrative. Satisfied its work was done, I put my manuscript behind me. At that stage I decided it should remain as private circulation among family and friends – I simply could not face the wrath of the Exclusive Brethren if I published my story.

I then channelled my energies and passions into social activist causes such as the 'GetUp!' group, of which I had been a member since the 2007 Federal Election campaign. This organisation has achieved outstanding success in bringing controversial issues to the notice of Government, consequently making real policy changes happen.

In the September 2013 Federal Election I was appointed by GetUp! as Booth Coordinator for my local Electorate polling station. It was a hectic and rewarding experience to be a part of a campaign to raise awareness of issues prioritized by the public, but ignored by Government.

I also trained as a volunteer teacher for Primary Ethics, which has given me immense personal satisfaction. This programme gives parents the option of enabling their children to learn philosophical ethics in schools, instead of attending Non-scripture. It runs alongside faith based lessons. The Ethics programme was approved by Government and rolled out in NSW Primary Schools in 2012.

Most fortunately for me, an Ethics Volunteer was needed at my grandson's Primary School; it has been a delightful experience to be his class teacher. I will never forget when the topic of Ethics came up when I was out on a family visit with my grandson. His uncle asked him 'What is Ethics, Justin?' I held my breath in the ensuing pause. After a few moments Justin replied: 'It's thinking about the hard questions about right and wrong so people can be better'. What an answer from an eight-year-old child – I couldn't have put it better myself!

One fine day in 2012, I was near Wollstonecraft Station, with a few minutes to spare before an appointment. It was a typical Sydney day – glorious sunshine, gentle breeze. I walked along a tree lined street, past substantial Federation homes, my meanderings leading me to Carpenter House in Shirley Road. Almost 40 years had passed since I was last here – as a new mother with a premature baby admitted to the care of the Tresillian nurses who ran the establishment at number 25.

Carpenter House was unaltered, with its gracious architectural style and tranquil setting among spacious lawns and shady trees. It was no coincidence that today was Anthony's 38th birthday – an opportune moment for me to pause and reflect on my life's journey to this point. When I returned home that evening, I felt a deep sense of peace when I realised I no longer struggled to find my identity. The soul-searching that has been a consequence of revisiting my past to write my story could now be put to rest.

In 2013 the alarming prospect of my big seven zero birthday in June loomed. When I was growing up in the Exclusive Brethren, the thought of reaching 70 was frightening. This was not merely because 70 seemed incomprehensibly ancient to a young girl, but once again the terrors of believing in literal interpretations of the Bible had a hand in my disquiet. The culprit in this case was in the form of a verse from Psalm 90:10 King James Version (KJV) *"The days of our years are threescore years and ten; and if by reason of strength they be fourscore years, yet is their strength labour and sorrow; for it is soon cut off, and we fly away."* It was hammered home to us that living beyond 70 would definitely be by the grace of God. For a sinner like me I knew if and when I attained that venerable age, there would be an axe hanging over my head.

So there was nothing for it but to organise a big party and thereby put another ghost to rest. Most fortuitously, the Sydney Philharmonia Festival Chorus and Orchestra had planned a performance at the Sydney Opera House on the weekend of my birthday. It was advertised

as *'A Birthday Celebration for Verdi (b.1813), Wagner (b.1813) &
Britten (b.1913)'*. As I am in the Choir, it was a great opportunity to
ask my friends to come along. It was a pretty impressive concert, but
the most special thing for me was my birthday celebration afterwards
in the northern foyer of the Opera House. The beautiful backdrop
of Sydney Harbour was particularly spectacular, being the closing
night of Vivid Sydney, with the foreshore buildings lit up by dazzling
displays of technicolour laser beams. It was a happy and memorable
night. I've come a long way from my first birthday in a Bristol bomb
shelter to this I thought. It's now over to me to make sure every year
henceforth is a bonus.

A bitter-sweet footnote to the night was the unexpected attendance
of my son Anthony and his new wife Mega, who were in Sydney on
a flying visit. Anthony's father was gravely ill so they decided on the
spur of the moment to come from Hong Kong to see him. Never for
a moment had I dreamed Anthony would be here for my birthday.
Sadly, only days later Norman passed away – another closure in my
life's journey.

I guess I've come full circle. Recently I had urgent need of
a JP's signature. I was at work and time was of the essence, so I
tracked down a colleague. As I approached his desk, my dreaded
full moniker leapt out at me! I hastily tried to fold the paper so the
offending name would not show, but being the conscientious JP he
is, my colleague refused to simply 'sign here' when I asked. Instead,
he unfolded the document with a flourish and roared with laughter
when he saw 'Myrtle Joy Nason'. I threatened him with all sorts of
dire retributions should he ever reveal my true name, but he couldn't
help himself – my secret was out.

Now, every time I arrive at work, his cheery greeting is 'G'day
Myrt'! And do you know what? I don't mind one little bit. I think
it's rather cute.

Around this time, the old French proverb: *'the more things change,
the more things stay the same'* proved a truism. I could not ignore
reports continuing to surface in the media of Exclusive Brethren
plots and ploys. Even though I had called it a day on my EB activism

and had distanced myself from anything public in this regard, these reports disturbed me greatly. They're up to their old tricks again I thought.

I had heard about a severe EB crisis in 2012, when the UK Charity Commission refused to grant charitable status to the Preston Down Trust, which the Brethren had formed to manage a meeting room in Torquay, Devon. The Commission's decision letter stated, *"As a matter of law, we are not able to satisfy ourselves and conclusively determine that Preston Down Trust is established for exclusively charitable purposes for public benefit and suitable for registration as a charity."*

A familiar pattern was emerging for me. Once more my hopes were high. I believed such a high level Government investigation as the UK Charity Commission would reveal the truth that the Brethren were indeed not charitable in any sense of the word.

I also had a personal interest in a claim that at the time of the Charity Commission Inquiry, the Exclusive Brethren attempted to discredit the London Counselling Psychologist Jill Mytton's research *'An Inquiry Into The Psychological Consequences of being Raised In And Leaving High Demand Groups; The Case of the Exclusive Brethren.'* Jill and I were the 'highly commended Diligent Gleaners' in those far off days of our EB childhood innocence. I had completed questionnaires to assist her research and felt a sense of outrage that the EB might go to such lengths to disrupt this professional work Jill had compiled over several years for her Doctoral studies.

I decided to ask Dr Ian McKay of Glasgow, who I knew was a prominent researcher of Exclusive Brethren history, about recent EB developments. As a result, Ian compiled *'The End Times'*, an enlightening document appended as Annexure 2. Ian has previously written mainly about biomedical sciences and statistics, but since retiring from academic life he has been studying oppressive, harmful forms of religion, trying to discover how they work, why they exist, what motivates their leaders and adherents, how their harm can be reduced, and how best to care for their victims.

While *'The End Times'* may appear to have a UK slant, anyone with even the smallest knowledge of the EB, will understand there is only one person who pulls the strings. Bruce Hales and his henchmen at the helm in Australia rule their universe with an iron hand. Make no mistake, what happens in the UK goes under the microscope in Sydney, the effect being felt internationally wherever there is a gathering of Exclusive Brethren, now operating as the Plymouth Brethren Christian Church.

Those who have suffered at the hands of the Exclusive Brethren, will not be surprised at the lengths the EB hierarchy will go to manipulate not only their faithful flock, but Governments as well. However, they will read Ian McKay's *'The End Times'* with mounting incredulity. They will reach the account of the Brethren's negotiated compromise with the Charity Commission, resulting in the revision of EB meeting room Trust Deeds to include a statement called *'Faith in Practice'*.

They will come to these lines:

'... the Brethren agree that it is acceptable for Brethren to socialise with ex-Brethren and to allow the continuation of family relationships where a family member has left the community, including providing access to family members'.

The document goes on:

'Where a person within the community dies, the principle of separation allows members of the extended family of the deceased, including former Brethren, to attend their funeral service.' Ian comments: *'How different from past practice, which was to delay telling relatives that their loved one had died, or to give them false information about the funeral to prevent them from attending.'*

At this point in *'The End Times'*, the reader will be overwhelmed with bitter-sweet emotions. It will be a poignant moment. They, like me, will be filled with the deepest sense of grief that the human tide of misery and suffering, endured in the name of this so-called Christian movement since the 1960s, could have been stemmed by the stroke of a pen. Too late for my family. Too late for their fathers, mothers, brothers, sisters. The reader may pause and reflect that at last the suffering has been vindicated, good has triumphed over evil.

Then will come the reality check. Where is the evidence of actual change in practice? They will search and the Brethren may be found wanting. The realists will conclude this is yet another cruel hoax perpetrated by the EB hierarchy, motivated by greed. The EB *'Faith in Practice'* charter may only be worth the paper it is written on. History will be the judge.

In concluding 'The End Times' account, Ian McKay observes:

'Brethren supporters and Brethren critics share a belief that the troubles of the last few years may be a sign of the "end times," though the phrase means different things to the two camps. According to Brethren folklore, the world is getting worse and worse and is ripe for destruction, and they are experiencing the persecution that is to be expected in the End Times. On the other hand, the troubles may be a sign that Hales Brethrenism is on its last legs, in its end times, and does not have what it takes to continue indefinitely. To both camps, the belief in End Times offers a glimmer of hope in an otherwise tragic scenario.'

The history of the Berlin Wall is analogous. In recent years, even the smallest victory over the Exclusive Brethren, or any concession wrung from them, represented to me another chink in the physical and psychological barricades surrounding the EB. As US President Ronald Reagan famously declared at the Brandenburg Gate near the Berlin Wall on June 12, 1987:

'This wall will fall. Beliefs become reality. For the wall cannot withstand faith; it cannot withstand truth. The wall cannot withstand freedom.'

A turning point for me had occurred on Tuesday May 6, 2014, when Australian TV Channel 9 A Current Affair ran a story *'Exclusive*

Brethren's tax-free millions revealed'. The by-line was: 'After years of bad press, the EB is on a major public relations offensive. They've got a new name and a new approach to charity, but it's not just about helping others. ACA lifts the lid on the secluded sect's cunning new plan'.

Then came the catalyst. On Monday August 11, 2014, Channel 9 ACA aired a further documentary *'The Exclusive Brethren Exposed'* concerning Craig Stewart, a former EB who was prevented from attending his mother's funeral, although the EB strenuously refuted the claim. I watched this emotional interview and I saw Craig's pain. I felt Craig's pain. I was back on the rocky outcrop at Balmoral, watching the waves breaking as my heart was breaking, when my mother was buried by the EB all those years ago and I was denied my right to be there.

I knew that despite the cleverly-packaged public persona they now presented in order to maintain their charitable status and keep their tax-free millions, the EB had not changed. This should come as no surprise, when you consider the closing pronouncement of an EB elder, Athol Greene, in an interview with David Marr, (Sydney Morning Herald July 11, 2009). The article, headed *'The Exclusion Brethren'* investigated the claim that 'A father's price for quitting his marriage was to lose contact with eight children left behind in the Exclusive Brethren'. In measured, clearly enunciated tones, Mr Greene declared: YOU. WILL. NOT. CHANGE. US.

Now I understood I must once more step out of my comfort zone and put up my hand to be counted. In the immortal words coined for the 1972 election campaign by the late lamented Gough Whitlam, former Prime Minister of Australia: *'It's time'*. The time is right to share my story.

If I needed any further motivation, there was a clarion call in the inspirational words of the investigative journalist Michael Bachelard, in his opening address to the CIFS (Cult Information and Family Support) Conference at Parliament House, Canberra, November 2, 2011. Michael's full speech transcript is appended as Annexure 1. Michael said:

'To make sure the power of cults is undercut takes two things: brave
former members or families of members who are prepared to stand
up and tell their stories; and a place where those stories can come out.'

I believe the place for my memoir 'Joy and Sorrow' is in the public arena, not hidden as a private account through fear of retribution from the Exclusive Brethren, now operating under the guise of the Plymouth Brethren Christian Church.

I have experienced so many joys, my sorrows have been far outweighed. It reminds me of the ancient Egyptian ritual of the Scales of Justice, where the heart was weighed against an ostrich feather. If the heart was lighter than the feather, eternal life was the reward. Miraculously my hand of cards in life has played out, with the balance tipped in my favour.

The Chinese Proverb *'One Joy scatters a hundred griefs'* was a guiding beacon for me when compiling this memoir. If by reading this, you have seen a light shining for you through the darkness, then telling my story has been a success.

I am happy with the person I feel I have become. I am comfortable in my Secular Humanist skin, borrowing from the Bible and borrowing from Buddhism. I have found inner peace and the joy of happiness that comes from within. On my desk as a daily reminder, I have written the inspirational words of Matthieu Ricard, from *'The Art of Happiness'*:

"Happiness does not come automatically. It is not a gift that good fortune
bestows upon us and a reversal of fortune takes back. It depends on us –
alone. One does not become happy overnight, but with patient labour. In
order to become happy, we have to learn how to change ourselves."

As for the faceless, nameless men of the nightmares in my Prologue – I always knew they represented Elders from the Exclusive Brethren church, come to mete out the punishments they prophesied so long ago. My nightmares have been banished and the EB cannot reach me now. I have consigned their false prophecies to the mythical flames of Hell where they belong.

Photos Part 4

1993 50th Birthday gift caricature of Shellcove Road girls in 1970

Fenghuang, Hunan Province, China, 2008. Joy with Anthony, Justin and Justin's
Chinese grandparents, Waigong and Waipo

1999 Joy and Pete at Gretna Green

2013 70th birthday party – Ant, Mega, Justin, Joy and Pete

Epilogue

At a recent Meditation class I attended, a poem was read out to us which left a deep impression on me. It is called 'Fire' by Judy Brown:

What makes a fire burn
is space between the logs,
a breathing space.

Too much of a good thing, too many logs packed in too
tight can douse the flames
almost as surely
as a pail of water would.

So building fires
requires attention
to the spaces in between
as much as to the wood.

When we are able to build open
spaces
in the same way
we have learned
to pile on the logs,
then we can come to see how it is
fuel, and absence of the fuel
together, that make fire possible.

We only need to lay a log
lightly from time to time.

A fire grows simply because the space is
there with openings in which the flame
that knows just how it wants to burn
can find its way.

Against all odds and despite the Exclusive Brethren, my life's fire was never extinguished. On the contrary, by finding its own way, it still burns bright.

Annexure 1

CIFS (Cult Information and Family Support)
Conference. Parliament House, Canberra,
Australia. November 2, 2011.

Opening Address: Michael Bachelard

Michael Bachelard, author and journalist for the *Sunday Age* and
Sydney Morning Herald, recounted his difficulties faced in reporting
abuses and irregularities perpetrated by cult-like groups. He spoke
of the harassment and hounding he had personally endured, and
greeted the Middletons' lawyer in the audience contracted by the
Exclusive Brethren to monitor him. Mr Bachelard also shared
how he had been personally uplifted by helping expose the abuses
of cults and the many people who have been heartened by his
public acknowledgment of their harsh treatment - including forced
separation from their friends and family.

Reporting on Cults; Rewards and Punishments
Michael Bachelard:

I have been writing about and thinking about cults since the morning
in late 2006 when my editor came to me and asked me to write a
story about the Exclusive Brethren.

'Who are *they*?' I asked.

It was a fateful question, both for me and, I suspect, for the Exclusive Brethren.

It turns out that, for a former political reporter recently promoted to *The Age's* investigative unit, the process of finding out about the Exclusive Brethren was very interesting indeed.

At that time, in New Zealand, this separatist little offshoot from nineteenth century dispensationalism was busy hiring private detectives to tail the Prime Minister, Helen Clark, and helping spread rumours that her husband was gay.

They had previously undertaken a shady, undisclosed attempt to manipulate the result of the 2005 New Zealand election, and install a Prime Minister who would have owed them big time.

Thanks largely to the work of a New Zealand journalist, their interference was uncovered, and the intended beneficiary of their assistance, National Party leader Don Brasch, unexpectedly lost the election and then his leadership.

And in Australia, it turned out, they had mounted a similar, though more successful, attempt to swing an election in favour of their candidate. In 2004, John Howard had received significant advertising support, as well as boots on the ground in his own electorate at least, to help him win that year's Federal election.

But it was not until two years later, in around 2006 that this involvement started to be revealed.

That's where I joined the story. Others had done much of the heavy lifting to identify the Exclusive Brethren's secretive hand in Australian and New Zealand politics to that point, and I was simply asked to find out if they would be intervening in Victorian state politics at the 2006 election.

Very quickly I was able to find out that they had already taken steps to help candidates at that election. They had met with at least one state MP on the conservative side of politics to test his views on certain issues.

I wrote the story; it was printed on page 1 - an early indication of the rewards one could expect when writing about such a strange and compelling group.

There's nothing an investigative reporter likes more than a secret, and exposing them clearly had its rewards when all their efforts were being expended to fly 'under the radar'.

Further potential rewards were immediately revealed to me. I was literally flooded with correspondence from former Exclusive Brethren members urging me to investigate further. Warren McAlpin, who was to become my guide through the convoluted world of Brethrenism, was important among those early calls.

It was at Warren's suggestion that I visited the Brethren's main compound, in a bleak part of suburban Melbourne, one night in that first week, and tried to make the case as to why they should let me in to view their church service.

"It's a public place of worship," I argued, "It's got a rate exemption hasn't it?"

My arguments fell on stubborn ears. The keepers of the locked gates refused me entrance, saying, "You might be the most corrupt man in Melbourne". But even if I'd been George Pell they would not have let me in. They're not called "exclusive" for nothing!

When I tried to ignore these gatekeepers and assert my rights by walking down the driveway, I was confronted by four burly men, who emerged from the shadows to block my way. They threatened me with trespass, so I withdrew to watch from across the road.

Awaiting me the following day was a legal letter accusing me of all sorts of things, and threatening various kinds of legal action, from trespass to defamation suits.

It was to be the first of many legal letters I have received from the Exclusive Brethren. Punishment, or the threat of it, turned out to be swift.

But that threat, like all the rest, simply served to encourage me. My two day excursion into their world turned into a month, then six months, then a year. I wrote dozens of stories about them - their cruelty towards their own flock, the financial trickery that goes to enrich them, and to fund their separatist schools; their hidden manipulation of the political system to their own ends, and even their mistreatment of child sexual abuse victims in Albury.

Ultimately I ended up writing a book about them, Behind the Exclusive Brethren, which drew all of this together in one handy compendium.

It must have become clear even to the Brethren at some point that the legal threats were not working. It didn't stop the threats arriving, but they added another weapon to their armoury: they hired a very expensive public relations firm, to try to spin their side of the story more effectively.

Jackson Wells, the team that also looks after the Church of Scientology, has taken on the Exclusive Brethren as a client.

And as my book was being published, suddenly they were opening up the doors of Brethren schools to my competitors to tell the world at large how nice it all was, what a wonderful place it was to grow up. They also put out a blizzard press releases to tell the world – before it was even released – that my book was a "work of fiction".

I accept all this. Journalists are involved in a robust public debate, often throwing barbs at other people, and we should accept that some will come back our way.

I do not believe that all speech, no matter how inaccurate, should be free. I accept there are limits on it. I am happy to operate within those limits because, I believe, my own credibility and that of the stories I tell, will suffer if I stray outside them.

Both the defamation law and the operation of public relations professionals calling my work into question, are two ways in which those limits on free speech are enforced, and I believe they are a part of legitimate public debate.

And so to the representative of the Exclusive Brethren's law firm who is listening to this speech, and presumably taking very careful notes, I say welcome to Canberra. I hope you're staying somewhere nice.

The Exclusive Brethren is just one cult. There are many. But they all share common characteristics.

I know this because my work on the Brethren has broadened out into an interest in other such groups, religious or otherwise.

My writing in *The Age* and *Sunday Age* has also touched on the activities of various cults, including the Jesus People, Kenja, Scientology, one other which, for legal reasons I will not mention today. I regard it as a privilege that I have been able to attain some expertise in this area.

A very small number of Australians are caught up in cults at any given time, but the damage that can be wrought on them and their children is deep. The damage can be financial, psychological, physical. But in most cases it lasts a lifetime, and longer.

I'll never forget the woman who approached me after my book launch in Melbourne in 2008 and said that her family had left the Exclusive Brethren when she was three years old, but the shadow of it had hung over her childhood – the missing aunts and uncles, the black holes in the life of her parents that they would not speak about.

This woman had never within her own memory belonged to that group, but still it had damaged her life to the point where, 35 years later, she was motivated to come to the launch of a book on the subject.

One of the things that all cults share is that, through their leader or leaders, they can control the lives of their members. They even seek to control the lives of their former members, and in that context, I would like to pass my very best wishes to our friend Warren McAlpin who cannot be here today for very complex reasons.

Cults and their leaders are control freaks. They set the rules that all must follow then they use the pressure of the group, and the threat of various punishments, to enforce those rules.

This means that the thing they hate most in the world is someone from outside, who is not subject to their rules or vulnerable to their techniques of manipulation, looking at them and exposing their beliefs and practices to the outside world.

When this happens the cult and its practices become part of the chaotic public conversation, subject of free speech and the cleansing power of daylight. It's totally outside their control, which is precisely where they don't like it.

That is why it's crucial that journalists continue to do this work, and why politicians continue to take notice of it.

Cults dress themselves in all the protections they can to mask their activities - religious freedom and its legal protections being a favourite.

But exposing Kenja as the controlling cult that it is, and not a simple counselling and circus arts group was crucial.

Undressing the religious pretensions of Scientology and revealing that at its heart lay Xenu and the Galactic Confederacy was an incredibly powerful act. It has not cured the world of Scientology, far from it, but it's certainly improved the weapons that can be used against it.

And showing the politicians in Canberra what these quietly spoken men in brown trousers and short sleeved shirts from the Exclusive Brethren really do behind their locked gates will hopefully mean that Bruce Hales and his "priests" have much less political power in future.

To make sure the power of cults is undercut takes two things: brave former members or families of members who are prepared to stand up and tell their stories; and a place where those stories can come out.

And so to the real rewards I have enjoyed for reporting on cults. Those rewards are in the people I have met and worked with. People like Warren McAlpin and Alison Alderton and her daughters, who revealed to me the horror of their life stories, and through them, the barbarism inherent in the doctrine of separation as practiced by the Exclusive Brethren.

Madeline Hardess, once of the Jesus People, Adrian Norman, who escaped from Kenja, and many others I cannot name have trusted me with their stories in a way that I hope has made some difference to them, and to the world at large.

To feel trusted with these stories is its own reward. And with luck, telling them will resonate with others who have suffered similarly.

And perhaps then the children, husbands and wives, partners, relatives of those who have left a cult can see that story and say "Yes, that's why you're like you are".

I have spoken to other journalists who have covered cults: Quentin McDermott from Four Corners, Rohan Wenn formerly of Channel Seven, and Brian Seymour of Today Tonight, and they agree: if our reporting brings just a few more people to their senses, draws some out of their high demand organisation, that would be the ultimate justification for our work.

But ultimately the biggest difference will be made if the criminal activities of cults, the psychological assaults they commit, can be identified, revealed and stopped.

That change will take more than a journalist's skill. That will take political will.

And if we can achieve that, it really would be worth all those legal threats and the spin doctors sneering at us and questioning our motives and professionalism.

That would be the biggest reward of all.

Thank you.

Annexure 2

Exclusive Brethren 'The End Times', Dr Ian C Mckay, Glasgow, Scotland

The End Times

The few years from 2012 to 2015 following the end of Joy's narrative have been turbulent enough among the Hales sect to put its continued existence at risk.

In June 2012 the Hales Brethren in England were thrown into a crisis that sent shock waves throughout their fellowship and eventually forced them to agree to substantial changes in their practices. The Charity Commission refused to grant charitable status to the Preston Down Trust, which the Brethren had formed to manage a meeting room in Torquay, Devon. The Commission's decision letter stated, "As a matter of law, we are not able to satisfy ourselves and conclusively determine that Preston Down Trust is established for exclusively charitable purposes for public benefit and suitable for registration as a charity."

No one had expected this. In the previous 12 months 1175 religious organizations in the UK had applied for charitable status and all had been successful. The Preston Down Trust is the only one that was refused. Even the Druids got charitable status, as the Brethren pointed out indignantly.

It was generally recognised that this was a test case, and the outcome would affect the many trusts through which the Brethren channelled large sums of money from their businesses and from individuals. Charitable status was of great financial importance to them because of the tax concessions that go along with it. In a public letter dated 27 September 2013 written by Peter Trevvett, a senior member of the sect, he said that loss of charitable status would threaten the survival of the Brethren. I do not think he was exaggerating. Some of us suspect that without its tax concessions the Hales sect would have lost one of its main reasons for existing.

This crisis had roots that went back as far as 1974. According to a speech by Malcolm Rifkind in the House of Commons as reported in Hansard (1st August 78), "In 1974 the Commissioners appointed Mr Hugh Elvett Francis QC to conduct an inquiry under the Charities Act into the doctrines and practices of the Exclusive Brethren. Mr Francis submitted a report in 1976 recommending that, pending a decision by the courts, the Commissioners should not register any meeting house of the sect which had adopted the doctrine of 'separation from evil' as practised by the followers of James Taylor Junior."

Mr Hugh Francis came to the following conclusion: "The doctrine is harmful and calculated to disrupt family ties and perfectly normal and proper business relationships. It has caused widespread distress and anguish among many deeply religious and decent people and is against the true interests of the community."

However, at that time there was considerable lack of clarity in UK Charity law. Charities were required to be of public benefit, both in their purposes and in their effects, but none of the statutes ever defined "public benefit," and religious organisations were automatically assumed to be of public benefit. That dispute between the Brethren and the Charity Commission was not settled until 1981. You can read about it in "The Report of the Charity Commissioners for England and Wales for the year 1981." Although the Charity Commission had collected lots of allegations about detrimental effects of the Brethren's practices, they had not collected hard evidence of this in the form of witness statements that could be presented in court. In the absence of clear evidence, the statutory presumption of charitable status for religious organisations weighed in the Brethren's favour, and they won their case.

This changed 32 years later when the UK Charities Act of 2006 abolished the presumption that religious organisations are charitable, and it put them on the same footing as any other organisation claiming charitable status. From now on they would have to show that they exist purely for the public benefit.

I don't think the Brethren noticed this change in the law until it began to hurt them, and then they went into crisis mode, swinging into action on several fronts and spending millions of pounds on a campaign to defend their charitable status and its associated tax concessions.

To begin with, they announced in July 2012 that they would take the Commission to the Charity Tribunal to appeal against the Preston Down decision, a process that they began on 14 August 2012 (Appeal no. CA/2012/0003) and on 3 December 2012 a preliminary sitting of the First Tier Tribunal took place, presided over by Principal Judge Alison McKenna, at which she refused to consider transferring the case to the Upper Tribunal, a decision that upset the Brethren because it meant they would have no right of appeal within the UK if the case went against them. Various dates were set by which evidence was to be exchanged, and it was decided that the main hearing would take place during 5 days starting on 25 March 2013. A UK Brethren leader, Mr Garth Christie of Leeds, later added that they would take the case all the way to Strasbourg if necessary (a very expensive process likely to take at least seven years).

On 22 November 2012 there was a debate about religion in the House of Lords, and Baroness Elizabeth Berridge made a speech describing abuses of religion by Exclusive Brethren that she had witnessed and experienced, and calling for a church-led inquiry into their sect. Some ex-Brethren who had suffered from such abuses reacted with tears of relief on hearing their concerns being publicly articulated at last. On Web sites there was an immediate outpouring of passionate approval and gratitude for her speech.

Towards the end of 2012 the Brethren hierarchy appointed emergency teams of Regional Coordinators and Local Coordinators to plan and execute a strategy to hold on to charitable status. They decided to conduct a massive Parliamentary lobbying campaign with the intention to see every MP and every member of the House of Lords. Peter Bone MP was persuaded to sponsor a Private Member's Bill to restore the presumption of charitable status for religious organisations, and a letter to the Prime Minister was drafted, to be signed by as many MPs as could be recruited, asking for the Charities Act 2006 to be changed.

This massive campaign had not the slightest chance of succeeding, except perhaps as a publicity exercise. A large majority of MPs voted in favour of Peter Bone's bill on its so-called first reading, but none of them had actually read it by that time. It had not yet been printed. Its opponents in Parliament didn't even bother to speak against it, because they knew that when its effects were understood, support for it would melt away without their having to raise a finger. Even as a publicity exercise, its effects were mixed. Some MPs were thoroughly irritated by the relentless lobbying. One of them complained that he had been approached by Brethren more than 50 times.

The Brethren also drew up a document denying point by point nearly everything Baroness Berridge had said in her speech to the House of Lords, and it was decided to send this document to every member of the House.

The Brethren asked the Attorney General to intervene in their dispute with the Charity Commission, but predictably he refused. It would have been quite improper for any Government Minister to intervene in a judicial process.

Brethren also sent a letter to other Christian groups asking for their support, and they arranged a meeting for 15th January 2013 on the terrace of Westminster Palace to provide hospitality for MPs and tell them about the Hales Brethren. They also decided to examine Jill Mytton's research (described below) minutely with a view to discrediting it. Plans were drawn up for "Pie Days" to be held at many of the Brethren's local meeting rooms, where local residents would be invited for 1 hour to receive a free lunch and a free bible, not in the meeting room but in the car park or a tent.

A slide show on a DVD was created very professionally using Microsoft PowerPoint and shown to the Brethren at all meeting rooms. Its purpose was to explain to them how urgent the crisis was, and to motivate them to take part in the various campaigns. One of the alarming points made in the course of the slide show was that for any existing Brethren charity, being de-registered would be disastrous, because all its assets such as cash or meeting rooms would then have to be transferred to some other charity, out of the Brethren's control.

Towards the end of 2012 Brethren also approached several academic researchers who had expertise in the history, sociology or psychology of religion, and offered them financial support to conduct research into the Hales Brethren, with a view to appearing as expert witnesses at the Charity Tribunal. But it soon became apparent that the Brethren wanted to choose the sources of the researchers' information in such a way that the proposed "research" would fall far short of the standards of objectivity, balance and honesty that are usual in academic work. The academics that I know of were too honest to take this bait, and turned down the offer. In fact, one of them offered to appear as a witness for the Charity Commission instead, and without any financial incentive.

A meeting of the House of Commons Public Administration Committee was held on Tuesday 30 October 2012 to consider Regulation of the Charitable Sector and the Charities Act 2006. Several lawyers specializing in Charity Law, and two leading members of the Exclusive Brethren were present to give evidence, a Mr Bruce Hazell and a Mr Garth Christie. The legal experts gave an interesting account of the essence of charity law, how it had developed, and the difficulties and ambiguities in applying it, and the Brethren gave a long list of charitable activities that they claimed to practise, and described their difficulty in being granted charitable status for the Preston Down Trust. Two of their statements particularly stuck in my memory.

First, Mr Bruce Hazell said their denomination was called the Plymouth Brethren Christian Church. That was the first time I had ever heard them called that, and it soon became apparent this was the start of a re-branding exercise, an attempt to change their name and their public image. Around the same time, the Brethren's own Web site, theexclusivebrethren.com, disappeared, and a new one appeared with their newly adopted name. Large newspaper advertisements appeared, telling everyone how charitable the Plymouth Brethren Christian Church (PBCC) is.

The name was misleading, because the Hales fellowship is only a very small fragment of the Plymouth Brethren movement, which is the usual collective name for more than a dozen separate denominations that have evolved from what was once only one. For the Hales fellowship to call themselves the Plymouth Brethren Christian Church is a bit like the British nation deciding to call themselves the Human Race. In a very limited sense it is true, but it exaggerates their relative importance and overlooks others as if they don't count. It was possibly an attempt to shelter under the relatively respectable umbrella of the much larger Plymouth Brethren movement, which has always been active in evangelism, charity and missionary work.

In giving evidence, Mr Christie's final words were, "We welcome scrutiny, that is not a problem to us. . . . We have nothing to hide." This contrasted strikingly with the Brethren's longstanding culture of extreme secrecy, and their habit of branding as traitors those who communicate the contents of their ministry to non-members. Mr Christie also confirmed that a Jewish MP would be welcome to attend the Brethren's Sunday morning meeting, which completely contradicts what the Brethren ministry says, and what the brethren have practised since the 1960s.

A video recording of the Public Administration Committee meeting can be seen at http://www.parliamentlive.tv/Main/Player. aspx?meetingId=11642 and a transcript of the proceedings can be read at http://www.publications.parliament.uk/pa/cm201213/ cmselect/cmpubadm/c574-iii/c57401.htm

Later, the Charity Commission formally complained that something the Brethren said to the Committee was seriously misleading, and this was a serious matter. Mr Christie replied with a letter of apology.

However, the Brethren did have one clear success. The Public Administration Committee agreed that when the charitable status of an organisation is in doubt, the only way at present of settling the question through the Charity Tribunal and courts is too slow, too arduous and too expensive.

In December 2012 the Brethren's universal leader advised that they should put extreme pressure on Mr William Shawcross, chairman of the Charity Commission, to review the Commission's decision without going to Tribunal, so in February 2013 they approached the Charity Commission with a request that the Tribunal be postponed to give time for negotiations, and on 5 February the Judge granted a three-month stay of the proceedings. The reason the Brethren gave was that a Tribunal would be expensive, and it would be better to see if they could come to some agreement out of court. Legal expenses had never been much of a deterrent to Brethren in the past, but perhaps part of the reason for their change of plan was the fact that many credible witnesses had come forward with a mountain of damning evidence that was all going to come out publicly in court. It would be vitally important to avoid this very public display of dirty laundry. Besides, if the Brethren lost the case, as seemed probable at that time, there would be no right of appeal within the UK.

One postponement was followed by another, then another, and finally the Brethren negotiators and the Charity Commission reached a provisional compromise. The Brethren agreed that the Trust Deeds of their meeting-room trusts would be rewritten to include a statement of *Faith in Practice*, which renounced most of the detrimental and harmful practices that they had been accused of, and they agreed that the new Trust Deeds would be approved by unanimous agreement of each congregation. The statement radically contradicted several major teachings of Brethren ministry during the previous 50 years.

It amounts to abolishing most of the emotional and practical barriers that make it difficult and traumatic for individuals to leave the church, and they now on paper agree that it is acceptable for

Brethren to socialise with ex-Brethren and to allow the continuation of family relationships where a family member has left the community, including providing access to family members, in particular children.

It says, "The principle of separation outlined at paragraph 2 above involves drawing away from the world in a moral sense, rather than in a physical sense." This contradicts the ministry of Mr James Taylor Jr.

It also says that members will be excommunicated against their will only "as an extreme or last resort measure for serious misdeeds wholly at odds with basic scriptural teaching." So for example, the Brethren would be breaching this principle if they excommunicated someone merely because he disagreed with B. D. Hales. This amounts to a really radical change, at least on paper, because since the 1960s the main criterion for qualifying for membership of the fellowship has in effect been agreement with and obedience to the universal leader.

The Statement says, "We are expected to care for those who are receptive to such care in our own community, but then also in the wider community (including former Brethren), to the best of our abilities and within our resources." How different from the teachings of James Taylor Jr., who thought those who did not toe the line had to be abandoned.

It says, "Within the parameters set out above, the principle of separation permits inter-personal communication and social interaction with non-Brethren (including former Brethren) . . ."

"Our adherence to these principles should never stop us offering to the wider public (including former Brethren) the opportunity to attend and benefit from our system of Christian worship." How different from past practice, which was to reserve the meetings for members only, and especially the one meeting per week that was primarily for worship!

It says, "Where a person within the community dies, the principle of separation allows members of the extended family of the deceased, including former Brethren, to attend their funeral service." How different from past practice, which was to delay telling relatives that their loved one had died, or to give them false information about the funeral to prevent them from attending.

The statement of *Faith in Practice* starts on page 47 of the Charity Commission's full report, which you can access from https://www.gov.uk/government/publications/preston-down-trust

In return for these radical undertakings, the Charity Commission agreed on 9 January 2014 that it would provisionally enter the Preston Down Trust on its Register of Charities, and the decision would be reviewed in about a year's time. It was understood that other meeting room trusts would be treated similarly if they signed up to the new Trust Deeds.

One source of information that upset the Brethren badly during 2012 was the research conducted by Jill Mytton, a counselling psychologist working in the London area. Jill specialises in caring for those who have been psychologically damaged by their experiences in high-demand organisations, popularly called cults. Part of her doctoral research project was to use various established and validated questionnaires designed to measure various kinds of psychological disturbance, and compare ex-members of the Taylor/Symington/Hales sect with the published norms for these existing questionnaires. She reported her findings at several meetings of learned societies.

By these methods she produced a description of the extent and prevalence and kinds of psychological problems among a self-selected group of ex-Brethren members, mostly finding the kind of results that cult experts would expect, but she also found something disturbing that she did not expect. A disturbingly large number of the respondents said they had been sexually abused as children. In one survey it was about 30 per cent, and in a later survey about 26 per cent. Not all of these cases involved rape, of course. If my own straw poll among personal ex-Brethren friends is anything to go by, I would expect only about half of these cases to involve rape.

By 2012 it was well known that sexual abuse of children has been shockingly prevalent in some religious bodies, particularly those with an authoritarian, patriarchal power structure and those with a culture of secrecy, so it should not have been entirely unexpected to find evidence of historical child sexual abuse among the Exclusives, who are certainly marked by a patriarchal power structure and a culture of secrecy. We should perhaps have foreseen this, because some ex-Brethren authors have mentioned sexual abuse in their biographies, many ex-members have reminisced about it, and some Brethren members have been convicted of sexual offences against children.

What was surprising though, and to me disappointing, was the Brethren's response to Jill's research. One might have expected that they would take a careful look at their safeguarding policies, if they have any, and see if they were fit for purpose, and make sure that all their members knew about the policies, how to reduce the risk, and what to do if a child disclosed any kind of ill-treatment. And they might have reviewed their policy on sex education to make sure their children knew how to recognise the danger signs, how to avert unwanted sexual advances, their right to be protected and how to seek help.

But that is not the response that we saw. That was not even part of it. At the time of writing (February 2015) I still don't know if the Brethren even have the legally obligatory written safeguarding policy, and none of the members that we have asked seem to know either. What we saw instead, starting in October 2012, was a series of increasingly intimidating lawyer's letters from an expensive law firm acting for a number of leading Brethren in England. Some of the letters were sent to Jill, and some were letters of complaint sent to various institutions that she was associated with, such as the Metanoia Institute, Middlesex University, Bournemouth University, and the Healthcare Professions Council. The Brethren also hired three academics to examine and criticise Jill's work, and then on 12 July 2013 when Jill was presenting her work at the Division of Counselling Psychology Annual Conference, two Brethren members turned up and distributed leaflets aimed at discrediting her. The Brethren also posted comments on their own Web site with the same apparent purpose.

These activities caused inconvenience, distress and delay in Jill's research, but I don't think the Brethren succeeded in stopping her research or damaging her reputation. However, they damaged their own. Members of the Psychology profession would be left with the impression that the Brethren were frantically trying to suppress or deny research findings.

In January 2013 the Web site known as peebs.net, which was by far the main route through which damning evidence against the Brethren was disseminated by ex-Brethren, disappeared from view without any explanation. Many users of the site tried to contact Tim Twinam the Webmaster asking for an explanation, but he did not reply to any such requests. It was widely rumoured by usually well informed people that the Brethren had given him a large bribe to close the site down. He had very large, urgent, unforeseen expenses at the time, so maybe a large bribe would be difficult to refuse. The Brethren had previously attempted to force the closure of Peebs.net by a long-running, very expensive lawsuit that started in 2009 and finally failed. In the emergency circumstances of 2012 it must have been obvious that a bribe might be much quicker, more dependable, possibly cheaper, and more importantly could be done covertly, avoiding the enormously damaging publicity that had attended the previous litigation. We may never know for sure.

But fighting the Internet, whether by bribes, threats or litigation, is a bit like fighting the legendary Hydra. Every time you chop off one of its heads, another two sprout up in its place. In this case there were many more than two. A blog run by Councillor Richard Stay became for a while the main public forum for discussing the problem of Hales Brethrenism, and a new Web site called WikiPeebia opened up, similar to Peebs.net. So did Friends-Alive, which specialised in catering for those who have been psychologically damaged by cults. Richard Stay's very active blog was soon replaced by Laurie Moffitt's very active blog, and several private Web sites, Facebook forums and email groups opened up too, some of them with access largely limited to ex-Brethren. The Internet became the Brethren leaders' nightmare. Indeed, it has made life very difficult for tyrants of all sorts, both religious and political.

Brethren members often contributed fiercely to the discussions on these blogs, apparently trying to defend and support Hales Brethrenism, but seldom used anything more than empty assertions unsupported by evidence or argument, interspersed with *argumentum ad hominem*. Or in English, if they couldn't discredit the message, they would attack the messenger. Or sometimes they would warn him that he was heading for eternal torment in Hell.

The whole of 2014 was a tense time for the Hales Brethren, especially in the UK. They were on probation, as it were, and conscious of being under the scrutiny of their critics and the Charity Commission. They had signed up to a statement that they couldn't possibly live up to without trashing some of the core messages of the previous 50 years of ministry. If they tried to live up to their promises, they might be in trouble from their own leaders; if they didn't try they might be in trouble from the Charity Commission. So they tried a little. A whole lot depended on it. One of their critics, after looking at a collection of company accounts, estimated that to lose charitable status for all their trusts would cost them something like £100,000,000 per annum in the UK alone.

During the crisis, the Brethren spent a great deal of money and effort to convince the public and the Charity Commission that they were a charitable organization that existed purely for public benefit. For the first time in their history they began to raise money for non-Brethren charities, such as the British Heart Foundation. In some of the towns where they lived they set up an organisation called the Rapid Relief Team, which turned up at conspicuous disaster areas where there had been floods, fires or motorists stranded in snow. There they served food and refreshments to the firemen and others, often from tents and vehicles and with high-visibility jackets all conspicuously decorated with their logo. These and other charitable deeds were frequently brought to the attention of the public and the authorities.

They also began to relax some of their more oppressive rules. For the first time in decades, Brethren have been seen shopping on a Sunday, allowing their children to play in a playpark on a Sunday, and visiting beaches. It is not clear whether the Brethren hierarchy allowed this relaxation as a policy decision or whether they are merely beginning to lose control.

Many of the changes in behaviour were striking and unprecedented among the Brethren, but they were not the changes that the Charity Commission had asked for. When it came to the treatment of dissenters and ex-members, many observers have said there has been very little change. The radical statements of *Faith in Practice* appeared to have had little effect in practice.

One of the problems that the Charity Commission was originally concerned about was the ban on members attending university, but the Brethren negotiators would not make any concessions on that one, so the ban remained. The statement of *Faith in Practice* did not commit them to changing this rule. However, some of the brethren now get permission to undertake further and higher education, but only by distance-learning methods and only in a very restricted set of subjects, usually related to business.

Towards the end of the probationary year the Brethren showed signs of worrying about whether their show of charity would stand up to scrutiny. An email was sent to UK businesses and individual brethren by a Campus Business Manager for the brethren's Universal Business Team for Europe. It contained an urgent request from PBCC Central Team for "the saints" to ramp up their "Bag It Beat It" campaign effective immediately (i.e. fill charity bags of stuff for the British Heart Foundation). The reason given for the special request was that "the Charity Commission have been asking questions recently and the Brethren are under immense scrutiny as to the amount of public benefit provided."

Towards the end of the probationary year of 2014-15, just as the time was approaching for their charitable status to be reviewed, at the worst possible time for the Brethren, two other problems arose that put them at further risk, the last of which looked potentially very serious and provoked unprecedented reactions from the hierarchy.

First, the UK public and Government became aware that some schools were promoting or at least permitting the spread of some very anti-social ideas, such as narrow religious allegiance, distrust and antipathy to other religious traditions, disapproval of democracy, disapproval of free expression and denial of human rights such as sexual equality, thereby potentially turning out a population that would tend to damage social cohesion and would be unable to contribute constructively to British society.

The Education Secretary and the Prime Minister both made speeches about the need for all schools (not just state-funded schools) to actively promote "British values." Ofsted, the body that inspects schools, published new regulations setting out revised or clarified criteria by which schools would be assessed. You can read one of these official policy documents at http://tinyurl.com/nd5d2c2

While the Brethren have serious difficulty in accepting modern liberal views about democracy, individual liberty and freedom of expression, the part of these official policy documents that will be most difficult for Brethren schools to implement is that independent school proprietors are required "to actively promote the fundamental British values of democracy, the rule of law, individual liberty, and mutual respect and tolerance of those with different faiths and beliefs."

A Government consultation paper published in June 2014, explaining the new rules, makes clear that even taking children on trips to different places of worship would not be enough to be judged compliant.

Later in 2014 it was reported in the Daily Telegraph that an unnamed Christian school had been downgraded and could even be closed for failure to 'actively promote' harmony between different faiths because **it had failed to bring in representatives from other religions.**

So can you imagine a Brethren School bringing in Imams or Rabbis to conduct religious education classes or school assembly? Or even a Roman Catholic or an Anglican representative? For anyone familiar with the Taylor/Symington/Hales tradition of extreme sectarianism, this requirement actively to promote mutual respect and tolerance of those with different faiths and beliefs seems almost unthinkable. How can the Brethren teach their children anything of the sort when their ministry for more than 50 years has strenuously taught the exact opposite?

Again, on 20 Jan 2015 it was reported that a Christian free school in Durham was to be closed after inspectors said that its pupils risked developing prejudiced views against other faiths. The inspectors accused governors of hiring staff based on their religious credentials rather than their teaching ability and said that children risked becoming prejudiced towards other religions. "The curriculum does not help students to understand fundamental British values or prepare them well for life in modern Britain," their report said. You can read that OFSTED report at http://reports.ofsted.gov.uk/provider/files/2448202/urn/140005.pdf

Respect for the Equality Act 2000 will also be very difficult for Brethren children to accept or Brethren schools to teach. Expressions of racism, sexism and homophobia have often been seen among Brethren children and their parents, and attempts to promote the principles of equality are often dismissed as "political correctness" or something evil and Satanic.

This is not only a cultural problem. It is also a financial problem. The UK Brethren have been trying strenuously to get government funding for their private schools, hoping to have them classified as "Free Schools." But with these new regulations, any misplaced hopes in that direction are fading fast, and the prospect of having to shoulder the heavy burden of the school costs indefinitely is being greeted with dismay.

And then came the final blow.

On 21 Jan 2015 the Charity Commission published a policy paper with the title *Charity tax reliefs: guidance on Charity Commission policy*. Among the subjects it deals with is tax avoidance.

The new document gives examples of tax avoidance methods that have been considered to be in breach of a charity's trustees' duties and responsibilities. These include "serial and contrived financial transactions involving charities and companies which seek to disguise what may have been a taxable transaction."

Suppose, for example, that an independent school collects fees from the parents but calls them charitable donations, or collects them indirectly through another charitable trust, and collects a proportion of the donations as gift-aid from the Treasury. The net effect is that the parents will not need to pay as much as they would have done if the payments had been called fees. Such an arrangement seems as if it might fall into the category that the Charity Commission is warning us about.

One criterion by which such unacceptable arrangements are identified is based on whether their principal aim is to confer advantage on private businesses or individuals, with any benefit to the charity being a by-product of the scheme rather than its principal aim.

Suppose, for example, that a charitable trust collects donations from church members along with gift-aid money from the Treasury and uses some of the proceeds to make payments described as gifts to private wealthy individuals. That arrangement also looks as if it might fall into the same category.

This all passed with little comment for a week or so, and Brethren defenders kept on asserting stoutly that the Brethren don't practise tax avoidance and always pay not only their fair share, but more tax than they legally have to.

But early in February 2015 we began to hear independent reports from several different Brethren members suggesting that the sect was back into full crisis mode again. It is alleged that Her Majesty's Revenue and Customs has taken exception to the financial arrangements by which their schools are funded. A letter has been circulated from the Universal leadership putting the blame for the trouble on the UK Brethren, and telling them that until further notice they are not to travel to other cities for "fellowship meetings" or "three-day meetings."

If the UK Brethren are landed with the blame for just doing as they were told, and landed with a big tax bill, and landed with a major increase in their already burdensome school fees, then discontent is likely to erupt. Maybe that is the reason for the ban on travelling to meetings in neighbouring cities. This ban is unprecedented. It is reminiscent of what is known in the Prison Service as "lock down", which is a precaution that is applied when there is a perceived risk of sedition or riots. Maybe the purpose is to prevent conspirators from meeting one another and planning a rebellion.

Brethren supporters and Brethren critics share a belief that these troubles of the last few years may be a sign of the "end times," though the phrase means different things to the two camps. According to Brethren folklore, the world is getting worse and worse and is now ripe for imminent destruction, and they are experiencing the persecution that is to be expected in the end times. But according to the Brethren's victims and critics, it is only Brethrenism that has been getting worse and worse, and the troubles may be a sign that the Hales Group is on its last legs, in its end times, and does not have what it takes to continue indefinitely. To both camps, the belief in end times affords a glimmer of hope in an otherwise tragic scenario.

© Ian C. McKay,
February 2015

Acknowledgements

To my husband, Peter, for his unquestioned support; to my cousin Liz for kindly supplying information from my mother's side of the family; to my sister Beryl and brother John for recollections of life in Coventry and Bristol and to all who have been part of my life's journey – thank you for providing the inspiration. I am indebted to my friends Jenny and Maureen for undertaking the work of professionally formatting my manuscript and seeing the project through to the end. Finally, heartfelt thanks to Ian, Peter and Naomi of the ex-Exclusive Brethren community; without their solidarity and encouragement, this book would not have been written.

References

1. Die Bible:The Luther Bible is a German language Bible translation from Hebrew and ancient Greek by Martin Luther.The New Testament was first published in 1522, and the complete Bible in 1534.

2. Peter Plowman, 2006, *Australian Migrant Ships* 1946-1977, Rosenberg Publishing

3. Susan Chenery, 2011, '*Stolen Childhoods*', Sydney Sun Herald, 12 June

4. John Nelson Darby, 1962, '*Spiritual Songs for The Little Flock*' – selected 1856 latest edition 1962

5. David Tchappat, 2009, *Breakout: How I escaped from the Exclusive Brethren*, New Holland Publishers

6. *Four Corners Separate Lives*, 2006 ABC TV

7. Bertram Russell, 1927, "*Why I am not a Christian*" lecture on March 6, 1927 to the National Secular Society, South London Branch, at Battersea Town Hall.Published later that year in pamphlet form.

8. George Orwell, 1945, *Animal Farm: A Fair Story*, Secker and Warburg, London

9. Andrew Loyd Webber, 1970, *Jesus Christ Superstar*, Arock opera

10. Norman Adams "*Goodbye Beloved Brethren*" Impulse Books Aberdeen, 1972

11. Fran Taylor, 2008, *Wind in my Wings: Running Away to Sea in the 20th Century*, Albatross Press, South Perth

12. Kazuo Ishiguro, 1990, *The Remains of the day*, Vintage International

13. Ken Follett, 1978, *Eye of theNeedle*, Penguin

14. Joy Nason 2000, www.Peebs.net posting December 2000

15. The Council for Secular Humanism, quoted http://www.pluralism.org/resources/tradition/atheism.php 2014

16. Robert Jay Lifton, 1961, *Thought Reform and the Psychology of Totalism*, Norton, New York

17. Raphael Aron, 1999, *Cults: too good to be true*, Harper Collins Publishers

18. Ngaire Thomas, 2004, *Behind Closed Doors*, Random House New Zealand

19. Michael Bachelard, 2008, *Behind the Exclusive Brethren*, Scribe Melbourne

Printed in July 2019
by Rotomail Italia S.p.A., Vignate (MI) - Italy